Policies To Boost Australian Saving:

How? and Why?

Edited by
Owen Covick
(For the South Australian Centre for Economic Studies)

Wakefield Press

First published in 2002
Wakefield Press (Aust) Pty Ltd
17 Rundle Street
Kent Town SA 5067
AUSTRALIA

National Library of Australia
Cataloguing-in-publication data

Policies to Boost Australian Saving: How? And Why?

Bibliography.

ISBN 0 9586395 2 3

1. Saving and investment – Australia 2. Australia – Economic policy – 1990 - 339 430994 I. Covick, O.E. (Owen E)

Contents

Preface

The work of the South Australian Centre for Economic Studies has in recent years involved a number of studies which have examined issues associated with national saving. The aim of this book has been to bring together the key themes that have emerged during that work (whether written-up at the time or not) and present that material in a coherent way that is accessible to all who are interested in the policy issues surrounding the topic – whether professional economists or not. The body of the book attempts to present fairly the different interpretations of facts and of 'economic' behaviour that make up the policy debate over national saving in Australia, rather than to push one particular line. The concluding comments chapter, however, presents the editor's assessment of what seems to emerge as having weighed most heavily in the scales of persuasiveness, as far as future policy action is concerned.

The year 2002 represents a particularly appropriate time for this work to be put before a wider audience. On 1 July, the minimum standard prescribed by Australia's compulsory saving scheme for wage and salary earners (the SGC arrangements) reached 9 per cent, having been adjusted upwards by the last of the increases scheduled in the original legislation in 1992. Thus 2002 seems a 'natural' time to reflect on the wisdom of the SGC arrangements as originally conceived, and now in full operation – and to ask where do we go from here. It is probably no coincidence therefore that the May 2002 Commonwealth Budget saw, for the first time, publication of the *Intergenerational Report* as Budget Paper No. 5. The focus of the report is on the implications of Australia's aging population for the Commonwealth's longer-term fiscal outlook, and for Australia's national saving position more generally. At the Annual Australian Conference of Economists being held in Adelaide this year, the Business Symposium segment is devoted to the topic 'The Economic and Business Implications of the Aging Baby-Boomers'. Publication of this book has been timed to coincide with that symposium.

The editor and SACES would like to make the following acknowledgements. We thank Beverley Vickers, Jim Hancock and Cliff Walsh both for their direct contributions, *viz* the chapters bearing their names, and also for their 'less-direct' contributions via comments/criticisms/discussions etc. of the overall emerging work. Paul Kenny of Flinders University also provided helpful comments. We thank those clients and corporate members of SACES whose financial support allowed the work reported here to be carried out and written up. Particular thanks are due to the South Australian Government's Department of the Premier and Cabinet, the Credit Union Services Corporation of Australia Limited (CUSCAL), the South Australian Department of Industry and Trade, and the Productivity Commission. The last mentioned should also be thanked for permission to use those parts of Chapter 5 which have been drawn from work previously published in Covick (1997a). The Editors of *Economic Papers*, we thank for their permission to include as Chapter 6 here a revised version of Covick (1996). Janine Molloy expertly converted large bodies of numerical information into intelligible charts and diagrams (a task she has performed with excellence for over twenty years at SACES). Cheree Metcalfe expertly converted large bodies of Owen Covick's unintelligible hand writing into elegant print. Michael Bollen from Wakefield Press guided us through the whole process with tact, consideration and urbanity.

Adelaide
August 2002

Contributors

Owen Covick is Associate Professor in the School of Business Economics at Flinders University, Adelaide, and Deputy Head of the Faculty of Social Sciences. He was economic advisor to a series of senior Cabinet Economics Ministers in the Federal Government from 1986 to March 1996: Peter Walsh, 1986 to 1990; Kim Beazley, 1990 to 1992, and again from 1994 to March 1996; John Dawkins, 1992 to 1993; Ralph Willis, 1994. A member of academic staff at Flinders University since 1973, he has been involved in the activities of SACES since April 1983. His academic publications are principally in the areas of productivity analysis, labour costs and finance. As a member of the INDECS team of economists he was co-author of the best-selling *State of Play* series of books on Australian economic policy.

Jim Hancock is the Deputy Director (Projects) at SACES. He has a background in macroeconomic monitoring and economic evaluation. Since joining the Centre Jim has worked on projects in a range of areas including macroeconomic performance and growth, cost-benefit analysis, environmental evaluations, competition policy, regulatory issues and public finance. Prior to joining the Centre, Jim worked in the South Australian Department of Treasury and Finance. His work there covered a range of areas including macroeconomic monitoring and forecasting, tax policy issues, evaluation methodologies and market structure issues.

Beverley Vickers is a lecturer in Business Economics and Associate Head (Academic) of the Faculty of Social Sciences, at Flinders University. She collaborated with Owen Covick in producing the Report *Saving in Australia* commissioned from SACES by the Credit Union Services Corporation (Australia) Limited for the National Saving Policy Forum held at University House, ANU in December 1995.

Cliff Walsh has recently been awarded the title of Professor Emeritus, Adelaide University following ten years as Professor of Economic Studies, a joint appointment of Adelaide and Flinders Universities. Cliff has a long history of involvement in policy analysis and policy development and in the review of administrative and bureaucratic approaches to policy, program and project delivery. He has extensive experience in advising National, State and Local Governments, Ministers and CEOs. Most recently this has included being a Member of the State Audit Commission for South Australia (1994); a Member of the Local Government Reform Board for South Australia (1996-1998); a Commissioner for the Commonwealth Overseas Aid Review Committee (1996-1997); and a Member of the Task Force on Regional Development in South Australia (1998-99). He is currently a member of the Australian Government's Foreign Affairs Council and its Aid Advisory Council.

The SA Centre for Economic Studies

The SA Centre for Economic Studies was established in 1983 as a joint venture of Adelaide University and the Flinders University of South Australia. Since 1983, the Centre has built a strong reputation for the quality of the research and consulting services it offers.

The Centre is a source of applied economics expertise. Its principal role is to review, research and provide expert analysis and advice on economic, fiscal and public policy issues. This is particularly in respect of issues of relevance to South Australia, although the Centre has also regularly undertaken research and consultancies on national issues, and for interstate and overseas clients. The basis for the Centre's activities in providing consulting services and in commenting on economic issues is the independence, integrity and expertise expected of a University-based operation.

While being university based, the Centre is nevertheless required to be fully self-funding. It derives its income and pursues its roles and objectives principally through:

- offering consulting and advisory services in specialist areas of applied economics to private and public sector organisations;
- offering a Corporate Membership program which provides exclusive access to regular detailed assessments of the Australian and South Australian economies;
- providing public commentary on economic trends and policy issues; and
- undertaking, promoting and disseminating the results of independent applied research, particularly on issues relevant to regional and national economic growth.

For more information about the Centre, please contact its Director, Mr Michael O'Neil.

The SA Centre for Economic Studies
PO Box 125
RUNDLE MALL SA 5000
AUSTRALIA
Telephone: (+61-8) 8303 5555
Facsimile: (+61-8) 8232 5307
Internet: www.adelaide.edu.au/saces
Email: davina.dolman@adelaide.edu.au

1 Why is Australia's National Saving an Issue?

Owen Covick

Debate on national saving in Australia is closely intertwined with debate over government spending and taxing. Since the middle 1980s calls for greater government spending on services provision and/or for lower levels of taxation in Australia have faced the increasingly vigorous response that the imperative of increasing Australia's national saving level means overall tax revenue levels must be guarded from erosion, and overall government spending levels *decreased* rather than increased. This type of response was initially most audible in the context of debate over the Commonwealth government's outlays and revenues, but by the early 1990s it had also become a standard feature of debate and commentary regarding State and Territory budgets and budgetary strategy. The key connecting link from national saving to government budgets is the arithmetic fact that national saving is the sum of two parts: what the government sector 'saves', and what the rest of the Australian community saves. If the aggregate of the two combined *must* be raised, and if effective policies to raise the non-government component are either non-existent, unwise or politically non-implementable, the task clearly *must* fall on the government sector's own saving level – meaning policies to reduce public sector deficits or increase public sector surpluses. And even if effective policies to raise private sector saving *are* available, there may be a case for using such policies in combination with 'direct action' on the government sector's own saving level.

Discussion of what governments *can* do to promote higher levels of saving in the private sector is commenced in Chapter Two, with the following three chapters examining the pros and cons of the principal policy approaches of this type that have been presented as possibilities. The task of this chapter is to tackle the logically prior question of *why* Australian governments should see increasing the level of Australia's national saving as an issue.

What is saving?

Income has two possible uses. It can be applied to *current* purposes, to meet immediate needs and lift living standards today. Alternatively it can be set aside, at least in part, and added to the stock of wealth that is carried forward into tomorrow. The portion of each period's income that is used to gratify immediate needs and wants is termed 'consumption spending' by economists. The portion that is set aside for the future is termed *saving*. This applies for individuals and families. It also applies for business corporations, for non-profit organisations, for governments in all three tiers of government, for government agencies, and so on. It applies for the Australian community as a whole. The consolidated total of the portions of disposable income being set aside for the future by *all* persons, private sector organisations and government bodies in Australia is termed *national saving*.

In everyday language it is common for people to use the words saving(s) and investment(s) interchangeably. The portion of current period disposable income that is saved is added to the various *savings* one has accumulated in the past, and then often described as representing one's *investments* for the future. That is perfectly logical. But economists have for a long time preferred to define *investment* as something much narrower. In their definition, and in the various official statistics, *investment* is the amount of money actually spent in a particular period on the creation or purchase of new physical assets (such as business plant and equipment, schools, office blocks, factories, shops and houses) or on building up holdings of goods awaiting sale or processing, or in the process of production. This narrow definition of investment has recently been modified for official statistics purposes to include also money spent on the production of certain intangible assets such as film originals, computer software and information on mineral resources. (See ABS, *The Australian National Accounts: Concepts, Sources and Methods*, Cat. No. 5216.0, 2000 edition).

By defining *investment* in this way, economists draw a distinction between the act of refraining from spending one's current income today (*saving*) and the act of devoting economic resources today to the purpose of building up real physical assets for use tomorrow (*investment*). A person, or business, or government body that is saving a greater amount this year than they are spending during the same period on investment purposes will be building up holdings of *financial* (or 'paper') assets, or reducing the level of financial liabilities carried into the future, from the past. Arithmetically each period's money has to go somewhere. Saving minus investment must equal an increase in a person or entity's net financial assets position.

Conversely an entity that is spending more on investment than it can cover through its own saving will need to draw down on its holdings of financial assets carried into the present from the past, or incur additional financial liabilities. In this case the money has to come from somewhere. Since every financial asset in existence has to be a financial liability to some counter-party, and vice versa, the net increase in demand for financial assets from those with saving exceeding investment must be matched, dollar for dollar, with the net increase in demand for financial liabilities from those with investment exceeding saving.

When we take the consolidated total of all the investment spending being carried out in Australia by all Australian residents, all resident companies, all Australia's government bodies and so on in a given year, we can compare that figure with Australia's *national saving* in that same year, and immediately see whether as a nation we have needed to draw on loanable funds from the rest of the world in that period - and if so, to what extent.

Chart 1.1 presents the relevant data for the period since 1959, the first year for which ABS quarterly national accounts figures exist. Australia's gross national saving as a percentage of gross domestic product (GDP) is the dark line. Total investment spending in Australia, as a percentage of GDP is the lighter line. It is clear that from the mid 1970s a persistent gap opened up between saving and investment in Australia, with the former falling short of the latter by an average of 4.7 percentage points of GDP over the last fifteen years. While national saving had fallen short of investment spending during the 1960s, except for the odd quarter or two, the gap during that period was smaller, an average of 2.6 percentage points of GDP.

Chart 1.1
National Saving and Total Investment Spending in Australia
1959-2001

Source: Australian Bureau of Statistics, *AusStats*, National Accounts.

Australia's saving-investment 'imbalance'

As explained above the saving-investment gap represents the call for 'outside finance' by the Australian community in the aggregate - public sector as well as private sector, business enterprises as well as the household sector. That aggregate call for outside finance manifests itself in the current account deficit in Australia's balance of payments with the rest of the world. On five separate occasions since the beginning of the 1980s, Australia's current account deficit has spiked upwards to near or above 6 per cent of GDP (see Chart 1.2). Each year Australia's current account deficit is of that dimension, there is a significant increase in the Australian community's level of net financial liabilities towards the rest of the world, and (unless reductions in world interest rates come to our rescue) a significant increase in the overall costs of servicing Australia's net financial liabilities towards the rest of the world.

Chart 1.2
Servicing Australia's Net Foreign Liabilities

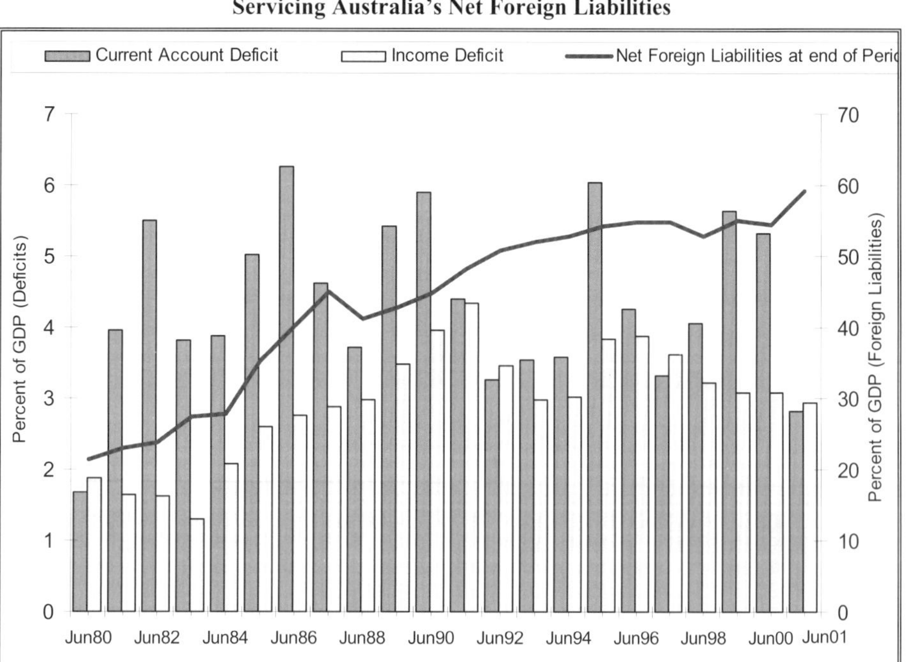

Source: Australian Bureau of Statistics, *AusStats,* Balance of Payments and International Investment.

In the financial year 1999-2000, 57 per cent of Australia's $33.7 billion current account deficit represented the costs of paying interest and dividends etc. on foreign investment in Australia net of the same types of income receipts from Australian investments overseas. Over the three financial years 1995-96 to 1997-98, almost all of Australia's current account deficit had represented these costs - costs which are themselves the direct consequence of previous years' current account deficits, of previous years' shortfalls between Australia's own national saving level and the level of investment spending in our country. See Chart 1.2.

It should be stressed that it is not always a sign of imprudent behaviour for saving to be below investment spending. At the individual level, circumstances can arise where it is appropriate for current purpose (or *consumption*) spending to exceed disposable income in a period, so as to give a *negative* level of saving - which is sometimes termed dissaving. The retiree taking a well-earned and long-planned-for major holiday is one example. A young adult giving up their job for a period to complete an educational qualification, and drawing down savings to hold up their standard of living during that period would be another. A farmer on land prone to drought might have virtually no income in drought years, but needs to spend enough to keep 'body and soul' together (and the farm functional) in those years, using funds shifted forwards or backwards from the better-than-normal years. When the economy as a whole is in recession, it can be appropriate for governments to allow their current-purpose spending to exceed their current period receipts to keep the community as a whole's 'body and soul' together (and the economy functional), again using funds shifted forwards or backwards from better-than-normal years.

But in all of these cases the test of prudence is whether the dissaver can *afford* to be dissaving to the degree observed. Are the savings brought forward from the past plus the level (if any) of future saving that can reasonably be anticipated sufficient to render that dissaving tenable? Sometimes the would-be dissaver and those being asked to provide loans (or to provide more time to repay existing loans) take quite different views on that question. When the lenders take more pessimistic views, and the would-be dissaver is unable to persuade them otherwise, the consequences can range from new debt being only available at higher interest rates (incorporating a loading or 'premium' to assuage the lender's perception of risk), through new debt being rationed by the lender(s) and subject to conditions placed on the borrower's spending behaviour, to more severe consequences such as the refusal of new debt and/or foreclosure. Where a dissaving strategy involves simply the running down of financial asset holdings previously acquired, the would-be dissaver has far greater freedom of manoeuver, far greater autonomy, than when outside borrowings are required. This is sometimes known as 'the golden rule' - those with the gold, rule.

Similar considerations are relevant where saving is positive, but falls short of covering an investment spending programme that the saver has sought to carry through. A young family may wish to build a new house in a particular period, at a cost which considerably exceeds their planned saving in the period of construction, but which they feel confident they can cover by saving out of future years' income. A business enterprise may wish to expand the scale of its operations by installing major new items of plant and capital equipment, at a cost which exceeds the retained profits which the business 'saves' while the expansion programme is unfolding, but which the firm's owners and/or managers feel confident can be covered comfortably out of the additional future profits generated by the expansion programme. A government contemplating a major public works scheme such as a new urban mass-transit system may feel it would be unjust for today's taxpayers to foot the full capital costs 'up front' during the construction phase, and may seek to spread the costs so that future years' tax payers (who are by then enjoying the benefits) share the costs with today's taxpayers.

In these cases too the test of prudence is whether the investor can *afford* to be investing in excess of their current period saving to the degree observed. Are the savings brought forward from the past plus the level of future saving that the investor can reasonably anticipate sufficient to render the investment project tenable? If the investor has sufficient financial asset holdings carried forward from the past to mean that incurring increased financial liabilities is *not* required, the investor is free to be their own judge. It is only their money that is on the line. But if outside financing is required, the lenders (or equity investors if equity type finance is involved) have to be consulted. If they are anxious or worried about the financial figuring, they have to be pacified. They are likely to be the more anxious, the greater the net financial liabilities the would-be borrower is already carrying. If that level is already regarded as high, in the perceptions of the lenders, 'pacification' is likely to require a higher risk-loading in the interest rate, or borrower acceptance of conditions more onerous than those accorded to borrowers who lenders perceive to be low risk.

It is for these reasons that the picture of Australia presented in Chart 1.1 aroused such concern on the part of economic and financial analysts. The gap that opened up between national saving and total investment spending in Australia up to the early

1990s was a matter of our national saving performance slipping rather than investment spending in Australia rising relative to our GDP. If the gap had widened through investment spending in Australia surging upwards and national saving rising only modestly in its wake, it would have been easy to present the likely cause as international recognition of the attractiveness of investment projects in Australia, with overseas wealth-holders happy to buy into Australian assets so as to tap into the benefits (either directly or indirectly) from the expected returns from the new investment spending. But with the increase in Australia's net external liabilities being apparently used to finance additional domestic consumption spending rather than additional investment spending in Australia, the question was increasingly asked during the 1980s: does the saving-investment gap represent an 'imbalance' – some failing in the way the aggregate of Australian saving decisions were being made – suggesting that consideration should be given to possible remedial actions/policies on the part of government?

An issue of public policy?

For economists inured in the profession's intellectual mainstream (the *neo-classical* approach), the appropriate first response to concern raised about reduced Australian national saving levels and a widening saving-investment gap was, it would seem, to throw the question back at those raising it: 'If each Australian entity seeking to incur increased financial liabilities believes it is acting in its own best interests in doing so, and if various overseas wealth-holders are happy to enter into the various arrangements on the basis of their own assessments of the pros and cons, why should any Australian government do anything more than police against fraud and provide appropriate legal frameworks for the handling of default, insolvencies, unconscionable treatment etc?' It is easy to lampoon this type of question as Panglossian, as implying that since, under free markets, we live in 'the best of all possible worlds' why fuss? At another level though, the question is both more interesting and more useful. It forces us to question whether the social framework of late twentieth century/early twenty-first century Australia encourages individuals and families to opt for personal saving levels which, while they might seem the best strategy to each decision-maker taken one-by-one, nevertheless in aggregate turn out to produce a community-wide outcome which is 'sub-optimal' – in the sense that the overall welfare of the community (now and into the future) is held back below where it could be. The process of identifying the sources of any such failures in the free market mechanisms may also assist in pointing to types of policy initiative which might help ameliorate the problem.

This whole issue is considered more thoroughly in Chapter Two. But at this stage it may be useful to foreshadow some of the conclusions of that discussion. Much of the private sector saving occurring in private-ownership free-enterprise economies since such economic systems first evolved, appears to have been driven by the three motives of: personal provision for consumption needs after retirement from work; personal precaution against the financial vicissitudes of life; and reaction to deficiencies in capital markets in the sense of their failing to provide access to loan-funds on 'appropriate' terms as and when required. The spread of State provision of income-support schemes and service-delivery schemes for citizens in need, particularly where such schemes are provided under means-testing arrangements, may have significantly muted the first two of those three motives – especially among persons in that part of the spectrum of lifetime–means where the means-testing might be expected to bite hardest (i.e., neither the poorest nor the most well off). The financial market liberalisation of many countries in recent decades may have significantly muted the third of the three listed motives, with the effects concentrated on those who under previous arrangements would have been most affected by quantity rationing re loans they were demonstrably capable of servicing and repaying: once again neither the poorest nor the most well-off in the community.

With the three motives listed becoming muted in these ways, the asset-holdings to income ratio which the individuals and families in the community choose to maintain is reduced. Other things being equal, in a closed economy that would put downward pressure on the level of the capital stock and consequent upward pressure on rates of return from asset-holding. In an open economy interacting commercially with countries with less well-developed State income-support schemes and less liberalised domestic banking systems, other things being equal the result would be more of your country's capital stock coming to be owned (or debt funded) by citizens of those other countries, and more of your country's GDP being devoted to servicing the associated net external liabilities.

Two further layers of complexity need to be added to the story above. Firstly the preceding paragraphs have implicitly suggested that the State income-support and service-delivery programmes referred to are being run on a pay-as-you-go basis. That means with the public sector *not* altering its net-worth position as members of the private sector reduce their holdings of 'visible' assets in response to being provided with a new 'implicit asset' in the perceived value of the stream of future benefits anticipated from the programmes. If the demographic structure of the community means that the pay-as-you-go arrangements will require higher levels of taxation revenue in the future, at the same time as the future level of citizens' private incomes from asset-holdings is being reduced, this is likely to cause a problem for the society over time, particularly if many citizens' act today on the basis that it is going to be somebody else's problem tomorrow, and therefore make no provision for future increased tax levels.

Secondly there is the matter of the currency a society uses and the foreign exchange value of that currency. When residents in community-X are incurring financial liabilities towards residents of another community (community-Y) and both communities use the same currency, the case for the *caveat emptor*/not-a-public-policy-issue proposition is far stronger than when community X has its own currency issued subject to the control of its own public authorities. In the common currency situation, if more 'foreigners' want to exit their holdings of instruments issued by residents of community X than there are immediate buyers for, the prices are likely to fall: pain is experienced by the vendors; the community X residents who issued the original instruments may face difficulties in making new issues on terms they feel comfortable with; and that is probably as far as the ripples spread. But in the same type of case but with the foreigners seeking to exit instruments designated in community X's currency there is the additional consideration of the downward impact of this on the foreign exchange value of the community X currency. This is likely to affect the perceived attractiveness to foreigners of *all* instruments designated in community X's currency and *all* new issues. It may also have disruptive effects on trade in goods and services between residents of community X and foreigners, where the buyers and/or sellers have any unhedged foreign exchange exposures during the period between production and settlement. The bottom line is that where a community has its own currency, fluctuations in the foreign exchange value of that currency can become a vehicle through which the 'under-saving' actions of some of that community's residents visit external costs across broader segments of the community. There is also the possibility of foreign investors perceiving a community's government as having public finance problems and their assessing a likely response as being an increased willingness by that government to tolerate domestic inflation (and associated currency depreciations). This would be likely to lead to increased risk-premiums becoming built into the prices and yields on all instruments designated in that country's currency. The greater the volume of a country's net external liabilities and the greater its current account deficit, the more scope there is for this type of effect (and volatility therein) to have disruptive effects on the country's trade in goods and services – with consequences which spread to affect virtually all residents.

To sum up, a country's national saving level is likely to pass the neo-classical economists' test for being a public policy issue under either of the following two scenarios: if the government sector's own saving level is incompatible with future levels of taxation and services-provision which the country's citizens/taxpayers regard as acceptable *and* are making private provision for; or if the private sector's saving level is being distorted below the social optimum by some type(s) of market failure, and the government sector's own saving level is not already 'compensating' for this.

The broad statistical picture

We have already noted from Chart 1.1 that a gap opened up in the mid-to-late 1970s between the national saving level and total investment spending in Australia. The gap persisted through the 1980s pushing the level of Australia's net financial liabilities to the rest of the world from 21 percent of Australia's GDP to over 50 per cent by 1991-92 (see Chart 1.2). The major recession of the early 1990s saw the saving-investment gap narrow substantially, but with reduced investment spending the decisive factor behind that outcome (see Chart 1.1). The focus of economic commentators' concern then shifted. It was no longer a matter of: how do we get the current account deficit down to manageable proportions? Instead it became: how do we get investment spending up to levels consistent with long-term community prosperity and reduced unemployment without blowing out the current account deficit in the process? The question had changed but the conclusion remained the same: 'increase the level of national saving'.

During the opening period of the twenty-first century, Australia's national saving level, at around 20 per cent of GDP has recovered by almost five percentage points of GDP from its 1991 low point. But it is below its average level for the 1980s and remains well short of the levels of the 1960s (see Chart 1.1). In a year of depressed investment spending within Australia such as 2000-01, we have sufficient national saving for our current account deficit to raise few eyebrows on world financial markets. But in a period of more buoyant domestic investment activity such as 1999-2000, we still experience a substantial saving-investment gap. Hence Australia's national saving level continues to be an issue, for the same reason it first became an issue in the mid-to-late

1980s. The stabilisation of Australia's net foreign liabilities level relative to GDP since the middle of the 1990s has taken some of the 'heat' out of the issue. But that stabilisation has occurred at a level much higher than that of twenty years ago and with a servicing requirement which now absorbs some 3 per cent of Australia's total GDP each year.

In 1999-2000, the most recent year for which fully detailed national accounts data are currently available, Australia's gross national saving was recorded at 19.7 per cent of GDP. Of that total, some 3 percentage points were contributed by general government sector – meaning the aggregate of those parts of the public sector which operate on a 'non-commercial' basis in the sense of making no direct charges to the users or beneficiaries of their services, or levying only clearly sub-economic (or 'token') such charges. By sub-economic we mean not set so as to recover any substantial portion of their costs of operation. A further percentage point was contributed by business enterprises owned by Australian governments (but excluding financial enterprises). The Australian 'household sector', which includes non-profit organisations which serve persons (e.g., churches, charities, trade unions, etc.) and business enterprises which are not incorporated (sole traders, partnerships and trusts) contributed about 7 percentage points. Non-government owned corporate business enterprises (excluding financial enterprises) contributed 7.5 percentage points. This five-fold breakdown of national saving provided by the current National Account framework, cannot unfortunately be provided for the full period 1959-2000 on a statistically consistent basis, because of various changes that have occurred in National Accounts concepts and methods during that period. A threefold breakdown on a consistent basis *is* however available and that is provided in the three panels of Chart 1.3. The general government sector and the household sector are separately identified but the three 'enterprise' sectors are aggregated together. Investment spending data on this same threefold breakdown are also provided, being the lighter line in each of the three panels.

Panel b of Chart 1.3 is probably the most startling of the three. Total investment spending by the Australian household sector, principally on the construction of dwellings (including extensions and alterations thereto), and on business structures, plant, equipment and stocks for use in unincorporated enterprises has been fairly stable at from around 8 to 11 percentage points of GDP throughout the last four decades. Up to the mid 1980s gross household saving (which includes the Statistician's estimates of economic depreciation on dwellings owned by persons and on the business assets of unincorporated enterprises) averaged about 4 percentage points of GDP more than that. Up to the middle of the 1980s, Australia's household sector cannot be regarded as being directly responsible for the widening of a gap between the nation's saving level and total investment spending. Direct statistical responsibility for that is to be found in panel a, with the general government sector. But from the mid 1980s onwards, Australian household sector saving has edged down. For most of the 1990s it has not exceeded household sector investment spending. In the early 1990s this was not reflected in the aggregate national saving figures because of an upsurge in 'enterprise sector' saving (see panel c of Chart 1.3). During the latter part of the 1990s the general government sector's own saving-investment gap was removed, but the 'enterprise sector': shifted back to a more 'normal' pattern of seeking significant finance from other sectors to cover its investment spending. In terms of the threefold breakdown presented in Chart 1.3, Australia's lower level of national saving at the beginning of the twenty-first century, compared with the 1960s and early 1970s, is statistically the result of reduced household sector saving, and is not *directly* statistically attributable to either of the other two sectors.

Clearly, however, the Australian household sector owns and controls a significant segment of the 'enterprise sector' as defined in Chart 1.3, as does the Australian general government sector. Even where the enterprises operate at arm's length from their legal owners, with salaried managers exercising significant delegated powers and 'autonomy' in day-to-day decisions on investment spending and profit retention versus dividend distribution matters, one would expect some interaction between the saving decisions made by the legal owners of the enterprises and the saving decisions being made 'on their behalf' within the said enterprises. It would be useful therefore if we could convert the threefold breakdown of Australia's national saving developments presented in Chart 1.3 into a two-fold breakdown, consolidating the government-owned portion of the 'enterprise sector' with the general government sector and the remainder of the 'enterprise sector' with the household sector into a more broadly defined 'Australian private sector'.[1]

Such a private-sector/public sector dichotomy would also help us overcome the problem presented by the statistical effects of private business enterprises 'migrating' from the household sector to the corporate sector (and, potentially at least, vice versa) during periods when the relative attractiveness of company structures alters markedly in a society. It needs to be stressed that the distinction in the national accounts between the 'household sector' and the remainder of the private sector provides only a fairly rough guide to trends in saving being carried out at the *personal* level rather than within privately owned business enterprises. It would be attractive if we could split the two apart so that we had the gross saving of the economy's business enterprises separately distinguished from 'true' personal saving. But in practice, the source data from which national accounts are complied do not permit this. Data do exist which allow the ABS to attempt to separate out the activities of *incorporated* business enterprises. But the retained earnings of most small unincorporated enterprises are in practice indistinguishable from the personal saving of the individuals or families who are their proprietors. As far as the National Accounts are concerned, therefore, *gross household disposable income* is defined as gross private sector disposable income minus the gross saving carried out by non-government owned corporations and financial enterprises in Australia. And *gross household saving* is defined as gross household disposable income minus private sector consumption spending.

An important upshot of this is that if something happens in the economy which makes it attractive for previously unincorporated enterprises to transform themselves into companies, then some saving which would previously have been recorded as household saving will start to be recorded as corporate saving. Even with all fundamental economic behaviour unchanged, there would be a tendency under such circumstances for recorded household saving to fall. The introduction of the Australian dividend imputation system in 1987, by removing the traditional 'double-taxation' of company

1 Note that this terminology ignores the fact that some of the enterprises in that sector are overseas owned and controlled.

Chart 1.3(a)
The General Government Sector

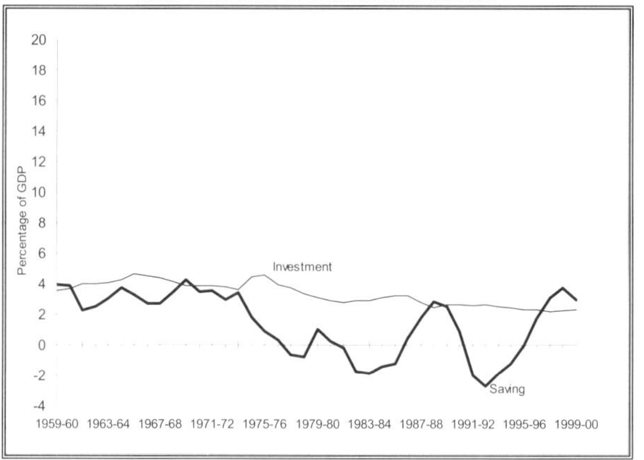

Chart 1.3(b)
The Household Sector

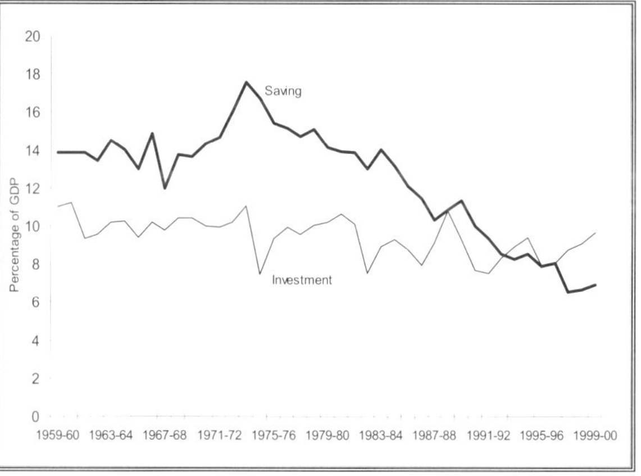

Chart 1.3(c)
The "Enterprise" Sector (Public and Private Combined)

Source: Australian Bureau of Statistics, *Australian National Accounts*.

income, could be expected to have made company status relatively more attractive than it had previously been. The picture is muddied by the fact that removal of the 'double taxation' system's disincentive to company dividend distributions combined with the introduction of the capital gains tax would have caused enterprises already incorporated to reduce their retained earnings as compared to previous behaviour. The 'new incorporations' effect would have boosted recorded corporate saving while the second effect would have worked in the countervailing direction.

The May 1988 announcement of a cut in the company tax rate to 39 cents in the dollar, by opening up a ten-cent gap vis-à-vis the top marginal personal tax rate which the personal income tax cuts announced in April 1989 did little to close, would have provided added encouragement to incorporation and to the retention of company earnings. This process was reinforced by the cut in the company tax rate to 33 per cent from July 1993. Although the company tax rate was raised to 36 per cent with effect from July 1995, and remained thus until 30 June 2000, there has clearly been a significant gap since 1988-89 between the tax rate collected on income directly saved by an Australian company and income saved by top-marginal-rate personal income taxpayers out of income distributed to its proprietors by the same company – or by the same business enterprise operating without the benefit of a company structure.

It is likely therefore that the 1990s may have seen some direct substitution of private corporate sector saving for household sector saving, either through more businesses becoming companies, or through already existing companies holding back more of their proprietors' profit-income, and those proprietors then making adjustments for that fact when determining their own personal saving from the income that *is* passed directly into their hands. This matter was discussed in 'The Measurement of Saving in Australia' in the Commonwealth Treasury's *Economic Round-Up* of Spring 1999 (pp. 21-50), which noted:

> …recent decades have seen a significant trend towards corporatisation by Australian business. This can be illustrated by the steady increase in the proportion of gross profit earned through company structures and the corresponding decline in the proportion earned by unincorporated businesses (p. 27).

Chart 1.4 is an updated version of the diagram used by Treasury to illustrate this point. With such a dramatic shift in the proportion of Australian business enterprise profits from being recorded within the household sector in the National Accounts to being recorded outside that sector, there is clearly the potential for an approach which takes the household saving picture from Chart 1.3 at simple face-value to be misleading.

If we could consolidate the *private* enterprise components of saving and investment spending from the 'enterprise sector' panel of Chart 1.3 with the household sector data that would seem to provide a straightforward means of dealing with this problem. Unfortunately the major changes to the Australian National Accounts methodology which occurred when the new internationally agreed system (SNA'93) was introduced (with effect from the 1997-98 figures) mean that it is no longer possible to derive a private/public sector breakdown of national saving and investment spending directly from ABS data. It is possible to use the ABS data compiled and published under the previous international system (SNA'68) to provide such a breakdown for the period up to 1996-97. But those figures are not compatible with the figures for the more recent period or with the more *aggregate* level national accounts figures published by the ABS for earlier years, which have been revised to render them compatible with the SNA93 methodology. (It is those revised aggregate level data which have been used in Charts 1.1 to 1.4 above). In the 1999 study already referred to, Commonwealth Treasury presented their own 'best estimates' of total private sector saving in Australia for the period 1962-63 to 1998-99 based on assuming the private/public split of financial enterprise saving to be the same in 1997-98 and 1998-99 as it was in the SNA68 figures for 1996-97 and splicing the SNA93 based figures into the long runs of SNA68 based figures.[2] The Treasury figures are reproduced in Chart 1.5. Because the "fixed 1996-97 split" assumption becomes increasingly questionable for each year beyond 1996-97 for which it is employed, we have not sought to update this Treasury Chart.

Chart 1.4
Share of Gross Profit – Corporate and Unincorporated Enterprises

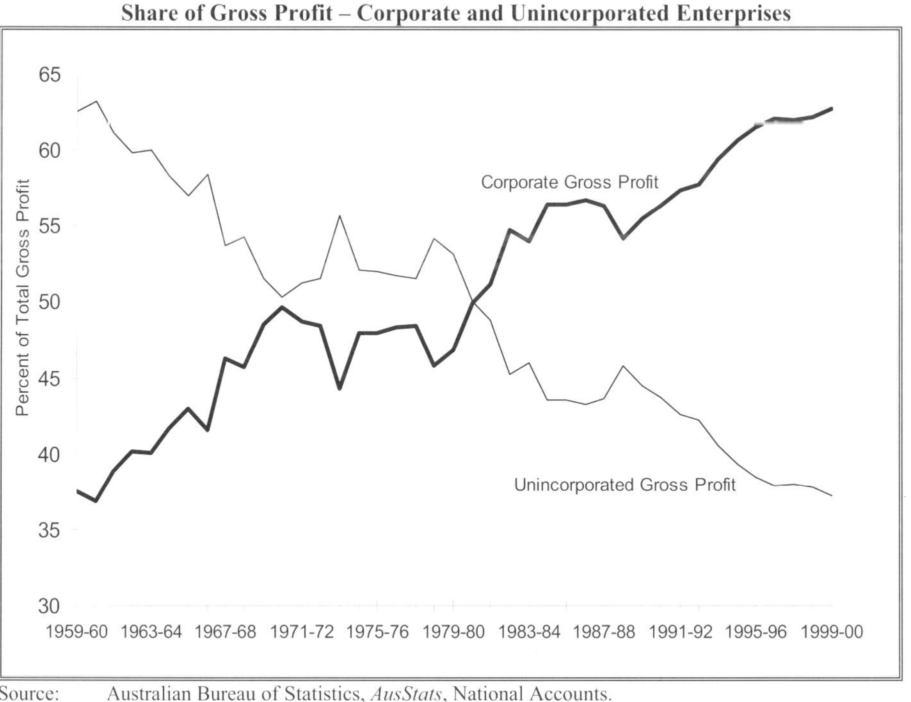

Source: Australian Bureau of Statistics, *AusStats*, National Accounts.

Two points seem to stand out from an examination of Chart 1.5. During the mid to late 1990s the corporate segment of the Australian private sector has been saving at a much higher level than was recorded through the 60s, 70s and 80s, this increase representing around 3 percentage points of GDP per year. But this increase in saving in the corporate segment of the sector has not fully compensated for reduced saving within the "household" segment of the private sector. Compared with the 1960s and 1970s, total private sector saving in Australia as a proportion of GDP in the latter 1990s is down

[2] The methodology is explained further in Appendix A of Commonwealth Treasury *op. cit.* (pp. 44-45), together with comments on limitations therein.

about 4 percentage points of GDP. The decline in total private sector saving since the beginning of the 1980s evident in Chart 1.5 is thus not so marked as the decline in household sector gross saving, particularly in proportionate terms. But a decline is there nevertheless. And as privatisation and related 'outsourcing' developments have progressed, a greater share of the nation's investment spending responsibilities are being borne by the private sector. A greater slice of the nation's profit share from owning and operating business enterprises is accruing to the private sector. Depreciation allowances and retained profits of entities such as the Commonwealth Bank, which for earlier decades would have been part of the public sector, are helping to push up the latest observations for private sector saving in Chart 1.5. On the other hand it could be argued that the Commonwealth Bank (*et al*) would not be operating in such a way as to generate those large retained profits if it had not been for the shift into private ownership. The effects of privatisation on national saving are the subject of a separate chapter (Chapter Six).

Chart 1.5
Components of Gross Private Saving

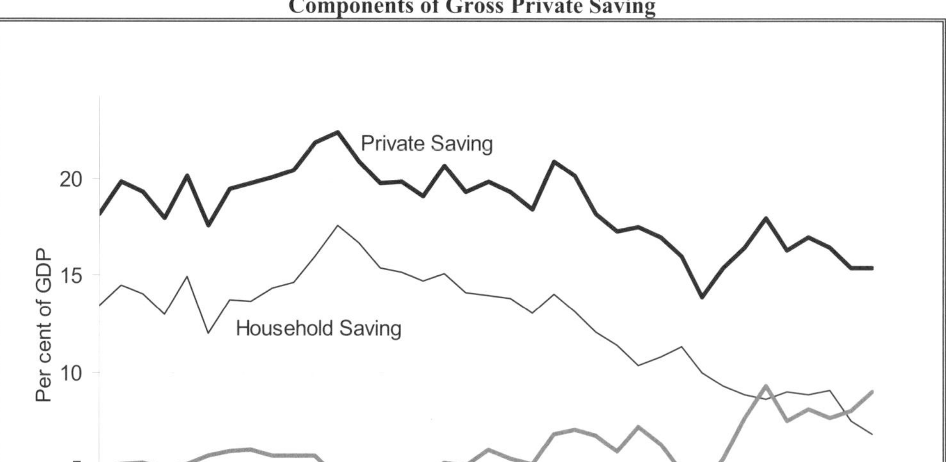

Source: Commonwealth Treasury, *Economic Round-Up*, Spring 1999, p. 31.

From this brief review of the broad statistical picture, it would seem that whereas in the mid 1980s there seemed a *prima facie* case for regarding Australia's reduced national saving level and widened saving–investment gap as the direct result of the Australian general government sector shifting to a lower level of saving, the situation in the more recent period is more complex. Fiscal consolidation strategies across the public sector as a whole (State and Commonwealth), together with a shifting of significant investment spending responsibilities out of the public sector into the private sector, by the late 1990s had lifted the level of general government saving significantly and largely eliminated any *direct* contribution from the public sector to Australia's overall saving-investment gap. Within the private sector, it is personal (or household) decision-making that is crucial in the saving versus consumption-spending choice. Companies may choose to withhold a smaller or greater proportion of their earnings accruing to their shareholders, but if the preference of those shareholders is to spend (and save) different proportions of that money, it is typically available to them to rearrange their affairs to give effect to that preference. If all else fails, they can sell down shareholdings in 'hoarding' companies and/or purchase additional shareholdings in companies with 'generous' distribution policies. Dividend re-investment plans and bonus share plans have made the latter type of approach more administratively convenient for shareholders during the period since the dividend imputation system was introduced in Australia. When shareholders adjust their personal saving/consumption decision in light of the size of the corporate earnings their companies save on their behalf(s), this is know in the jargon of economics as *seeing through the corporate veil.*

How do Australian households save?

The answer many households would no doubt give to this question would be 'with great difficulty'. That answer focuses on the *flow* concept of saving which is a matter of maintaining a gap between one's flow of income over a period and one's flow of consumption spending over that same period, with the level of the former exceeding that of the latter. But there is another dimension to the "how" question which involves: what 'vehicles' for saving are used? what types of asset-holdings make up the household sector's balance sheet? Table 1.1 is an attempt to summarise the main available information on that last question for the Australian household sector as a whole. When SACES first attempted to put together such a table (in 1995, in work for the Australian Credit Union movement) the ABS had not published balance sheet data for Australia's household sector, though it did publish early in 1995 'experimental estimates' of Australia's balance sheet at the nation-as-a-whole level for the years 1989-1992 (See ABS Cat. No. 5241.0). The Reserve Bank had published in the November 1991 RBA *Bulletin* an estimated balance sheet for the Australian household sector as at June 1989, which was juxtaposed with a comparable set of estimates for June 1981. But the RBA has not published revised or updated data since that time. The data prepared by SACES were intended to be an update of the RBA's 1991 methodology, but with an expansion of that approach so as to take account of the assets owned by the household sector through non-corporate business trading enterprises. That category of assets was ignored in the RBA's November 1991 estimates. The ABS does now publish balance sheet data for the Australian household sector as part of the Australian National Accounts (ANA) but the data for physical assets such as houses and for unincorporated enterprises business assets in those ANA tables are not on a market value basis. They are essentially estimates of dollar historical cost adjusted downward for depreciation on the basis of average expected asset lives, with those depreciated figures then adjusted upwards to allow for price increases in 'replacement' assets. For this reason (and for two others explained in the notes to Table 1.1) SACES has used the new ANA balance sheet data directly for the entries in the upper half of Table 1.1, but has attempted to provide market-value basis figures in the lower half. The data for 1989 to 1995 prepared by SACES in 1995 are reproduced in the appendix to this chapter.

The gross saving of Australia's household sector during the course of the 1999-2000 financial year was, according to the Australian national accounts, $43.8 billion. That represented an increment of only 1.9 per cent to total household sector net worth as at June 30, 1999 as reported in Table 1.1. The fact that household sector net worth is recorded in Table 1.1 as having grown by the much greater amount of 11.0 per cent between June 1999 and June 2000 is attributable to three factors: errors and omissions in national accounts statistics for income and consumption spending; errors and omissions in the wealth figures; and holding gains (or losses) on the household sector's assets. It has sometimes been argued that the experience of such holding gains (or losses) impacts significantly on the saving versus consumption decisions made by the household sector. This matter is returned to in Chapter Two. Indeed if a "true and comprehensive" concept of income were being used, these holding gains would form part of that income, and to the extent they are *not* spent, part of the flow of household saving.

The single biggest item in the Australian household sector's balance sheet is clearly net equity in housing. At 30 June 2000 this accounted for some 48 per cent of household sector net worth, down only slightly from the around 49 per cent recorded for 1995. The available ANA data suggest that about four fifths of the personally owned housing stock is owner-occupied. If one assumes the same gearing ratio of owner-occupied housing as for the total personally owned stock (a fairly 'heroic' assumption), it can be said that just under 39 per cent of the Australian household sector's total net worth is held in net equity in owner occupied housing. This is the 30 June 2000 figure. The second biggest "single" item in the household sector's balance sheet is superannuation scheme and life insurance policy assets (including the actuarial value of memberships of unfunded occupational superannuation schemes run by Australian public authorities) which represented almost 25 per cent of total net worth in 2000.

Net equity in housing which is rented out accounts for about 10 per cent of household net worth, about the same as the portion in cash and deposits, and a little ahead of net equity in unincorporated enterprises (9 per cent) and holdings of company shares and units in equity trusts (9.1 per cent). That leaves 2.2 per cent of total household sector net worth as the proportion held in other financial assets (which includes government bonds), and a sum equivalent to about three per cent of household net worth representing (with a negative sign) personal loan liabilities to financial enterprises.

For each $100 held by the household sector in cash and deposit-type-assets at 30 June 2000 some $75 was held in deposits at banks, some $21 at deposit-taking financial institutions other than banks, and a little over $4 in notes and coins. These three categories combined, cash plus deposits at all deposit-taking financial institutions, are usually referred to as monetary assets. The proportion of total household sector net worth held in monetary assets has been drifting downwards. Over the last five years it has fallen by more than one percentage point. This is a trend one would expect to see continue. It explains why Australia's banks have been so keen to move into providing funds-management services more broadly-defined and why they argued during the Wallis Inquiry that the regulatory framework should be adjusted to accommodate that.

Although building up net equity in housing is the single biggest item in the household sector balance sheet for Australia and *ipso facto* in aggregate terms the single greatest vehicle for household sector saving, it should be remembered that additional spending

Table 1.1
The Assets and Liabilities of the Household Sector
($ billion)

	June 1995	June 1996	June 1997	June 1998	June 1999	June 2000
Monetary Assets						
Notes and coin	8.6	8.8	9.2	9.7	9.9	10.6
Deposits at banks	148.3	159.1	171.0	176.8	180.6	185.0
Deposits (other)	30.6	33.4	36.3	44.1	49.1	51.9
	187.5	201.3	216.5	230.6	239.6	247.5
Superannuation & life insurance funds	281.2	314.2	367.3	403.7	450.3	510.6
Unfunded superannuation	104.2	114.6	119.5	122.8	125.8	129.1
Shares and other equity	92.5	93.4	131.7	146.2	193.7	236.7
Other financial assets	33.9	48.7	59.1	57.2	57.0	58.2
Net Equity in Housing						
Dwelling assets	1,017.3	1,058.4	1,110.2	1,229.8	1,341.1	1,518.1
Less Housing loans	-156.0	-173.0	-189.1	-207.6	-229.6	-263.9
	861.3	885.4	921.1	1,022.2	1,111.5	1,254.2
Net Equity in Unincorporated Enterprises						
Uninc. Ents. assets	287.2	287.4	295.3	326.3	343.2	367.7
Less "Other loans"	-56.9	74.1	-83.6	-101.9	-113.5	-133.9
	230.3	213.3	211.7	224.4	229.7	233.8
Less Personal loans	-44.6	-47.9	-52.3	-58.3	-66.5	-72.0
Net Worth	1,746.3	1,823.0	1,974.6	2,148.8	2,341.1	2,598.1
Consumer Durables	103.9	108.7	109.5	114.3	118.9	123.3

Source: The key source for this table is the Household sector balance sheet table from the *Australian National Accounts* (ABS, Cat. No. 5204.0, 1999-00, Table 43). The figures published in that table do not however provide current market price estimates for housing assets or unincorporated enterprise assets (the "produced assets" figures are on what is essentially replacement cost basis); the land which houses stand on is not identified separately from land occupied by unincorporated enterprises; and the household sector's debt liabilities are not broken down between housing debt, personal debt and other. For the entries in the bottom half of Table 1.1 therefore, the following approach was used:

(a) The dwelling assets estimates have been drawn from p. 148 of the article "Australian net private wealth" in Commonwealth Treasury, *Economic Round-Up*, Centenary Edition, March 2001, pp. 137-152. Those figures are on a market value basis and include the land on which the dwellings stand. Three per cent of the Treasury's "total private sector" estimates are excluded in each year to make rough allowance for dwellings owned by private sector companies.

(b) The national accounts figures for the assets of unincorporated enterprises (excluding land) were scaled up using the factors derived from comparing the dwellings figures derived as described in (a) with the national accounts figures for household sector dwelling assets (excluding land). This methodology means that these figures are subject to much greater likelihood of error than the rest of the data presented in Table 1.1.

(c) Data from the Reserve Bank *Bulletin* (Table D2) were used for the housing loans and personal loans rows in the table. Entries in the "other loans" row were derived by subtracting these RBA-sourced figures from the total household sector liabilities estimates provided in *National Accounts* Table 43.

(d) The consumer durables figures were taken from page 148 of the Commonwealth Treasury publication cited in (a).

on the construction of new housing and alterations and extensions to existing houses represents additional investment spending in the economy. Any additional saving via the housing vehicle which was matched dollar-for-dollar by additional investment spending on housing construction would *not* therefore have any direct effect on the nation's saving-investment gap. It is not surprising therefore that successive Commonwealth governments have resisted the argument that a good way to boost Australian household saving would be to make it easier for families to get their hands on enough money to pay the deposit on a house, and to do this by allowing households to draw down their accumulated superannuation savings. Any measure which had the effect of increasing the size of any one of the financial asset entries in Table 1.1 simply by running down one or more of the other financial asset entries by the equivalent amount (or by running up one or more of the financial liabilities entries by the equivalent amount) would clearly leave household net worth and household saving unchanged. And any measure which lifted household saving but simultaneously lifted household sector investment spending by the same amount would leave the household sector's direct contribution to the nation's saving-investment gap unchanged. These points need to borne in mind when we ask what *can* governments do to lift national saving in the next chapter. But before focussing on that question, a brief look at the situation overseas is useful.

How does Australia's saving level compare internationally?

Tables 1.2 and 1.3 provide the data which allow Australia's saving performance to be compared with saving levels and recent trends in saving levels in other countries of the world. Table 1.2 is reproduced from a major OECD report on saving published in late 1994, and provides data for OECD member countries. The OECD secretariat took great care to ensure that these figures as far as possible represent comparable data for OECD member countries. And that 1994 work remains the most comprehensive study of this type. Truly comparable data for countries outside the OECD are typically not available. But Table 1.3 sets out the data that are available for the major Asian economies (excluding Japan, which appears in Table 1.2), as compiled and published by the Asian Development Bank.

Australia's national saving as a proportion of GDP fell by 4.1 percentage points between the average for the 1960s and that for the 1980s (see the last but one column of Table 1.2). Most of that decline occurred between the 70s and the 80s. From Table 1.2 it is clear that the great bulk of OECD member countries experienced declining national saving rates between the 70s and the 80s. Only Norway and Turkey are exceptions. Norway appears to be a special case because of the rapid development of its oil riches during that period, providing a significant surge in national income. Turkey is usually ranked with Portugal as a less mature economy than the bulk of the OECD membership. Portugal is the only OECD member other than Norway and Turkey which is recorded as having increased its national saving level between the 1960s and the 1970s.

From Table 1.3 it can be seen that while the bulk of OECD member countries experienced reduced levels of national saving between the 1970s and the 1980s, the opposite is true of the dynamic economies of East Asia. All eight economies listed increased their national saving performance between the 70s and the 80s, some substantially. And all except Taiwan and Indonesia experienced further increases in their national saving to GDP ratios between their 1980s and 1990s averages.

Focussing on saving levels, Australia's national saving to GDP ratio for the average of the 1980s, at 20.6 per cent, was only a little below the (unweighted) average for the OECD as a whole (21.3 per cent), but markedly below all the East Asian economies listed in Table 1.3. Australia's total private sector saving, at 18.6 per cent of GDP for the average of the 1980s compares with a figure of 20.9 per cent for the average of those OECD member countries with a public sector/private sector dissection of their saving data available. During the opening years of the 1990s, Australia's national saving performance slipped relative to the OECD average (17.9 per cent compared with 20.8 per cent), which means an even wider gap has opened between our national saving rate and the rates of the dynamic economies of East Asia.

It is probably unwise to attempt to read too much into comparisons of the household sectors' saving performance across the various OECD member countries. Different institutional arrangements mean that incorporation is more extensive in the business sectors of some countries than of others. And in some countries retirement income arrangements involve the public sector directly collecting compulsory contributions from workers and their employers, with those contributions *entitling* the relevant workers to receive a pension on retirement, paid to them *by* the public sector. In the OECD's statistical conventions, any national saving which occurs through this route is recorded as public sector saving rather than household saving, even though the households concerned might view their building up of an entitlement to a retirement pension as a form of personal saving.

To summarise the OECD data for the 1980s, Italy has the highest gross private sector saving ratio but its heftily dissaving public sector pulls its gross national saving performance back towards the middle of the pack. At the other end of the gross private saving scale, Iceland is in the opposite position, a strong positive public sector saving level lifting its gross national saving performance up the OECD ladder. In gross national saving terms, Denmark and the U.K. are lowest, Japan and Switzerland highest. On both counts Australia ranks in the middle of the OECD pack, but below the OECD averages. From Chart 1.1 it can be seen that Australia's national saving slid to 15.5 per cent of GDP in late 1991 and has recovered by only about four percentage points since then. The 1993 FitzGerald Report (discussed below in Chapter Four) argued that a national saving goal of 22 to 23 per cent of GDP should be set, and set not just for the peak years of the economic cycle, but for Australia's 'average' performance over the course of future cycles. (See V.W. FitzGerald, *National Saving, A Report to the Treasurer*, AGPS, Canberra, 1993). FitzGerald argued that we need to be a percentage point or so ahead of the OECD average national saving performance because of the greater investment spending needs of Australia's higher population growth, and structurally adjusting, economy – combined with a desire to limit the growth in Australia's overseas indebtedness, and hence the Australian community's exposure to the vagaries of world capital markets. From Tables 1.2 and 1.3 it can be seen that FitzGerald's goal is not intended to put us among the world's high-flyers in terms of national saving.

Table 1.2
Gross Saving as a Proportion of GDP
OECD Countries

	Average in the 1960s	Average in the 1970s	Average in the 1980s	Average 1990-1992	Change between the average in the 1980s &: Average in the 1960s	Average in the 1970s
Australia						
National of *which*	24.7	24.1	20.6	17.9	-4.1	-3.5
Public	--	2.8	1.9	--	--	-0.9
Household	--	13.2	10.9	--	--	-2.3
Corporate	--	8.1	7.7	--	--	-0.4
Austria						
National of *which*	27.7	28.0	24.3	25.8	-3.4	-3.7
Public	7.2	6.2	2.7	2.5	-4.5	-3.5
Household	5.4	6.2	6.4	8.4	1.0	0.2
Corporate	15.1	15.6	15.2	14.9	0.1	-0.4
Belgium						
National of *which*	22.4	23.1	16.9	21.3	-5.5	-6.2
Public	1.2	0.0	-6.0	-4.3	-7.2	-6.0
Household	9.8	15.1	13.1	15.3	3.3	-2.0
Corporate	11.4	8.1	9.7	10.3	-1.7	1.6
Canada						
National of *which*	21.9	22.9	20.7	15.4	-1.2	-2.2
Public	3.6	2.7	-1.4	-3.1	-5.0	-4.1
Household	7.8	10.4	12.2	10.7	4.4	1.8
Corporate	10.5	9.7	9.9	7.8	-0.6	0.2
Denmark						
National of *which*	23.3	20.9	15.4	18.6	-7.9	-5.5
Public	--	5.4	0.4	-0.1	--	-5.0
Household	--	--	--	--	--	--
Corporate	--	--	--	--	--	--
Finland						
National of *which*	25.4	26.7	24.2	17.3	-1.2	-2.5
Public	7.3	9.0	7.3	3.6	0.0	-1.7
Household	6.4	7.3	7.6	8.2	1.2	0.3
Corporate	11.6	10.3	9.3	5.4	-2.3	-1.0
France						
National of *which*	26.2	25.8	20.5	20.7	-5.7	-5.3
Public	--	3.6	1.4	1.2	--	-2.2
Household	--	13.6	10.2	8.7	--	-3.4
Corporate	--	8.5	8.7	10.6	--	0.2
New Zealand						
National of *which*	21.2	22.2	20.1	18.1	-1.1	-2.1
Public	--	--	--	--	--	--
Household	--	--	--	--	--	--
Corporate	--	--	--	--	--	--

Table 1.2 (Continued)
Gross Saving as a Proportion of GDP (OECD Countries)

	Average in the 1960s	Average in the 1970s	Average in the 1980s	Average 1990-1992	Change between the average in the 1980s &: Average in the 1960s	Average in the 1970s
Norway						
National of *which*	27.4	26.8	27.7	23.5	0.3	0.9
Public	6.5	7.9	8.6	--	2.1	0.7
Household	--	5.9	4.1	--	--	-1.8
Corporate	--	12.7	15.0	--	--	2.3
Portugal						
National of *which*	23.1	26.0	24.3	25.9	1.2	-1.7
Public	--	-0.4	-1.7	--	--	-1.3
Household	--	--	25.4	--	--	--
Corporate	--	--	0.6	--	--	--
Spain						
National of *which*	24.7	25.5	21.1	20.9	-3.6	-4.4
Public	--	--	0.4	--	--	--
Household	--	--	8.6	--	--	--
Corporate	--	--	11.9	--	--	--
Sweden						
National of *which*	24.0	21.1	17.7	16.5	-6.3	-3.4
Public	--	--	2.1	--	--	--
Household	--	--	3.1	--	--	--
Corporate	--	--	11.9	--	--	--
Switzerland						
National of *which*	29.4	28.6	28.5	30.2	-0.9	-0.1
Public	4.5	3.9	3.6	1.2	-0.9	-0.3
Household	7.9	8.9	9.1	--	1.2	0.2
Corporate	17.1	15.9	15.8	--	-1.3	-0.1
Turkey						
National of *which*	14.8	17.1	19.3	19.8	4.5	2.2
Public	--	--	--	--	--	--
Household	--	--	--	--	--	--
Corporate	--	--	--	--	--	--
United Kingdom						
National of *which*	18.4	17.9	16.6	13.8	-1.8	-1.3
Public	3.6	2.6	0.5	-0.1	-3.1	-2.1
Household	5.4	6.2	6.2	7.1	0.8	0.0
Corporate	1.7	9.2	10.1	6.7	8.4	0.9
United States						
National of *which*	19.9	19.6	17.7	15.1	-2.2	-1.9
Public	1.9	0.4	-1.9	-2.9	-3.8	-2.3
Household	9.3	10.7	10.6	9.1	1.3	-0.1
Corporate	8.7	8.5	9.0	8.9	0.3	0.5

Source: OECD, *Taxation and Household Saving*, OECD, Paris, 1994, pp. 21-24.

Table 1.3
Gross Domestic Saving as a Ratio of GDP
Selected Asian Countries

	Average 1971-80	**Average 1981-90**	**Average 1991-2000**
China, People's Rep	32.5	33.7	40.3
Hong Kong	27.5	30.5	32.0
Indonesia	22.6	31.8	29.6
Korea (Rep. Of)	22.3	31.8	34.8
Malaysia	30.4	33.2	41.4
Singapore	30.0	42.3	49.5
Taipei, China (Taiwan)	32.2	32.9	26.0
Thailand	21.5	24.5	33.4

Source: *Asian Development Outlook*, 1991, 1998, 2001.

Appendix to Chapter One

The Assets and Liabilities of the Household Sector
SACES 1995 Estimates ($ billion)

	June 1989	**June 1990**	**June 1991**	**June 1992**	**June 1993**	**June 1994**	**June 1995**
Monetary Assets							
Notes and coin	6.2	6.6	7.5	7.6	8.1	8.9	9.3
Deposits at banks	99.5	115.4	117.9	122.5	136.4	146.8	149.4
Deposits at NBFIs	29.9	30.5	31.2	32.1	25.8	27.4	29.2
Other Financial Assets							
Public sector securities	9.2	7.4	6.7	4.4	4.5	3.6	4.6
Other interest-bearing	29.0	32.2	35.1	27.5	21.2	21.9	24.2
Superannuation & life ins.	138.1	156.4	168.7	190.2	204.0	218.9	231.0
Equities and units in trusts	61.0	58.6	55.1	69.1	93.0	117.2	113.1
Other	6.5	2.3	10.0	1.9	0.7	9.0	16.1
Net Equity in Housing							
Dwelling assets	743.9	787.1	820.1	844.9	884.8	967.2	991.9*
Less housing loans	-63.3	-74.8	-81.5	-91.3	-109.6	-134.8	-155.8
	680.6	712.3	738.6	753.6	775.2	832.4	836.1*
Net Equity in Unincorporated Enterprises							
Uninc. Ents. Assets	133.6	134.5	125.2	129.2	126.5	148.4	165.4*
Less 'other loans'	-51.0	-59.7	-63.5	-64.1	-63.0	-56.4	-57.5
	82.6	74.8	61.7	65.1	63.5	92.0	107.9*
Less Personal Loans	-44.8	-44.6	-42.3	-40.5	-40.4	-41.3	-44.8
Net worth	1,097.8	1,151.9	1,190.2	1,233.5	1,292.0	1,436.8	1,476.1
Memorandum Item: Consumer durables	79.5	86.0	90.0	93.1	97.8	102.7	n.a.

Notes: * The 1995 entries in these rows were imputed by adding 1994-95 gross investment to the 30 June 1994 stock of relevant assets (i.e., assumes away valuation changes and depreciation).

Source: Covick. O. and B. Vickers (1995), *Saving in Australia, A Report to the Credit Union Services Corporation (Australia) Limited*, South Australian Centre for Economic Studies, October.

2 What *Can* Governments do to Lift National Saving?

Owen Covick

Governments can act to boost the public sector segment of national saving *directly* by altering the settings of budgetary policies towards reduced current purpose outlays and/or increased current revenue raising. Provided the private sector does *not* respond to reduced government spending by increasing private spending dollar for dollar, and to increased government revenue raising by reducing private saving dollar for dollar, increased public sector saving should boost overall national saving though one would have to expect there normally to be some partial offset from private sector behaviour. That then leads to the question: are there any available types of policy initiative which could be expected to be effective in raising private sector saving? In order to answer that question we need first to ask *why* it is that people save. Only then can we sensibly consider what changes in circumstances would induce them to save more.

Why do people save?

'Consumption – to repeat the obvious – is the sole end and object of all economic activity'. Thus wrote Keynes in *General Theory*, chapter 8. If one defines 'consumption' sufficiently widely this statement is true but is a tautology. If one defines 'consumption' in the more everyday sense of *using up* available purchasing power, either now or in the future, in order to satisfy wants and needs (or to provide satisfaction or "utility", to use economists' jargon) one has to recognise that utility or satisfaction can sometimes be generated in other ways. Devoting one's labour to producing things often generates satisfaction or utility in its own right (i.e., over and above the utility from "consuming" the produced items oneself or consuming items bought from the sales proceeds of those items). In a similar way the possession of wealth can often generate a flow of satisfaction over and above any consumption services of the usually-recognised types that directly flow from the assets (spending the pecuniary yield, living in the house etc.), or from contemplation of the enjoyment of the future "consumption" of goods and services to be expected from exercising the spending power of that wealth. The outright miser simply enjoys counting and re-counting the dollars. The less eccentric derive pleasure from the freedom which wealth gives from the petty tyrannies of employers, landlords, bank managers, etc. Beyond some point freedom from the tyrannies of others merges into the ability to exert power, and perhaps exact various tyrannies on others, oneself. Perhaps also possession of a certain level of wealth affects how a person believes other people perceive them, and 'relate to' them. The level of 'respect' a person believes other members of their society have for them may be an important source of the satisfaction/*utility* they derive from life. Being perceived to be behaving well towards the members of one's family may represent an important part of that. Being perceived as the person who has created or built up the value of a widely-known asset (or even just as the good 'steward' who prevented the value being run down) may also play a role. These types of factors can lead individuals (or at least *some* individuals!) into viewing the accumulation of private wealth as an 'end and object of economic activity' distinct from and additional to *consumption* in the everyday sense of the term. It is, of course open to economists to define 'consumption' for the purposes of their studies sufficiently broadly so that the sentence at the beginning of this section is true. But then that statement does not seem to advance things very much, and may simply serve to mislead those who have not been 'let in' on the broadness of the definition.

In this book, we shall stay (except where specifically stated otherwise) with the definition of consumption (and hence of saving) which is embodied in the national accounts statistics discussed in Chapter One. It follows that one possible motive for some people's personal saving is the *direct utility from wealth* motive. Setting aside this motive for further discussion later, there appear to be three principal motives for saving which *are* consistent with consumption in the everyday sense of the term being the prime object of economic activity. Firstly there is the need to accumulate from current income the purchase cost of naturally lumpy items of consumption outlay – such as cars and other major consumer durables, weddings, trips to Europe etc. Such accumulation can precede the outlay, or can take the form of paying off in succeeding periods debts run up at the time of the outlay. Either way, it is saving.

Secondly there is a precautionary saving. In some occupations (farmers, entertainers, stockbrokers etc.) the inevitable but unpredictable ups and downs of life render it prudent to save from the income of the good times to even out for the lean The same applies to those working in industries in which a drying up of customary overtime, or short-time working, layoffs, redundancy and unemployment might be expected to occur in the face of cyclical downturns, disruptions from industrial disputes, sudden shifts in consumer fashions etc. Precaution against disruption to one's family finances from ill-health, accident, being a victim of crime or of natural catastrophe and so on also comes under this heading. Once again such saving can precede the occasions of *dissaving* (or negative saving) to which it relates – in this case the 'rainy days' – or it can take the form of paying off debts run up to cope with those rainy days. It can also take the form of paying regular insurance premiums - where the relevant insurance cover is available. Finally there is saving to provide for a reasonable standard of living after one's retirement - when current income from working can be expected to have largely dried up. Biology largely dictates that this third type of saving has to *precede* the period of dissaving to which it relates. The risk that one might live for a longer period after retirement than one had expected means that a precautionary cushion may be consciously built into this type of saving. Alternatively life annuities provide a means of insuring against this *longevity risk*.

Especially with the first of these three motives there will be a tendency over the course of any given period for the positive saving of some families to be matched by the equal and offsetting corresponding negative saving of others. For every ten families saving one tenth of the cost of a given lumpy outlay in a given period there is likely to be one actually making that type of outlay, thus generating the equivalent dissaving. This broadly applies provided economic circumstances are 'normal' (discussed further below). An interesting conclusion follows. A society which adheres to a very strict ethic that lumpy consumption outlays should always be financed by pre-saving will have exactly the same community saving-to-income ratio generated from this motive as a society handling the same volume of lumpy outlays via the alternative approach of post-saving or debt repayment. Transition from one community ethic to the other would alter the saving ratio during a transition period, however. And as it did so the ratio to income of the aggregate stock of net private savings assets held from this motive would shift.

The second motive, precautionary saving, provides the main explanation of *changes* in the private saving-to-income ratio from one year to the next. In years of economic boom, there is more saving taking place *for* a rainy day. In economic slumps there are more people experiencing a rainy day and consequently dissaving. The statistical record, both in Australia and overseas, shows that this effect usually overwhelms the tendency for people to defer postponable durable goods purchases when the economic outlook appears bleak and to bring forward such purchases when prospects look bright. Hence the sharp falls in the private saving ratio during the last two recessions (see Chart 1.1) and the subsequent increases in the ratio as the economy recovered. If we could statistically 'adjust' our figures for the effects of cycles of booms and recessions we would expect to find that most of the aggregate private saving occurring as a precaution against the effects of such cycles would disappear. Like the first type of saving it would net out to zero across the community and across time, for 'average' or 'normal' economic circumstances.

The interaction between the precautionary motive for private saving and the availability of voluntary-purchase private-enterprise-organised insurance cover is complex. If a person was certain that event x was going to happen to them *sometime* in their lifetime, impose a cost with a present value of $z on them at the time it did (with the timing of this unknowable), and with that representing a 'handle-able' amount in terms of their expected lifetime income from all sources, a little economic arithmetic would produce the following two conclusions: Firstly if the person were confident they could always borrow 'handle-able' amounts of money at roughly the same interest rate they can earn on their financial asset holdings, the person would be exactly as well off spreading the cost of the $z evenly across their lifetime, making positive personal saving of the appropriate fraction of that amount period by period, as they would be by buying 'actuarially fair' insurance; Secondly if part of the community took the one course and the rest took the other course, the overall saving of the community and the overall net financial assets to income ratio would be the same no matter what the breakdown was between the self-insure and the pay premiums segments. The greater a person's fear that they would not be able to borrow 'handle-able' amounts of money on reasonable terms, the greater the incentive *either* to plan to build up precautionary financial asset holdings sooner rather than later, *or* to be willing to pay 'actuarially unfair' insurance premiums for the relevant cover. Under those circumstances the greater the portion of the community opting to purchase insurance contracts of a given degree of actuarial unfairness, the smaller will be the community's overall net financial assets to income ratio even though the community's steady-state saving level is unaffected. If the available insurance cover were to become more actuarially fair, one would expect a transitorial period of reduced overall community saving as the net financial assets to income ratio shifted to a lower level, as more people took up the available insurance.

There is more to the story, however, than this. Some of the potential occurrences against which individuals would like to take economic precautions are such that if they did occur, the cost imposed by them on the individual would be very large relative to their expected lifetime income from all sources, quite possibly exceeding that. The subjective probability assessment made by an individual of the likelihood of such an event occurring to them, combined with their degree of aversion to risk might mean they are willing to pay for insurance cover at premium levels actuarially unfair to them in some given degree *if such cover is available*. But in an absence of such insurance cover being commercially available, there is in these circumstances no conceivable individual saving strategy that can act as a substitute. One could conceive of circumstances in which an individual's fear of this type of financial ruin led to a fatalistic 'spend-now', live-for-today personal economic strategy – involving the minimising of their personal saving and of their personal net wealth holding. Under those circumstances the opening up of opportunities for the person to buy the relevant insurance cover could mean that on taking up the cover there is an *increase* in their personal saving and personal net assets holdings outside the context of that insurance policy. If the insurer draws from the premiums to build up reserves against the risk of future claims this will represent a second boost to community saving generated by the inception of that insurance. There is of course another possibility – that those persons living in terror of financial catastrophe from uninsurable risks, instead of adopting the 'live-for-today' response, become hoarders – trying to build up the personal wealth holdings that would at least mitigate the full force of the feared catastrophe. If a sufficiently large proportion of the community were behaving in this way, the advent of insurance against the feared but previously uninsurable catastrophic risks (or the fairer pricing of such cover) could cause community saving to fall.

And the complications concerning the interaction between the precautionary saving motive and insurance do not stop there. When a financially catastrophic event afflicts a member of a community there will often be some sort of 'rallying-around' either by charitable-minded individuals or by more formal community organisations (including those funded from taxes), to ameliorate the lot of the victim(s). If there is a perception among the community that a person is more likely to be treated generously in such circumstances, the *smaller* the level of their net asset holdings, this might act as a disincentive toward the personal accumulation of such net asset holdings (particularly among those of modest overall means). It might also create an incentive to hold one's net wealth in some asset categories rather than others, if the means-testing arrangements treat some categories more generously than others. Under this type of scenario one can see how the introduction of legal compulsion to take up insurance against certain risks might alter these incentive patterns in a way that increased the overall level of community saving. But what if the compulsory insurance arrangements involve major cross-subsidies such that some persons are required to pay premiums only a small fraction of the 'actuarially fair' rates, with insurance reserves run down and liabilities to pay claims during future periods *accrued* now but not fully-funded? Once a type of insurance cover is made legally compulsory, the types of market forces one would normally expect to generate pressure towards 'actuarial fairness' and full-funding seem to become muted. (For further discussion of this matter, see Owen Covick, 'The Treatment of Casualty Insurers in the Australian National Accounts' paper presented to the 24th Conference of Economists, Adelaide, September 1995.)

Abstracting from these complications associated with the interaction of the precautionary motive with a society's prevailing insurance cover arrangements, it would seem reasonable to argue that it is the saving-for-retirement or *life cycle* motive (together possibly with *direct utility* effects) to which we must look in order to explain the *level* of the private saving to income ratio that prevails in a country on the average across macroeconomic cycles. It was for his work in this field that Franco Modigliani of the Massachusetts Institute of Technology (MIT) was awarded the 1985 Nobel prize. In the words of two other specialists in this field: 'The celebrated life-cycle saving hypothesis holds that aggregate savings arise because the dissaving of the retired population is exceeded by the saving of the more numerous and prosperous young' (Lawrence Summers and Chris Carroll, 'Why is US National saving so low?', *Brookings Papers on Economic Activity*, 2, 1987, p. 625). There is continuing debate about the extent to which the retired *consciously plan* to make bequests as distinct from leaving bequests as a by-product of factors such as precaution against living longer than expected. See for example William G Gale and John Karl Scholz 'Inter-generational Transfers and the Accumulation of Wealth', and the references cited therein, *Journal of Economic Perspectives*, Vol. 8, Fall 1994, pp. 145-160. And considerations regarding the *bequest motive* are clearly important to analysing the effect of inheritance taxes, and of possible changes in such taxation arrangements. But that is probably incidental to the main issue here. The level of the aggregate private saving to income ratio for an economy such as Australia's, smoothed for cyclical effects, is viewed by professional economists as overwhelmingly the result of decision making by persons of mature working age to accumulate wealth on a long-term basis with a view either to spending the money themselves in their retirement years, or to passing it on to their heirs as bequests.

The bottom line of this is that left to individual choice the level of the aggregate private saving to income ratio, smoothed for cyclical effects, depends mainly on the following types of factors: the number of years of retirement people expect to live for relative to the number of years they expect to spend in paid work; the extent to which national saving for retirement is handled via government-levied contributions and government-organised and administered pensions; the perceived strength of the *direct utility* effect from holding wealth in one's twilight years (i.e., the feeling of independence it gives and/or the power to secure satisfactory behaviour from one's children, grandchildren, carers, etc.); and the age structure of the population.

On the face of it, however, the four factors cited above do not seem to provide much scope for policy intervention aimed at boosting the private saving ratio. The last two of the factors are largely outside the hands of the government – though immigration policy could possibly provide some limited scope for boosting the proportion of the population in the highest saving age cohorts. Strong economic and social reasons unrelated to national saving exist for increasing the retiring age (or abolishing compulsory age-retirement altogether) rather than reducing it. And once a system of government-provided income support for the aged has been in existence for any lengthy period, policymakers in a democratic system face major constraints on any attempts to wind that system back. We return to government retirement incomes policy below, but another issue needs to be addressed first.

Increase the 'reward' for saving?

Most non-economists seem to think it would be straightforward for the government to induce the private sector to increase its *saving*. All that is needed is a 'carrot', they declare. And the 'carrot' usually consists of reducing the income tax levied on interest income. In the decade or so of popular debate on the saving issue in Australia, a variety of schemes have been put forward. Behind all these proposed schemes is a common thread of argument which can be summarised as: interest, after tax and adjusted for inflation, is the reward for saving; inflation causes the tax rate on real interest to be very high - possibly over 100 per cent; an increase in the after-tax real rate of interest will cause national saving to rise. Of these three statements the second is clearly valid. A taxpayer with a marginal tax rate of 50 per cent who received interest at a nominal interest rate of 8 per cent will be paying an *effective* tax rate of 100 per cent if the inflation rate were 4 per cent. The first and third of the statements require closer attention.

Interest is not the reward for *saving*. Interest is the reward for holding your *savings* in one form rather than another - in a bank account for example, rather than in the bricks and mortar of your own home, or in company shares etc. For the bulk of Australians the principal vehicles for long-term saving are paying off the house mortgage and accumulating superannuation scheme entitlements. Both these vehicles are accorded tax treatment which means the interaction of the inflation-compensation element of interest payments with the personal tax scale is of no relevance to the saver. Since capital gains were taxed on an inflation-adjusted basis from 1985 until indexation was 'frozen' in late 1999, this factor was also irrelevant to saving via company shares, real estate or building up the value of one's own business during that period. Under the new capital gains tax arrangements introduced from 21 September 1999, this continues *in essence* to be the case, provided there is no substantial increase in the rate of inflation. Nor is the inflation factor relevant if your saving takes the form of paying off consumer debts.

The upshot is that a proposal such as exempting from income tax the first $1,000 per year of interest income, or introducing special tax-exempt bonds, could be expected to have more effect on the mix of vehicles in which the nation's pre-existing stock of *savings* was held, than on the level of the flow of new *saving* being made. Those of reasonable net wealth who previously held very little in bank accounts would be provided with an incentive to shift some of their existing wealth into that form. Those of reasonable net wealth who previously had already been earning $1,000 p.a. in interest would be provided with no incentive to adjust their behaviour at all. Interest income subject to personal income tax can thus be regarded at most as the reward on only a portion of saving. Whether acting to lift that reward could be expected to have *any* effect on national saving is the next question to address.

Commonsense suggests that if after-tax real interest rates were to rise, this would make holding interest-earning assets a more attractive proposition and would induce households to substitute dollars away from current consumption and into saving. Similarly a drop in real after-tax interest rates would appear likely to cause households to save less. But there is more to this than meets the eye. Interest rate changes, as well as having a *substitution* effect as described above, have an *income* effect also. Tax breaks which increased after-tax real interest rates would increase the incomes of those individuals who are net creditors and would allow them to enjoy both more current spending and more current saving. If these gains were pushed mainly into current spending, it is quite possible for this *income* effect to outweigh the earlier *substitution* effect and give a reduced saving-to-income ratio. For net debtors the story is different, but in the aggregate the household sector of the economy is a net creditor.

Couched in terms of the three principal motives for saving discussed earlier: the higher the long-term rate of reward on saving is expected to be, the lower the proportion of current income which today's workers need to save to attain a given standard of living in retirement; the higher the return on saving the less of one's income one needs to save in order to obtain a given cushion of comfort from the precautionary motive; and the higher the rate of return the less current consumption you need to forgo to *pre-save* for a lumpy consumption outlay such as a car or overseas trip. Working in the opposite direction, higher interest rates make *pre-saving* relatively more attractive vis-à-vis *post-saving*, providing a tendency for durable goods purchases to be postponed and an incentive for the building of more sizeable precautionary cushions.

Careful study of the statistical record suggests that the *income* and *substitution* effects of changes in the reward for saving largely cancel each other out as far as the overall private sector saving ratio is concerned. Modigliani, in his review of the evidence, stated this as his 'provisional view' pending more convincing general evidence ("Life cycle, individual thrift and the wealth of nations", *American Economic Review*, June 1986, pp. 297-313). Other writers appear more convinced. A 1988 study by the Office of the Economic Advisory Council (EPAC) reported: 'Empirical research has not demonstrated any strong influence of rates of return on saving behaviour, except possibly in respect of short term effects of high interest rates on durable goods purchases' (*Trends in Private Saving*, Council Paper No. 36, Canberra, 1988). Summers and Carroll stated: '...the experience of the 1980s certainly creates doubt about the ability of economic policy to raise private saving by increasing the returns available to savers' (*op cit*, p. 625).

In November, 1994, the OECD published a major study *Taxation and Household Saving*, which re-examined the available evidence in this field. The study concluded:

> There is no clear evidence that the level of taxation, along with other factors affecting the rate of return, does generally affect the level of household saving.
> ...While a new tax relief for a particular type of investment may not affect the overall level of household saving, it is likely to increase saving in that type - particularly by those with higher incomes. If in fact overall saving remains largely unchanged...saving must decrease in other assets... An attempt to restrict tax relief to 'new' saving is likely to be very difficult to enforce.
> ...some of the schemes which are the most 'successful' in terms of take-up may well reduce total national saving, because they indicate that different forms of saving taxed at different rates may be close substitutes, rather than that consumption is easily reduced.

A summary of the findings of this OECD study was published in the Commonwealth Treasury's *Economic Round-Up* of December 1994.

The question of whether the present tax treatment of interest (and other forms of income from asset-holdings) is socially inequitable is considered further in Chapter Three. The question of whether the present tax treatment leads to distortions in decision-making, and allocative inefficiency is discussed in Chapter Four.

Compulsory saving

In discussing above *why* people save, we were careful to state that we were talking about the situation where people are able to act on the basis of their own individual choices. It is a fact of life however, that the market for loans is not like the market for potatoes. Before you can receive a loan you have to satisfy the lender that you are an acceptable risk, under the given loan terms. Where individuals whose personal rational choice it is to go into debt (to consume now and pay later) are prevented from doing so by lenders saying no, this clearly causes those individuals to incur lesser levels of financial liabilities than would otherwise be the case. Other things being equal that means that overall household (and national) saving is higher than it otherwise would be. Where individuals seek to alter the future behaviour of would-be lenders by demonstrably accumulating holdings of financial assets - when their first preference would be to go immediately into debt – this is likely to reinforce that result. In the jargon of economics these are called *imperfect capital markets* effects, or *liquidity constraint* effects. A more subtle form of the effect occurs when members of one generation deliberately set out to hold greater levels of financial assets than they believe they themselves directly need, in order that they can act as guarantors of loans for members of the next generation(s) of their families, who would otherwise be subject to liquidity constraint problems.

The bottom line is that many in our society are saving more than they would prefer (or *dissaving* less than they would prefer) as a result of the way our lending institutions operate. That is true today. But it was true to a much greater extent before the financial deregulation of the 1980s. Thus financial deregulation has been identified as one of the main factors responsible for many countries recording lower private saving ratios during the last twenty years or so than they had in the pre-deregulation period. The way financial deregulation has worked to reduce the private saving ratio is essentially that it has brought about a shift from pre-saving to post-saving (or debt repayment) in a number of areas of lumpy outlay - an important one of which is the purchase of one's first home. It needs to be stressed that these effects of a shift from pre-saving to post-saving on the *flow* of saving are transitional, as was explained earlier. The private saving ratio would be expected to recover (other things being equal) as transition to the new financial market situation becomes complete. In the new "steady-state", the stock of savings is lower relative to the income level, however. Nevertheless it remains true that a turning back of the clock on the regulation of credit arrangements would boost the private saving ratio - albeit only over a 'transitional' period.

Since most economists would regard that as a retrograde step the conclusion that is often drawn is that in seeking to lift national saving there is little a government can do that is 'prudent and reliable' other than to run 'chronic budget surpluses' and hence lift directly the public sector component of national saving. The Commonwealth Government accepted even while the 1990-92 recession was at its worst, the objective that its Budget be returned to surplus as the economy recovered from that recession. The Commonwealth government also embarked on a package of initiatives in the 'retirement incomes policy' area, which it believed would be effective in raising the private sector saving ratio over time. Foremost among these is compulsory superannuation, enforced by the Commonwealth through the *Superannuation Guarantee Charge* (SGC) legislation. To quote from *Budget Statement No.2* of 1994:

> Central to the Government's strategy of increasing national saving is the restoration of public saving. ...Private saving is more difficult to influence with public policy, especially in the near term. However, the Superannuation Guarantee is aimed at boosting private saving over time by extending superannuation more widely throughout the community.

The announcement that the SGC would be introduced with effect from 1 July 1992 was made in the August 1991 Budget. The SGC legislation provided for a prescribed minimum standard of employer superannuation contributions with this set to rise in stages to 9 per cent of each employee's wages or salary by July 2002. On top of this employer 9 per cent, in the May 1995 Budget the then Commonwealth government announced its intention to implement measures which would see a further 3 percentage points of each worker's wage/salary income compulsorily saved, with this additional 3 percentage points phased in over the period 1997 to 2000. The change of government following the March 1996 federal election meant that this additional element of compulsion was not brought into being.

The SGC is essentially a device for sidestepping the fact that the Constitution does not give the Commonwealth Government the power to make laws to compel employers to make contributions to superannuation schemes for the benefit of their employees. Under the SGC, the Commonwealth Government does not attempt to make such a law. Instead, it merely lays down a prescribed minimum standard of employer contributions and legislates for the imposition of a new taxation charge (the SGC) on any employers who do not satisfy that prescribed standard. The dollar value of the charge is equivalent to the cost of having met the prescribed standard (plus an adjustment for interest). But paying the charge is rendered less attractive than meeting the standard by the charge being non-deductible for income tax purposes. The same approach to sidestepping constitutional constraints on Commonwealth powers had been used from 1990 until its 'suspension' in 1994 with the Training Guarantee Levy. The purpose of the TGL had been to compel each employer to meet a prescribed level of expenditure on government-approved training programmes for their workers. The device embodied in the TGL withstood the test of High Court challenge. In the superannuation context, the Government's announcement of its intention to use this device followed the decision by the Industrial Relations Commission in the April 1991 National Wage Case, rejecting the ACTU's claim for a second round of 3 per cent employer superannuation contributions to be implemented via the *award* mechanism. That claim had been supported by the Commonwealth Government as part of its Accord Mark VI agreement with the Australian Trade Union movement.

In order to satisfy the SGC requirements, the superannuation entitlements building up through the prescribed employer contributions must be such that they remain the property of the employees if the employees leave their jobs (this is called full *vesting*).

But the employees must not be able to get their hands on that money and be able to spend it until they are over a prescribed age and retired (this is termed full *preservation*). One final important feature of the SGC policy is that the scheduled increases in employer superannuation contributions were *intended* not simply to be *add-ons* to the wage increases that would have occurred without the SGC. Rather the Government's *intention* was that they should substitute for the equivalent quantum of increases in more direct forms of pay. While the Accord arrangements were in place, the Australian Trade Union movement was committed to public support of that position.

The bottom line then is that the SGC is a programme designed to compel virtually every Australian wage and salary earner each to save at least a defined minimum from their overall remuneration from working, to save that money via approved superannuation funds, and to lock-up that saving in those funds until they reach retirement at or above a prescribed age (currently 55, but to rise to 60 by the year 2025). Some of the workers affected by this new compulsion may have been assuaged by the feature of the SGC which makes it appear that it is the employer who is being compelled to do something rather than the employee. But it was the *intention* of the SGC that those additional payments it requires employers to make should be fully offset by workers forgoing some of the pay rises they would otherwise have received directly. And even if that had not been the *intention*, the theory of markets suggests it would be the likely effective outcome anyway. This matter is discussed further in Chapter Five.

What effect can this new compulsion be expected to have had on national saving? According to some commentators, very little. Employees already in superannuation schemes with employer contribution rates at or above 9 per cent have been unaffected. And among employees directly affected by the SGC, those who were happy with their pre-SGC level of personal saving would face an incentive to respond to the SGC by saving correspondingly less through other saving vehicles, or by arranging deeper levels of personal and housing debt and/or slower rates of repayment of such debts.

But this argument overlooks the situation of those affected by the *imperfect capital markets* effects, or *liquidity constraint* effects, discussed above. A worker in that position and affected by the new compulsion of the SGC would *not* have been able to offset its effects through alterations to their non-SGC saving behaviour. In a 1991 study of this issue, FitzGerald and Harper concluded:

> There is a variety of evidence that low to middle income earners have very limited financial savings against which to substitute their superannuation saving. Their main saving is in the form of increasing equity in the family home... In other words for most households, particularly those with low to middle incomes with limited borrowing possibilities and limited savings, consumption is pretty much constrained by current income. Therefore for such households, any scheme of forced saving is likely to lead to increased net saving... Accordingly we believe that a net increase in aggregate private saving is a very likely result.[1]

---

1 V.W. FitzGerald and I.R. Harper, "Super preferred or 'level playing field', implications for saving and the financial system", paper presented to the Third Annual Melbourne Money and Finance Conference, Sebastopol, Victoria, December 1991.

More recent empirical work into the extent of apparent liquidity constraint effects on Australian households has suggested that about one third of the gross effect of the SGC is likely to be offset by adjustments to non-SGC saving.[2] While an offset of that order means the SGC can be expected to have a significant effect in terms of raising national saving, it does not automatically follow that the SGC represents good policy. Some might reasonably object to a system of compulsory superannuation being introduced in what is otherwise an increasingly market-oriented economy. Others might object that the people who the SGC actually *does* compel to save more are often people who 'shouldn't' be thus compelled - for example young couples with families and mortgages, and without well-off parents to act as loan-guarantors, or to borrow from. The new compulsion of the SGC, it could be argued, impacts most heavily on those who financial deregulation was supposed to benefit by freeing from the 'old compulsion' of loan rationing.

There is a possible counter-argument to such propositions about the 'social injustice' of the now compulsory saving. Chart 2.1 depicts the type of diagram economists typically use to analyse personal decision-making about allocating current period income between saving and consumption. The individual's expected lifetime is simplified into just two periods: a 'current period' in which an income from working of y_1 dollars is received and a 'future period' in which income from working is assumed to be zero. The decision problem facing the individual is to divide current period income between current period consumption (C_1) and current period saving ($y_1 - C_1$). Income which is saved attracts a rate of return of i so that the amount of future period consumption (C_2) which can be enjoyed is $(1+i)(y_1\text{-}C_1)$. The individual obtains satisfaction/utility from both current period consumption and future period consumption with the levels of such utility being depicted by a family of indifference curves (with $U_4 > U_3 > U_2 > U_1$ in the diagram). The utility maximising behaviour of the individual is to opt for the (C_1*, C_2*) position in the diagram – that being the point in the set of feasible choices (the triangle between y_1, the origin and $(1+i)y_1$) which yields the highest utility level. This is the type of diagram usually used to bring out the point made earlier about the income and substitution effects of an increase in the reward for saving. It is possible (indeed very easy!) to draw Chart 2.1 in such a way that when i increases (so that $(1+i)y_1$ shifts to the right) the new optimal choice involves higher levels of *both* c_1 and c_2 - implying a *lower* level of current period saving.

When a means-tested government-provided old-age pension is introduced into this type of analysis, the individual's choice set ceases to be a simple triangle and becomes the more complex shape depicted in Chart 2.2. If the person saves none of their current period income and enjoys current period consumption (c_1) at the level y_1, they can now have a consumption level equal to the old age pension rate (p) in the future period. This strategy is represented by point a in Chart 2.2.

Most means-testing arrangements allow a person to have some modest level of private means and still receive a full pension. In the diagram this 'free' (of means-testing) amount is denoted by f. A person can save some amount from current period income

[2] See O. Covick and B. Higgs, "Will the Australian Government's Superannuation initiatives increase national saving?". Paper presented to the 24th Conference of Economists, September 1995.

and earn *i* on that amount to provide spending power of *f*. They can then enjoy a future period consumption level of (*p*+*f*). This strategy is represented by point *b* in Chart 2.2.

If the individual opts for a saving level which (after interest) provides more than *f*, this triggers some claw-back in the amount of pension provided by the government. The slope from *b to d* reflects how 'tight' (or 'harsh') the claw-back rate in the means testing arrangement is. If it were dollar-for-dollar the *bd* section would be a vertical straight line. At point *d* the person is making current period saving exactly sufficient to preclude them from receiving *any* old age pension. Any decision to make additional saving above that level thus sees no further claw-back of pension occur – the consequences for future consumption of the choice would be the same as in Chart 2.1.

Looking at the shape of the choice set in Chart 2.2, it is easy to imagine the "corner" represented by point *b* touching an indifference curve representing the highest level of utility available to the individual. This will be the more likely to occur the more generous the level of *p* and *f* relative to the individual's pre-retirement income level, and the harsher the claw-back rate in the means-test.

A government programme aimed at assisting people to have satisfactory living standards in retirement might have the effect of causing some individuals to have worse living standards in retirement than if the programme did not exist at all. As depicted in Chart 2.2 such an individual is still better-off overall with the programme existing than without (a higher indifference curve is achieved) but Chart 2.2 has not attempted to depict the tax imposts levied on individuals in order to pay the pensions. Once this factor is introduced it is possible to imagine circumstances in which the effect of a means-tested old age pension programme of the type depicted is to reduce the community's current period saving, and to do so in a way which causes the overall welfare of the community (as measured by individuals' own utility levels) to be lower than it could be.

Chart 2.1
The Saving-versus-Consumption Decision

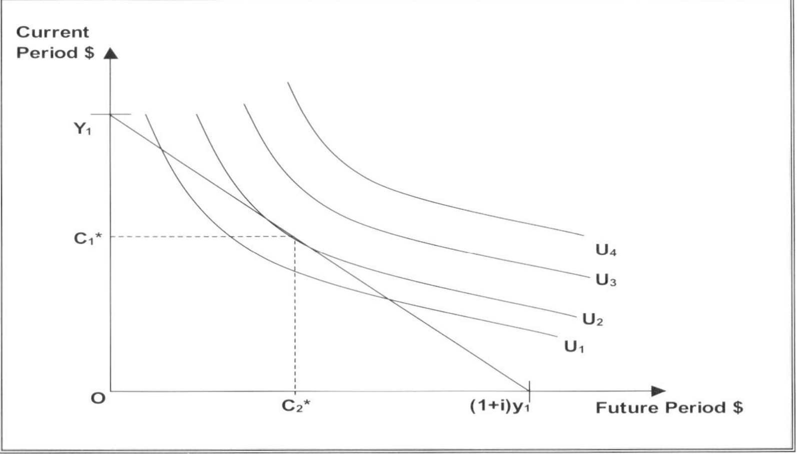

Chart 2.2
The Saving Decision with a Means-Tested O.A.P.

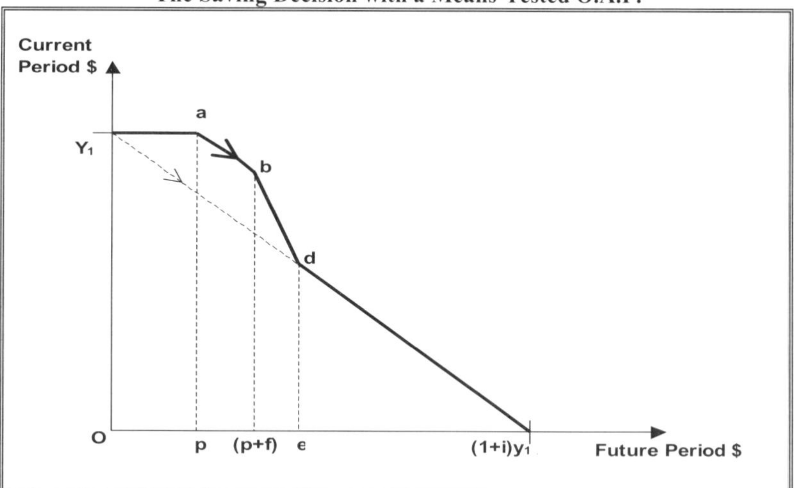

It may nevertheless turn out to be the case that a programme of this type is the only available way of providing socially acceptable post-retirement-age living standards for those in society with very very low pre-retirement incomes. A way of achieving this social justice goal while *at the same time* preventing the programme having the adverse consequences described in the preceding paragraph might be to add a new feature: a compulsory minimum private saving requirement for those who are *not* on *very very low* pre-retirement incomes. Under these circumstances, an interesting possibility arises. Chart 2.3 takes the diagram presented in Chart 2.2 and inserts a horizontal line at

Chart 2.3
The Saving Decision with a Compulsory Minimum

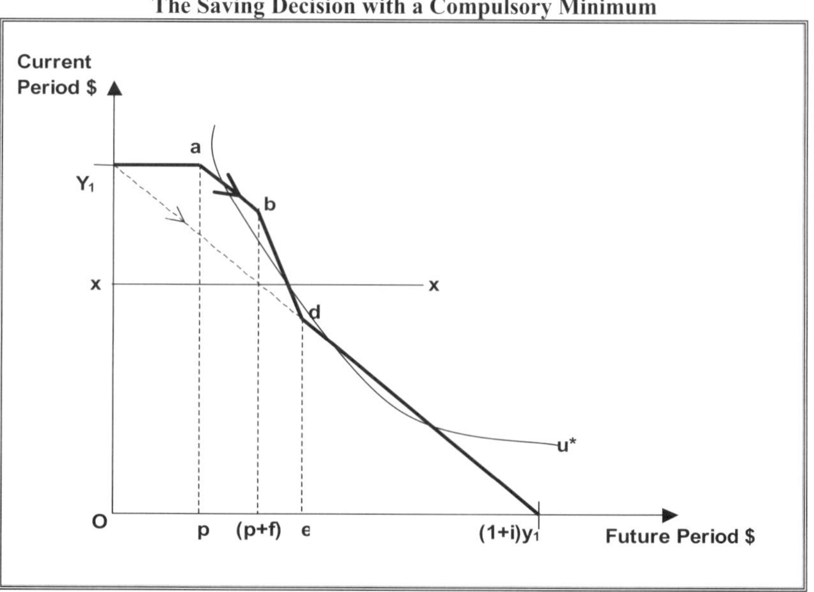

xx indicating the government-mandated compulsory minimum saving requirement. If the individual simply undertook that minimum quantum of saving, their utility level would be U*. But in Chart 2.3 they can attain a higher level of utility by undertaking some additional *voluntary* saving, over and above the compulsory minimum. It has traditionally been regarded by economists as something of a paradox when they have observed cases of compulsory saving apparently inducing persons to make additional voluntary saving which takes them to overall levels of saving beyond those which would have prevailed in the absence of any compulsion. (See Green (1981) and Green (1984) and references cited therein). It may be that complexities in the shapes of choice sets resulting from means-testing arrangements are the cause. But it could also result from liquidity constraints (if the fruits of the compulsory saving are completely inaccessible for a long period and thus do not adequately substitute for voluntary saving in helping combat such constraints) or from some sort of habituation (or 'addiction') effects. Habit effects are usually scoffed at by mainstream economists as requiring a conception of human decision-making that is at odds with *rational choice*. The final section of this chapter examines this further.

Policies other than compulsion

As was noted above, among professional economists the standard way of thinking about private sector saving behaviour is in terms of Modigliani's *life cycle* approach, modified for liquidity-constraint effects where appropriate - and sometimes for bequest-motive effects. In the context of that way of thinking, and with income and substitution effects from altering the general *rate of reward* from saving assessed as largely cancelling each other out, most professional economists are skeptical about the scope for policy initiatives to succeed in lifting national saving other than through the channels of direct public sector surpluses, or compulsion.

But the *life-cycle* approach does have its critics as an explanation of observed private sector saving behaviour. Writing in the prestigious *Journal of Economic Perspectives* in 1987, Richard Thaler stated:

> The life-cycle theory assumes that individuals solve for the optimal consumption plan, and then execute it with will of steel. In real life, people realise that self-control is difficult and so they take steps to constrain their future behaviour. One method is to take irreversible actions, such as joining a pension plan, or buying whole life insurance. ... The other method is to adopt internally enforced *rules of thumb*. Examples of such rules are: keep two months' income in [a reserve] account; do not borrow except to make durable goods purchases such as a house, car, or major appliance. Note that households following the latter rule might appear to be liquidity constrained, *unable* to borrow, whereas they are actually *unwilling* to borrow.

Thaler's approach brings together two ideas. The first is the idea that to act on the basis of a *habit* one has adopted *can* be more efficient than to attempt a rational thought process on each and every occasion when an option to act arises. As Hirshleifer wrote in the *American Economic Review* in December 1985:

> *Habit* is surely a way of economising on scarce reasoning ability. Indeed, in many contexts habit may be faster and more accurate than thinking; no-one can play the piano or drive a car effectively without engaging in a host of complex unthinking actions. (p. 61)

Thaler then pairs this with a second idea, based on there being more than one 'self' within each individual. In a 1989 paper in *Journal of Economic Perspectives* (with George Lowenstein) he asked rhetorically:

> Who is sovereign, the self who sets the alarm clock to rise early, or the self who shuts it off next morning and goes back to sleep? It is instructive that we normally see the far-sighted self take actions which constrain or alter the behaviour of the myopic self. Dieters pay money to stay on 'fat farms' ... smokers buy cigarettes by the pack (rather than by the carton which is cheaper).

Thaler sees the adoption of habitual ways of behaving in the saving/spending sphere as a means by which the far-sighted self can constrain the behaviour of the myopic self (or selves). The role of *habit* in saving/spending behaviour is something which earlier leaders of the economics profession had given more prominence than has been the case during the last thirty or forty years.

Irving Fisher, a leading force in America's economics profession during the early decades of the twentieth century, stressed the role of 'impatience' in determining saving.

> Impatience differs with different persons for the same income and with different incomes for the same person. The personal differences are caused by differences in at least six personal characteristics: (1) foresight, (2) self-control, (3) habit, (4) expectation of life, (5) concern for the lives of other persons, (6) fashion.
> (*The Theory of Interest*, p. 81)

Fisher went on to elaborate on the roles of the listed six personal characteristics. His comments on the second and third are relevant here:

> ... The effect of a weak will is similar to the effect of inferior foresight.
> ... The influence of habit may be in either direction. When those habituated to luxury suffer a reverse of fortune they often find it harder to live moderately than do those of equal means who have risen instead of fallen in the economic scale; and this will be true even if foresight and self-control are inherently the same in the two cases.
> ... Our thrift campaigns are designed to reduce impatience by cultivating certain habits of regular saving out of income. (pp. 83-84)

These types of arguments have been used by a number of economists to explain why statistical studies often show saving through different saving vehicles to be complementary activities, rather than substitutes. The British economist Francis Green has written extensively in this area. In the March 1991 issue of *Journal of Economic Issues*, he stated:

> The argument is reinforced by a ... proposition taken from behaviouralist psychology, which is that effort is intensified the closer one is towards one's goal.
> ... The idea is that if the attainment of a reasonable target level of retirement income seems remote, little effort will be made to approach this level, but that if the goal comes into sight and appears both concrete and attainable then people are stimulated to save in order to achieve it.

Economists have traditionally been skeptical about the capacity of campaigns of 'public education' to alter people's behaviour on any lasting basis. But the various writings cited in this section suggest that economists should perhaps think again regarding public education initiatives to lift private sector saving. Individuals may need assistance to develop a picture of their economic futures, and about the pros and cons of various behaviours for making their saving/spending decisions. Individuals may need assistance to ease themselves into habits which limit the risk of their making spur-of-the moment decisions which undermine their own longer-term preferred strategies for dealing with their financial circumstances. And individuals with no previous experience of holding wealth of any significant dimensions may need to be regularly reassured that they *can* succeed in implementing personal financial plans - at least up to the point where it is clearly evident that they are succeeding. Community organisations such as credit unions would appear to have a natural role to play in these types of initiatives. The ratings of the Channel 9 television programme *Money* would suggest that many Australians are keen to learn more about such matters of personal finance.

3 Policies on National Saving: Equity Considerations

Owen Covick and Beverley Vickers

Since the late 1960s, the Australian Bureau of Statistics has regularly conducted sample surveys of the Australian population in order to construct official estimates of the distribution of household income, and cross-tabulations of household income with various other household characteristics. But none of those surveys have sought to collect data on household net wealth, or the asset and liability types comprising it. Indeed the ABS has not sought to collect or publish official estimates of household net wealth since the wartime Wealth and Income Census of 1915. When the Australian Labour Party (ALP) won the Commonwealth election of 1983, it had as one of its policies the establishment of a national inquiry into wealth holding in Australia. This may have been inspired by the Diamond Royal Commission which Harold Wilson's government had established in 1975 to inquire into wealth in Britain. But whatever the original inspiration, the Hawke government's motivation apparently waned, and no such national inquiry was carried out in Australia. The upshot is that although the Australian Bureau of Statistics has an international reputation as a statistical agency that is second to none, our data on wealth distribution, wealth composition etc. across the Australian population lag behind what most other western developed economies have available.

The Commonwealth government's Retirement Income Modelling (RIM) Task Force has sought to address this data problem, mainly by attempting to *infer* figures on household wealth from other bodies of data, such as data on household income generated by income-earning assets and estimates of average yield levels on various broad asset types. Table 3.1 presents the data for wealth distribution across the Australian population as a whole, as estimated by the RIM Task Force on this basis from the ABS survey of income distribution for the year 1989-90. The bottom row of the table indicates that in 1990, Australians aged 16 and over held on average $9.1 thousand of 'ordinary' (or interest-bearing) savings, about the same value in equities, and $54.8 thousand invested in their own home. Note that these figures exclude many types of asset (such as equity in superannuation funds and life insurance, assets in unincorporated enterprises, shares in non-dividend-paying companies, cash) and net off only home mortgage liabilities.

Nevertheless, these data provide a valuable guide. The bottom 30 per cent of Australians aged 16 and over hold very little wealth at all, and the little they do hold is held in 'ordinary savings'. The next 10 per cent (decile 4) of wealth-holders have wealth holdings totalling on average a little over 60 per cent of their annual incomes, and hold some 43 per cent of that wealth in ordinary savings, and virtually all the rest in equity in their homes. Each of the next three deciles of wealth holders going up the wealth spectrum holds fewer dollars in ordinary savings than decile 4, and more in home equity - while still keeping largely clear of company equities. Only in the top 20 per cent of the wealth-holding population do holdings of equities start to become significant, with their significance sharply escalating within that top 20 per cent. Somewhere near 5 percentiles from the top, company equities holdings overtake holdings of interest bearing assets. It seems probable that higher still, within the top two percentiles, they overtake equity in the home.

Table 3.2 presents the same RIM data, but this time on an age group by age group basis. Total wealth-holding, as identified in the RIM approach, rises rapidly with age up to the 45-54 age group and then essentially plateaus. Many mainstream professional economists would find the over 65s figure surprisingly high, as the life-cycle theory of saving behaviour discussed in Chapter Two predicts the retired to run down their assets as they age so as to be able to enjoy higher levels of consumption spending than their post-retirement incomes can cover. To some extent the over 65s figure is probably a statistical artifact. Where one member of a retired couple dies and passes the bulk of their assets to their surviving spouse, this would tend to increase the 'average' wealth of the survivors. And the fact that the RIM approach fails to identify assets being accumulated in superannuation funds, but does typically succeed in identifying the assets once the super fund has handed the money over to the individual, would also work to disguise any underlying 'hump' in life cycle wealth-holding. Nevertheless Table 3.2 provides added support to the view that direct utility from wealth-holding and/or the desire to make bequests are important factors in explaining saving behaviour (see the discussion of this in Chapter Two).

Table 3.1
Distribution of Assets by Wealth Quantiles
All Australians Aged 16 and Over, 1990 ($ thousands)

Wealth Quantile	Total Annual Income	Estimate of Ordinary Savings	Estimate of Equities	Estimate of Equity in Home	Total Identified Wealth
0-09%	13.5	0	0	0	0
10-19%	15.1	0.1	0	0	0.1
20-29%	18.5	1.1	0	0	1.1
30-39%	19.9	5.2	.3	6.8	12.3
40-49%	19.3	3.2	.3	30.2	33.7
50-59%	18.3	3.5	.3	44.9	48.7
60-69%	18.9	4.7	.4	59.1	64.3
70-79%	19.5	7.3	.7	75.4	83.3
80-89%	20.1	13.7	1.7	102.3	117.8
90-94%	24.6	24.4	6.6	143.9	175.0
95-98%	32.8	56.6	60.6	199.2	316.5
99-100%	77.1	126.1	527.2	535.0	1,189.1
ALL	19.7	9.1	9.1	54.8	73.0

Source: Data supplied by Retirement Income Modelling (RIM) Taskforce; Commonwealth Treasury Building, Canberra.

Table 3.2
Distribution of Assets by Age Group
All Australians Aged 16 and Over, 1990 ($ thousands)

Age in Years	Total Annual Income	Estimate of Ordinary Savings	Estimate of Equities	Estimate of Equity in Home	Total Identified Wealth
16-24	14.5	1.6	0.7	7.2	9.5
25-34	21.7	3.6	6.5	29.2	39.3
35-44	24.9	6.9	12.3	62.7	81.9
45-54	23.9	9.3	17.6	78.0	104.9
55-64	17.6	17.6	8.0	79.7	105.3
65+	11.0	20.6	8.3	81.3	110.2

Source: Data supplied by Retirement Income Modelling (RIM) Taskforce; Commonwealth Treasury Building, Canberra.

Table 3.3 provides a more detailed picture of life-cycle wealth-holding in Australia. It is taken from work at the National Centre for Social and Economic Modelling (NATSEM) at the University of Canberra, published in 1998. This study took as its starting point the ABS data from the 1993 survey of income distribution and sought to make estimates of the asset categories missed out in the RIM figures – principally assets in superannuation schemes. The NATSEM figures focus on households rather than individuals, categorising households by the age of the oldest member. But as the figures are presented on an 'average assets per adult' basis, the surviving spouse effect referred to above would be present in the later rows of this table in the same way as in Table 3.2. The basic picture from the total wealth column is still one of personal net wealth holdings rising rapidly with age up to the early 50s and then essentially plateauing. The level of housing debt per adult is at its highest in households recorded in the 30-34 age group. In the next two rows we see the level of housing debt remaining fairly unchanged but the gearing represented by this falling as a higher gross value of housing is held. The housing debt level and the gearing it represents then both diminish age-group by age-group from the mid 40s upwards. Superannuation fund assets peak in the 50-54 age cohort, holdings of other non-interest bearing assets (principally company shares, units in unit trusts, and unincorporated enterprise net assets) somewhat earlier.

Holdings of company equities according to both tables appear to be concentrated in the 'middle aged' age groups. The category 'interest-bearing assets' rises with age. The fact that the elderly hold less in company shares than the middle-aged may indicate a greater degree of aversion to risk among the elderly. Or it may indicate a reduced willingness to devote time and energy to the management of a share portfolio. Note though that the equities column in Table 3.2 and the 'other assets' column of Table 3.3, to a greater extent than the other columns, are dominated by the behaviour of the highest wealth-holders in each age group. If the wealthiest 10 per cent of 45-54 year-olds are excluded from Table 3.2, the remaining 90 per cent have average holdings of equities of less than 500 dollars. That same 90 per cent of 45-54 year-olds' average equity in their homes is $36.0 thousand.

Table 3.3
Household Assets by Type and by the Age Cohort of Oldest Household Member
Average Assets per Adult: Australia 1993 ($'000)

Age Group of Oldest Member	Housing Gross	Housing Loans	Housing Net	Interest Bearing Assets	Superannuation Assets	Other assets	Total Wealth
15-20	0.7	0.3	0.4	1.2	0.7	0.4	2.8
21-24	4.2	2.4	1.8	4.0	4.2	4.7	14.7
25-29	20.8	10.4	10.4	3.6	10.7	8.9	33.6
30-34	39.6	15.9	23.6	4.9	16.4	13.8	58.7
35-39	53.5	14.9	38.6	6.9	23.5	16.4	85.3
40-44	77.0	14.9	62.1	9.5	29.6	31.1	132.2
45-49	79.7	12.8	66.8	11.4	35.1	22.1	135.4
50-54	76.9	7.2	69.7	16.6	39.9	29.4	155.6
55-59	73.5	4.4	69.1	14.8	23.9	26.9	134.7
60-64	80.4	2.2	78.2	23.6	15.9	21.3	139.1
65-69	80.1	0.4	79.7	36.1	8.0	17.7	141.4
70-74	82.3	0.5	81.8	28.9	7.8	12.9	131.4
75+	88.3	0.2	88.1	42.8	8.0	7.6	146.5

Source: Baekgaard, H., "The Distribution of Household Wealth in Australia, 1986 and 1993", National Centre for Social and Economic Modelling, Discussion Paper No. 34, University of Canberra, 1998, p. 27.

The fact that the highest wealth-holders hold their wealth in quite different ways to the great majority of the population in economies comparable to Australia, but with better wealth data, is well-known. Professor Tony Atkinson, in his highly-regarded survey of wealth in Britain (*Unequal Shares*, Penguin Books, 1974) wrote: 'The most striking difference was in the proportion of wealth held in company securities (quoted and unquoted). Over a third of the wealth of the man [sic] owning £250,000 or more was in this form.... The wealth of those in the bottom 90% was much more likely to be in the form of cash, bank deposits, building society deposits, and an owner-occupied house' (p. 30).

It makes sense for those with the lowest levels of wealth-holding to concentrate their attention on holding assets which can quickly, easily, and cheaply be converted into cash, and where you can feel confident that any attempt to convert quickly into cash will not trigger capital losses. That points the finger to deposits available at call (or on short notice) with banks or readily-accessible non-bank deposit-taking financial institutions. The rate of return on such deposits is likely to be low. But to obtain a higher return is almost certain to involve a situation where if encashment is suddenly and unexpectedly required, this is going to cause problems - perhaps delays and 'shoe leather' costs, or penalty charges, or the acceptance of 'firesale' prices for quick release into cash - perhaps some combination of all three. The lower and the more precarious your income is, and the greater your fear of unexpected and urgent spending requirements, the less rational it becomes to opt for return rather than risk-minimisation and liquidity.

There is an important exception to this broad-brush generalisation. In the paragraph above we have implicitly assumed that the level of income a person derives from working during their working years is largely *independent* of the mix of assets they opt for (including the amount of borrowings they incur in order to hold particular gross levels of various asset types). This is probably true for the roughly four out of five Australian workers who supply their labour as employees to employers which are at 'arms length' in the sense of not being close relatives, family-owned companies, family trusts or the like. The employee worker may need to hold some of their wealth in essential tools of their trade or profession, but apart from that, how they choose to hold their wealth probably has little significant interaction with their capacity to earn one level of labour income rather than another. This is typically *not* the case among the self-employed. One *can* find cases of self-employed people producing and supplying goods or services without any significant levels of tangible business asset holdings (the freelance writer or entertainer for example) or using only assets which they rent on short term operating leases (some taxi drivers). But across the broad bulk of the self-employed (and those who are 'employees' of family-owned companies, partnerships or trusts) the usual pattern is for production and income to be generated by the simultaneous supply of self-employed labour and self-employed capital with it being practically impossible to distinguish a quantum of labour income and a quantum of 'income-from-business-assets-holdings', which simply add-up together to a person's total income from self-employment.

The upshot of this is that many persons and families reliant for their labour incomes on the operation of self-employment based enterprises cannot sit down and make decisions on the mix of assets and liabilities to deploy their net wealth across without taking into account the interaction of this decision with the income level that can be expected to be generated by their labour. Under such circumstances it seems likely that some persons and families in this situation would judge that to achieve a 'satisfactory' level of overall income from self-employment requires them to hold large levels of *gross* business assets in their enterprises relative to their total net wealth positions, but that they are nevertheless willing to tolerate the associated 'distortions' in their balance sheets away from what (focussing on the balance sheet alone) would seem a prudent mix of assets and a prudent gearing ratio between debt liabilities and those assets. The likelihood of this happening would be greater where the persons making the decisions felt that their labour could *not* easily be redeployed into employee-status work with arms length employers at reasonable pay, congenial conditions, minimal family social upheaval etc. Where the perception was that major problems on these fronts would accompany any attempt to opt against self-employment status, a person might be willing to tolerate virtually their entire wealth being tied up in highly illiquid high-risk and very low return assets in their own business, basically to 'buy' jobs for themselves (and possibly for other close relatives). If being seen by other members of one's community to be in employment was a sufficiently strong motive, an individual might even be willing to pay dearly for such a job even though the income it generated was low and the work uncongenial and/or unhealthy. This is almost certainly a significant social problem in today's Australia, although our lack of data on the incomes and asset holdings of the self-employed makes this hard to investigate. It is discussed further in Owen Covick 'Self-Employment as Disguised Unemployment', in T. Lange (ed.), *Unemployment in Theory and Practice*, Edward Elgar, London, 1998.

When the SGC compulsory saving system was introduced in 1992, the self-employed were left outside the arrangements, except to the extent they have the legal status of employees of family controlled companies, trusts or partnerships. This was largely a byproduct of the Accord origins of the SGC which naturally focussed on employee remuneration, together with the nature of the legal device used in that legislation to render the 'compulsion' constitutional (see Chapter Two). The FitzGerald Report recommended that the compulsory minimum standard of superannuation contributions system should be extended to cover the self-employed, but the Government did not take up that recommendation (see 'FitzGerald Report on National Saving: release of Dr FitzGerald's policy proposals and government response', Treasurer Press Release No. 97, 17 August 1993). On the face of things it would seem inequitable for a self-employed person not to be subject to the compulsory saving requirements imposed on a person with the same lifetime working income who works in employee status. If both would prefer, given the opportunity, to opt for a strategy of high-current-period-consumption, take a free-ride on the taxpayer funded income-support system in retirement, why should one be legally compelled to refrain from that strategy but not the other? But that may not be the full story. At least some of the self-employed may already be subject to imperfect-capital market effects compelling them to save more than they would otherwise like to, with that saving *having* to flow into net equity in their own enterprises and generating as a 'by-product' adequate provision for post-retirement living standards. A truly equitable treatment of the self-employed vis-à-vis those in wage/salary earning employment would seem to require that there be recognition of this type of circumstance and that compulsory contributions to superannuation funds not be imposed when demonstrably equivalent financial provision for life in retirement is already being made. But if that approach were attempted, a different type of inequity would immediately emerge: why should the bulk of citizens be required to put their retirement savings into the custodianship of trustees subject to regulatory supervision over their adopting and maintaining *prudent* investment strategies whereas a largely self-selecting minority are permitted to commit *their* retirement savings to potentially very high risk strategies with the taxpayer-funded income support system limiting the exposure of the individuals concerned to the full downside consequences?

Setting aside these complications arising from interaction effects between asset-mix decisions and labour income levels among the self-employed, economists would normally expect to find that those with the lowest and most precarious incomes in our type of society, and facing the greatest risk of urgent and unexpected spending requirements tend to focus what (if any) wealth they possess into the holding of cash or near-cash equivalents at banks or other deposit-taking institutions. People with high incomes from working can have precarious incomes, of course. And people on high and not-so-precarious incomes have to face up to the possibility of urgent and unexpected spending requirements arising. In those circumstances there is a clear greater need for holdings of liquid and low-risk assets than would be the case for other persons of the same income and wealth. But for those whose income is above what is needed to cover consumption of what they have come to regard as the basic necessities, and where net wealth is above the very modest, then it is possible to accommodate these potential needs for ready cash by *either* holding some 'comfort-zone' amount of wealth in cash and near-cash equivalents, *or* by arranging short-term line-of-credit type facilities with various financial institutions. In the latter case the situation is essentially that you are allowed to borrow against the security of various less-liquid assets in your overall wealth portfolio, without any immediate requirement to cash-in those assets.

The overall picture that could be expected to emerge *if* we did have good quality data on wealth-holding in Australia would thus be as follows. Different categories of assets vary in the ease, speed and cost at which they can be converted into ready cash *and* at which ready cash can be converted into them. A spectrum can therefore be drawn up with assets displaying the greatest of those advantages at the left-hand end (deposits accessible by writing personal cheques), shading through term deposits at deposit-taking financial institutions as one moved to the right, to short-term government debt, bank-accepted bills and so on – until at the far right one found shares in unlisted and small (or foreign) companies etc. The market mechanism would tend to operate so that the asset categories at the far right of the spectrum carry the greatest expected return (weighted for risk), so as to persuade holders to forgo the advantages of being further to the left in the spectrum.

Setting aside the two *special cases* of home ownership and non-optional superannuation, we would expect to find individuals with low wealth and precarious incomes holding assets concentrated at the left-hand end of this spectrum. And as one focussed on progressively higher wealth-holding groups of the population, one would expect those left-hand-end assets to represent progressively smaller fractions of overall wealth held, and a shift in the 'centre of gravity' of the overall wealth held progressively towards the right of the spectrum. Extensive utilisation of trusts by the very wealthy in Common Law countries can serve to prevent the full flavour of this effect being apparent in wealth distribution statistics, however, unless attempts are made to adjust reported personal wealth for interests in trusts.

Taxation and non-superannuation assets

Australia's taxation system imposes different *effective* rates of taxation on the income flowing from the ownership of wealth, depending on *both* the details of the *way* in which the wealth is held *and* on other significant circumstances including the rate of inflation, the overall size of the wealth-holder's taxable income, sometimes their age, sometimes the time at which the particular wealth-holding was acquired, and so on. The system is complex. It undoubtedly creates a situation where some asset categories receive taxation treatment which is more lenient than other categories, in some cases irrespective of who is the asset-holder, in other cases dependant upon the circumstances of the asset-holder, or even of that particular asset-holder's holding of that particular asset. What can be said regarding the equity features of the present taxation regime surrounding saving and wealth in Australia?

In order to judge whether a particular piece of income is being taxed leniently or harshly, and to what extent, it is necessary first to define a benchmark. The benchmark most commonly used is that of a 'pure' (or 'comprehensive') income tax system, but with full adjustment to offset the effects of inflation. It should be stressed that no such system of 'pure' income taxation has ever existed in the world, or is ever likely to. And it is hard to imagine anyone seriously advocating implementing one. A 'pure' income tax would bring every cent of a person's true real income to account, in the period in which it accrued, and subject it to the published personal income tax rate scale. The principal alternative benchmark is that of a 'pure' expenditure tax (not quite the same as a consumption tax). That would bring to account every cent of a person's expenditure for consumption purposes, in the period in which it is expended, and subject it to a defined progressive rate scale. Mark Latham, the federal MP for Werriwa, devoted pp. 133-139 and 246-349 of his recent book, *Civilising Global Capital* (1998), to comments on expenditure taxation. The expenditure tax benchmark is useful because it removes the *double-taxation of saving* which is an inherent feature of a pure income taxation system.

That can be illustrated as follows. Consider a person with $200, contemplating saving it for a year, and facing an interest rate of 10 per cent and a pure expenditure tax at a flat rate of 50 per cent. Spending the money today means obtaining goods valued at $100 on a net of tax basis; spending the money next year secures goods valued at $110 net of tax. Now consider the same situation but with a pure income tax at a rate of 50 per cent. Spending today still obtains $100 of goods; but saving now means earning 10 per cent interest on only $100, and with that $10 of interest subject to tax also. So saving this year and spending next year now obtains $105 of goods. In the pure income tax system there is a penalisation of thrift because two layers of tax apply. Saving occurs out of after-tax dollars and the interest on savings is then itself subject to tax. If *one* of these two layers of tax were eliminated, the arithmetic on the reward for saving would bounce from $105 to $110. You would effectively have an expenditure tax treatment.

(a) Interest-bearing assets

Where a person directly holds an interest-bearing asset, the Commonwealth income tax applies to give a pure income tax treatment *provided* the inflation rate is zero. If the inflation rate is positive, the effective rate of tax is harsher than that, with the degree of harshness being greater the higher the rate of inflation *and* the greater the individual's marginal tax rate. If the inflation rate were ever to be negative, the effective rate would be more lenient than the benchmark. This result follows because the inflation compensation element of interest income is not a part of *true* income, but real-world income-tax systems can only recognise this at the cost of major added complexity. It should be noted that interest-bearing assets in the form of deposits with banks or NBFIs have typically attracted additional State taxation in Australia, either upon deposit or at both deposit and withdrawal. The impact of this on the overall effective rate of tax on the holder's interest income depends on the turnover level.

(b) Home ownership

In a pure income tax world, owner occupiers would be taxed on the imputed income they accrue from enjoying the benefits of occupancy without the requirement to pay rent. They would be able to claim income tax deductions for costs necessarily incurred in earning that imputed income – mortgage interest, local government rates, insurance premiums, repairs and maintenance costs etc. The Commonwealth income tax operated on that basis between 1915 and 1922, the British income tax until 1963. Today's Australian tax system neither taxes imputed income from home ownership, nor allows deductions for the costs incurred in earning that income. Against the pure income tax benchmark this is harsh to those with very large outstanding house mortgages. It crosses over to leniency at the point where the mortgage is low enough for the real interest on it, plus the various other necessary house-ownership outgoings, to exactly match the imputed rent. It then becomes more lenient the lower the outstanding mortgage, the lower the level of local government rates, and the higher the owner's marginal income tax rate. The fact that the principal private residence is exempt from capital gains tax is generous to those who experience a real capital gain on their homes. For everyone else it removes the paperwork burden associated with keeping track of the 'indexed cost base' – including adjustments for alterations and extensions etc.

The present Australian tax treatment of home-ownership is close to the expenditure tax model. Of the two layers of tax in the pure income tax model, the second is largely removed. The fact that local government rates can be viewed as representing (at least in part) a form of income tax on imputed home ownership income means this is not as clear-cut as it is sometimes claimed to be, however.

(c) Real estate that is rented out

Where a person directly holds real estate that is used to earn rental income, the Commonwealth income tax applies to give a pure income tax treatment *provided* that *either* no interest costs are chargeable as deductions against the property, *or* the inflation rate is zero. If the inflation rate is positive, the effective rate of tax is gentler than that, provided that debt is present, to a degree that is greater the higher the rate of inflation, the higher the individual's marginal tax rate, and the greater the ratio of debt to net equity. If the inflation rate were negative, the effective tax rate would be harsher than the benchmark. This is the mirror image of the interest-bearing assets case. The inflation compensation element of interest costs is not a deductible in the definition of *true* income, but real-world income-tax systems can only recognise this at the cost of major added complexity. Local government rates and State land taxes need also to be factored in when considering the overall tax treatment of income from this asset category. The alteration of Australia's capital gains tax arrangements with effect from 21 September 1999 means that the real capital gain element of the return from this asset category and the next two is likely to be taxed leniently unless there is a resurgence of inflation. This is discussed further in Chapter Four.

(d) Assets in an unincorporated business

Here the story is basically the same as in (c) except that various taxation concessions, particularly depreciation allowance arrangements, allow for a deferral of income tax. As well as being a benefit in itself, such deferrals might be susceptible to conversion into the 'goodwill' component of a capital gain on the sale of one's business. For small enterprises there is a concessional treatment of this element of capital gains. Because there is typically a 'mingling' of labour income and income from capital in a self-employment based enterprise there is often scope for income that is 'truly' the labour income of one individual to be removed from appearing as that person's income and represented as that of a family member with a lower tax rate. The benefits of this might be regarded as a 'bonus' to the tax treatment of 'asset-income' from assets in an unincorporated enterprise. The more otherwise-low-income persons over 18 one has in one's family, the more valuable this 'bonus' becomes.

(e) Company shares

Where a person directly holds shares in an Australian company, which pays Australian company tax on its income prior to making dividend distributions to shareholders, the effective taxation situation is more complex than it would be sensible to attempt to describe here. The principal sources of complexity relate to the roles played by: business tax concessions (particularly depreciation allowance arrangements); gearing; and company retained earnings. Where the shareholder has borrowed to buy the shares, and is claiming tax-deductibility of the interest, the gearing issue is the same as under (c). But where the company is claiming interest deductions, the company's tax benefits will eventually be clawed back when the proceeds are distributed to shareholders without franking credits. The same applies to company tax benefits from business tax concessions such as the 125 per cent Research and Development write-off. Where a company retains after-tax profits this means the shareholder's immediate effective tax-rate is held at the company tax rate, and persons with personal marginal tax rates above that rate enjoy a deferral benefit. But if such deferral is not unwound at some stage, it carries the risk of the shareholder being taxed on a capital gain against which an 'appropriate' franking credit is not available. The September 1999 changes to CGT serve to reduce the risk of this being 'harsh', provided the inflation rate remains low.

Further research on this issue, and public availability of the results, would clearly be welcome. One thing that should be stressed, however, is that the dividend imputation system is *not* a tax concession. Its introduction marked the removal of a major distortion from the Australian taxation system. Its continued operation allows many of the 'concessional' tax treatments embedded in company tax to be effectively clawed back, without the angst of attempting to pull them out by the roots. *In itself*, dividend imputation cannot be challenged as being unfair or inequitable.

When the inflation rate is positive, our taxation system taxes income from interest-bearing assets more harshly than income from company shares. This was formerly because our taxation of capital gains makes adjustments for inflation whereas our taxation of interest flows does not. It has nothing to do with the dividend imputation system. The greater our success in expunging inflation from our economy, the more that problem tended to solve itself. And if it were found that deferral of tax via the retention of company earnings were a significant problem, that again would not be an indictment of the dividend imputation system *as such*. It could be dealt with by a mechanism such as a reintroduction of an equivalent to the old Division 7 in the Income Tax Assessment Act. The changes in Australia's capital gains tax arrangements with effect from 21 September 1999 mean that the real capital gain element of the return from this asset category is likely to be taxed leniently unless there is a resurgence of inflation. This is discussed further in Chapter Four.

(f) Life insurance and friendly society bonds

Where a person *indirectly* holds a basket of underlying assets through the vehicle of a ten-year (or greater) 'bond' with a life office or a friendly society, special taxation arrangements apply. These consist of flat rates of tax. For friendly societies, the rate is at present 33 per cent with realised capital gains taxed on an inflation adjusted basis. For life offices the rate is 39 per cent, with capital gains taxed on a basis that is *not* adjusted for inflation. How this compares with the pure income tax benchmark depends on the rate of inflation, the asset holder's individual marginal tax rate, and (in the case of friendly societies) the debt-instruments to equity mix of the underlying portfolio.

(g) Other asset-categories

Categories (a) to (f) above by no means exhaust the range of non-superannuation assets. Employee share acquisition schemes (ESAS), shares in approved pooled development funds (PDFs), and the special arrangements for infrastructure borrowings all require special analysis. So also does the case of equity-type instruments held continuously since prior to September 19th, 1985. The direct use of one's own 'unpaid' labour to construct (or 'improve') assets either for own use or for sale (but not as a sale from conducting a business) is a further special case.

Taxation and superannuation assets

Superannuation is not so much an asset category as a vehicle through which a person can hold a basket of underlying assets. The Australian regulatory framework means that asset selection is required to serve the best interests of the superannuation fund's members, but gearing of investments is not permitted. Income which passes through superannuation funds is subject to special taxation rules which then interact with the taxation treatments accorded to the actual assets held by the fund. The relatively harsher tax treatment accorded to interest-bearing assets compared with company shares or real estate when the inflation rate is positive-but-modest applies also where the assets are held through super. But the special taxation rules applying to super serve to attenuate the relative harshness, particularly for individuals on high marginal tax rates.

The tax rules for superannuation are rendered complex by four factors: contributions paid by employers are treated differently from contributions paid by employees; benefits taken as lump sums are treated differently from benefits taken as pension income streams; there are grandfathering provisions; and there are special rules for unfunded schemes. The various possible permutations and combinations of these four factors make the full picture difficult to describe briefly. But at the core of the system there is a logical and coherent principle. Employer contributions to funded schemes from which benefits are taken as pensions are subject to two tiers of income tax: fifteen per cent when the money enters the fund (and when investment income is received by the fund); and then tax according to the scheme member's personal rate scale, but with a fifteen percentage points rebate, when the pension payments are made.

This represents a half-way house between pure income tax treatment and pure expenditure tax treatment. It is concessional compared with a pure income tax treatment on two counts: the individual's marginal tax rate is likely to be lower post-retirement than when working; and the fifteen per cent 'up front' tax rate means that more money stays in the fund to earn investment income than if the member's personal rate scale had been applied up-front. The fact that the up-front layer of tax is at a flat rate makes for administrative simplicity, as compared with attempting to apply each member's personal marginal tax rate to contributions made on their behalf. The latter would be particularly complex in the case of some defined benefit schemes.

As noted above, however, the tax regime just described is only part of the picture. Since August 1996 an additional 15 percentage points of tax (the superannuation surcharge) has been applied to employer contributions received by superannuation schemes on account of persons with incomes above a defined threshold. Employee contributions are accorded a tax treatment akin to the pure income tax model, but with investment earnings on those monies subject to the two layer, half-way-house arrangement. Benefits taken as lump-sums are taxed according to a scale which varies depending on whether the individual is under or over the age of 55. The scale contains elements of progressivity, but over a long range is (for the over 55s) a flat 16.4 per cent. This rate needs to be compounded with the up-front tax, and the resulting rate of 28.94 per cent (or 41.48 per cent for surcharge victims) compared with the recipient's personal marginal tax rate in order to assess the extent of generosity/harshness in the treatment. Clearly for persons on the highest marginal tax rate, the lump sum scale is likely to be advantageous. The reasonable benefit limits (RBLs) provide a cap to this concessional treatment. But grandfathering arrangements mean that some individuals have higher RBLs than the norm, and some are able to enjoy additional concessions in the treatment of benefits attributable to pre-1983 employment. Eventually of course, the complexities arising from today's grandfathering arrangements will work their way out of the system.

Taxation issues: overview

From the above it should be clear that different saving vehicles are subject to different effective rates of taxation, but that it is difficult to specify exactly what effective rates of taxation without additional information such as the rate of inflation, the personal marginal tax rate of the individual concerned, the manner in which a superannuation end-benefit can be expected to be taken, the extent to which equity-type investments are geared, and so on.

Tables 3.4 and 3.5 are taken from a paper published by McKissack and Sedgley in 1993, and provide a summary of the situation. Taxpayers with high personal marginal tax rates face a greater amplitude of differences in effective tax rates across the range of possible saving vehicles than do taxpayers on the lower personal marginal rates. They are particularly heavily taxed on interest-bearing assets when the inflation rate is significantly positive. They derive proportionately greater benefits from those special features of taxation arrangements which serve to attenuate the progressivity of the tax on personal income, when it is derived from particular sources, or through particular channels. Those on the lower personal marginal tax rates are in the reverse position on both counts.

A final word of warning needs to be stated regarding the interpretation of Tables 3.4 and 3.5, and of similar tables published by other writers. For many of the asset categories an important factor is omitted: the extent to which the relevant asset market *responds* to the tax benefits or tax detriments listed. Take the case of housing. If house-ownership is widely known to carry a favourable tax treatment on the return from the asset, and if that treatment is widely expected to continue through the foreseeable future, we would expect the price of houses to be bid up relative to the price of other assets whose returns are less favourably taxed. In effect the market's estimation of the future flow of tax

Table 3.4
Effective Tax Rates on Selected Saving Vehicles for a Top Marginal Rate Taxpayer at Zero and 3 Per Cent Inflation Rates

SAVING VEHICLE	EFFECTIVE TAX RATE (per cent)	
	Inflation = 0 per cent	Inflation = 3 per cent
Bank Deposit	48.4	77.4
Direct Equity - without Gearing	47.0	47.0
Direct Equity - Geared (75%)	42.9	-44.2
Owner Occupied Housing - without Gearing	20.0	20.0
Owner Occupied Housing - Geared (40%)	33.3	33.3
Investment Housing - Without Gearing	57.3	57.3
Investment Housing - Geared (75%)	84.2	-3.0
Superannuation - Employer Contributions	-53.2	-50.5
Superannuation - Employee Contributions	26.7	37.2
Life Insurance Bond	38.4	61.0
Friendly Society Bond	32.2	50.2

Source: 'The Effective Taxation of Personal Savings in Australia', by A. McKissack and P. Sedgley, 1993 Conference of Economists.

Table 3.5
Effective Tax Rates for Different Marginal Rate Taxpayers: (With Inflation 1.9 Per Cent Per Annum)

Saving Vehicle	Effective Tax Rate (per cent)		
	MTR = 21.4%	MTR = 30.4%	MTR = 48.4%
Bank Deposit	29.5	54.4	66.8
Direct Equity - Without Gearing	20.5	38.1	47.0
Direct Equity - Geared (75%)	-6.6	-10.7	-12.3
Owner Occupied Housing	20.0	20.0	20.0
Owner Occupied Housing - Geared (40%)	33.3	33.3	33.3
Investment Housing - Without Gearing	36.2	50.2	57.3
Investment Housing - Geared (75%)	56.3	37.8	29.0
Superannuation – Employer contributions	38.8	-16.5	-51.4
Superannuation – Employee Contributions	33.4	33.4	33.4
Life Insurance bond	52.7	52.7	52.7
Friendly society bond	43.6	43.6	43.6

Source: 'The Effective Taxation of Personal Savings in Australia', by A. McKissack and P. Sedgley, 1993 Conference of Economists.

benefits becomes built into the price of established houses. A new or recent buyer who has paid the full market price for an established house is *not* then enjoying a true tax benefit. The pre-tax *yield* on the house has been shifted by the market mechanism to offset the tax benefit.

Similar processes might be expected to operate in other asset markets. Imagine a deposit taking institution which used all the money deposited with it to make loans to unincorporated business enterprises. When the inflation rate is positive, as we saw above, the depositors find their interest income taxed at harsh effective rates, while the borrowers gain an effective tax advantage on their interest deductions. Under those circumstances one might expect the depositors to require higher pre-tax interest rates to continue playing the game, and borrowers to be willing to tolerate higher interest rates on their borrowings. It is possible to envisage the interest rate moving to a level which restores the after-tax yield earned by the average depositor to a figure which wipes out the effect of the tax detriment, by simultaneously wiping out the effect of the tax benefit on the borrower's side. In the real world, of course, this picture is muddied by some borrowers not being able to claim tax deductions on their interest costs, and by different borrowers and different depositors having different personal marginal rates. Still, the fact remains that if these market *responses* to tax benefits and tax detriments are ignored, data of the type presented in Tables 3.4 and 3.5 can mislead.

Compulsion

Mainstream economics views human behaviour as being in the main the behaviour each individual chooses to engage in. Furthermore economists typically assume each individual to be the best judge of what, at the direct personal level, is good for them. This leads to a basic presumption that compelling an individual to behave other than in the way they would personally choose is likely to make them feel worse off. Often, of course, this is overridden by considerations of the greater social good where choices made by one individual generate significant 'side-effects' for the welfare of others. Speed limits, for example, only directly constrain those who would prefer to exceed them. But that is widely regarded as an acceptable element of compulsion on that minority in order to make the roads safer for all.

Australia's new compulsory saving arrangements will not cause *all* Australians to behave differently from the way they would have behaved otherwise. The self-employed and those outside the workforce are outside the arrangements. Wage and salary earners in jobs (and with career prospects) which were already carrying occupational superannuation cover at or above the compulsory minimum are likewise unaffected. Those with significant net wealth and/or already intending to make significant saving from their incomes could be expected to rearrange their affairs to offset the effect of compulsory superannuation – if that is their choice. That leaves wage and salary earners in the lower income/lower net wealth categories as the main groups actually constrained by the new compulsory saving arrangements.

On the face of things that smacks of vertical inequity: those on the low and middle rungs of the wage and salary earning hierarchy face an effective compulsion to behave in a way that they would not choose, while those on the highest rungs face no such compulsion *in effect*. But the situation may not be so straightforward. The social security system of a society such as Australia's means that the individual who opts against personal saving is shielded from the full personal financial consequences (for themselves and their dependants) of that choice. The greater the number of persons who succumb to this temptation, and save little or nothing, the greater has to be the taxation burden borne by those of the same income who *do* save. The latter fact, when widely appreciated, can then become a further disincentive to personal saving. This is known to economists as the *moral hazard* argument. It provides the principal justification for compelling employers to take out workers' compensation insurance, for compelling vehicle-owners to take out compulsory third party insurance and so on. Some would want to argue that to compel to save those with the means sufficient to save in our society, is defensible on *moral hazard* grounds, and should not be viewed as inequitable treatment of the persons actually constrained to behave other than as they would freely choose.

4 Policies on National Saving: Economic Efficiency Considerations

Owen Covick and Jim Hancock

When economists speak of *efficiency* they are more often than not referring to *allocative efficiency*, which is not the same as *technical efficiency* – the thing that non-economists are usually referring to when they speak of efficiency.

- *technical efficiency* is present when a producer of goods, or a provider of services is producing as much output (of a given quality) as it possibly *can* from the actual quantities (and qualities) of labour, capital equipment and other inputs that it is using to produce that output. Saying the same thing a different way: technical efficiency is present when a producer of goods or provider of services is *not* using more of any one type of input than it strictly needs to, to produce the output it is generating, given the quantities (and qualities) of the other inputs being used.
- *allocative efficiency* is something it does not really make sense to define at the level of an individual producer. It is all about how the economy's labour, capital, and other resources are *allocated among* their various possible uses (typically in different places of production, producing different types of outputs). An economy could be producing each of two goods (guns and butter perhaps) at maximum technical efficiency, but might still be able to improve its welfare by cutting back on the production of one, and re-allocating the freed-up resources towards an increased production level of the other. Only when all possible welfare gains from that type of re-allocation have been achieved can an economy be said to have achieved *allocative efficiency*. It might be worth noting that the maxim 'there is no such thing as a free lunch' is true *only* if all possible gains in technical or allocative efficiency have already been achieved – a fairly sweeping premise.

The term economic efficiency embraces both technical and allocative efficiency. It also embraces the third member of this economists' trinity: *dynamic efficiency*. Creating and developing new products, new techniques of production, and new market opportunities all require that resources be diverted to those ends and away from uses with more immediate (and more certain) payoffs. The same goes for investments in skills and education. If too few of today's resources are devoted to these types of purpose, that is clearly a recipe for a tomorrow in which a society's welfare is lower than it could have been. But it is also possible to devote too many of today's resources to those types of purpose, or to plough too much into projects with low likelihood of payoffs great enough to justify the risk – as appears to have been the British experience with Concorde. In principle there ought to be some quantum of commitment of today's resources to the various types of research and development, education and skills formation etc., which is 'just right' in terms of securing the best possible *time-path* of advance in a society's material welfare. If it could be identified, that would represent dynamic efficiency. Whether some initiative is good or bad for dynamic efficiency is typically a harder question to answer than whether it is good or bad for technical or for allocative efficiency.

Allocative efficiency and the tax system

For the capital market to operate efficiently in its role as allocator of capital to different possible investments, it is necessary that effective tax rates be equalised across investments. This equalisation is the basic requirement for *neutrality* of the tax system. This is so because private sector investment decisions depend on expected after tax returns. Investors will seek the highest returns available (after allowance for risk). The system therefore tends to finance investments which exceed investors' required rates of return and not to finance investments which fall short of those requirements. The net effect, via this process of maximisation at the individual level, is to maximise after tax rates of return in an aggregate sense.

If tax rates are uniform across investments, then the maximisation of after-tax returns leads to a maximisation of pre-tax returns. However, this will not be so if effective rates of tax differ. This is easily illustrated by an example. Suppose an investor is considering two investments each with the same cost as the other. The present value of the first investment before tax (i.e., inclusive of cash returns and capital gains to the investor and payments to the tax office, all suitably discounted) is $100. The second investment has a before tax present value of $90. Assume as well that the tax structure imposes an effective tax rate of 30 per cent on the first investment and an effective tax rate of 10 per cent on the second investment. In that case, the after tax present values to the investor are $70 for the first investment, and $81 for the second investment. Consequently, the second investment will be selected, even though it has the lower pre-tax rate of return and hence lower aggregate return to society.

The capacity of the capital markets to bring about efficient allocation of resources is reliant on a tax system which equalises effective rates of tax across investments. For this to be achieved, it is necessary that tax and commercial values coincide. Of course in some instances a non-neutral treatment may be desired as a matter of policy. This can be introduced when appropriate, but does not diminish the weight of the neutrality objective in general terms. It may, in those instances, be preferable to achieve the desired result with explicit government subsidies rather than tax preferences which are unlikely to be targeted as effectively.

From the discussion in Chapter Three it will be clear that the Australian Taxation System is not *neutral* in the effective tax rates it imposes on incomes from different types of assets or investments. Four deviations from neutrality are particularly apparent:

- the special treatment of the return from owner-occupied housing;
- the special treatment of the element of return represented by real capital gains or real capital losses on assets;

- owners of depreciating assets are often permitted to claim depreciation deductions faster than the 'true' economic or commercial reality would warrant;
- where taxable income is not distributed from an incorporated entity, it is taxed at the company tax rate and shareholders on higher marginal tax rates gain a tax deferral (with consequent income benefits and reductions in effective tax rates).

The tax-treatment of capital gains

Joseph Minarik, in 'Capital Gains Taxation, Growth, and Fairness' (*Contemporary Policy Issues*, July 1992) argued that:

> The real issue is whether taxing some people at a different rate than others having the same income level is appropriate. Under the principles of comprehensive income taxation, a burden of proof rests with anyone who argues that one taxpayer should be charged a lower rate than everyone else at his income level. (p. 16)

Of course a proponent of preferential capital gains taxation might argue that the onus is on the critic of preferential treatment. The response would be that when capital gains are realised they deliver a dollar amount to their owner which is no less in purchasing power to a dollar derived from any other source. Arguments for concessional treatment of capital gains have typically been along two lines. The first relates to the so-called 'lock in' effect; the second to more general views that lower CGT offers a dynamic boost to the economy.

Lawrence Lindsey in 'Rates, Realisations and Revenues of Capital Gains' (in Martin Feldstein (ed), *Taxes and Capital Formation*, University of Chicago Press, 1987), defines 'lock in' as a situation where:

> … a taxpayer might defer selling one asset and purchasing another with a higher pretax return because capital gains on the sale make the tax unprofitable…

The effects of lock in are thus entirely the consequence of an earlier deviation from neutrality in the tax system – the failure to tax capital gain at the time of accrual, with taxation delayed until realisation. The Australian tax system allows certain types of rollover relief from CGT. These involve allowing the lock in period to be extended and, in practical terms, the tax cost to the taxpayer of unlocking actually rises, thus increasing the degree of lock in. If one seriously believed lock-in effects were producing major allocative inefficiencies in an economy, logic would seem to suggest that one should be arguing that capital gains be taxed to a *greater* extent on an accruals basis and to a *lesser* extent on a realisation basis. This would necessarily generate increased costs of tax compliance and tax administration, but if you seriously believed lock-in was a source of major allocative inefficiencies you would presumably be happy to view some additional compliance and administration costs as an acceptable price to pay for reducing those effects? To attempt to use lock in as an argument for zero or highly concessional effective tax rates on capital gains would seem 'extreme'.

The dynamic efficiency arguments for effective rates of tax on capital gains to be lower than on 'normal' income are more complex and much more difficult to assess. Trying to model the impact of differential capital income tax rates in a neoclassical framework is highly dependent on assumptions used as a starting point. However, it has often been suggested (without reference to a coherent economic framework) that lower CGT would boost activity, incomes, employment etc., Jane Gravelle's assessment of these arguments in the US context, was:

> …claims that a capital gains tax reduction is important for economic growth or for efficient allocation between consumption and savings appear unsupported by the evidence. The efficiency gains are probably small and a more direct approach of decreasing the government deficit would be more likely to succeed in increasing savings… (J.G. Gravelle, *The Economic Effects of Taxing Capital Income*, MIT Press, Cambridge Mass, 1994)

William Vickery, the winner of the Nobel Prize in 1996, argued that:

> Rather than cutting capital-gains tax, cutting the corporation income tax offers far better prospects for encouraging investment. (W.S. Vickery, 'Meaningfuly Defining Deficits and Debt', *American Economic Review*, May 1992)

Capital gains tax concessions could be expected to shift investment patterns away from investments which deliver returns in the form of current income towards those that deliver capital gains. This would imply that some capital gains intensive investments with lower before tax present values than alternative 'current income' intensive projects would go ahead, as their after tax present values would be higher by virtue of preferential taxation treatment.

One can imagine that buildings and structures might be advantaged while manufacturing might be disadvantaged. However, that is a generalisation. The real question is not just whether or not gains producing assets are likely to be deserving of special support, but also whether CGT preferences are a closely targeted means of achieving such an outcome.

Minarik (*op cit*) argued that:

> A capital gains tax break would increase personal saving infinitesimally if at all, while it would decrease federal tax revenues and thus decrease national saving. It would have little impact on total investment, but it would almost certainly shift investment into low-value commercial real estate and out of other, more productive uses.

It is sometimes suggested that preferential CGT is desirable because it supports venture capital. In assessing this argument it is important to focus on the underlying investment which it is intended that government policy should deliberately encourage vis-à-vis other investment types. In principle there may be a case to differentiate effective tax rates for certain types of investments. This would be so where the investments are thought to have 'spillovers' which deliver benefits (or impose costs) to parties separate from the investor. These spillovers drive a wedge between private returns (before and after tax) and social returns from the investment activity. The investor, with a focus on commercial after tax rates of return will not take into account these spillovers. However, if the effective tax rate is varied for relevant investments then it is possible to load allowance for the spillover into the investment decision.

The case for preferential tax treatment on the basis of spillovers (or externalities) needs to be treated very carefully. The knowledge requirements to establish the existence of spillovers are considerable, and may at times be only fulfilled in a loose way. In addition, the acceptance of a 'spillovers' case on the basis of imperfect information invites other vested interests to seek concessions on grounds which may be difficult to confirm conclusively or to refute. That said, the subject of spillovers has attracted very considerable attention in the economics literature. Spillovers are most often thought to exist with respect to:

- certain widely used infrastructure projects, where consumer valuations are diverse but access charges are standardised;
- investments in knowledge, as even where there is intellectual property protection via patents etc., a residue of knowledge flows to other parties at no cost; and
- investments in education and training.

There has been debate about what this means for research and development spending. Knowledge may be more relevant when it is created in workers who use equipment with a high embodied technology component. For instance, it may be more important to encourage companies to provide PCs to workers than it is to encourage a PC manufacturing sector with research and development concessions. In 1997 *The Economist* reported an OECD study, *Technology and Industrial Performance* (OECD, 1997), which found that invention of new products did not offer as much as diffusion of new technology through an economy. As *The Economist* put it:

> The OECD finds that in many industries, the purchase of technology has more impact on productivity growth than direct R&D spending by the industries themselves. Manufacturers' R&D spending does seem to explain most of their productivity growth. In services, however, the diffusion of technology matters much more. According to OECD estimates, the rate of return on 'embodied R&D', i.e., the purchases of R&D intensive equipment, averaged 190% in the 1980s, up from 130% in the 1970s. In particular, productivity growth in transport, telecommunications and financial services has benefited considerably from the purchase of computers and telecoms equipment.

In this context, technology take up might be regarded as an adjunct to skill formation – which has very well established connections with income and productivity growth more broadly. Providing concessional tax treatment on the capital gains element of return from all assets and all investments, or from all investments in business entities of certain legal types (e.g., companies with shares) would therefore seem an unlikely vehicle for securing for a community as a whole the allocative efficiency or dynamic efficiency gains associated with encouraging some types of investment initiatives vis-à-vis others.

Taxation and 'over-investment' in housing

It is frequently argued that the features of the Australian taxation system outlined in Chapter Three, together with the concessional treatment accorded to an owner-occupied home in the various means-testing arrangements that apply to government-provided pensions and benefit payments (and also to the provision of some government services) create incentives for a greater than warranted commitment of the nation's resources to the construction of housing (both new houses and extensions to existing ones).

As was noted in Chapter Three, the exemption from income tax of the imputed rental income from owner occupation affects different people in different ways. Those with low levels of net equity in their homes and large housing debt tend to be over-taxed. Those in the reverse situation tend to be under-taxed. The latter group are then willing to pay higher prices for houses than would be the case without the tax exemption for imputed rent. The former group may also be willing to pay higher prices if they anticipate being able to reduce their housing debt, become members of the advantaged group, and hold their houses long enough for the benefit of that status to outweigh the upfront tax disadvantage. The overall result is almost certainly going to be that the prices of established houses (inclusive of the land they occupy) are bid up above the levels that would prevail without the tax exemption for imputed rent.

The capital gains tax exemption on the principal residence, to the extent it provides any benefit at all, would tend to accentuate this – as does the omission of imputed rent from most income-testing arrangements, and the concessional treatment of the family home in the social security asset-testing arrangements.

The pressure for the prices of established houses to exceed the levels that would prevail without the tax exemption for imputed rent (and related effects) means in turn that there is an incentive for more new houses (and house additions) to be constructed than would be the case without the tax exemption (and related effects). How strong this effect is, depends on the extent to which the population regards newly constructed houses (and/or newly extended ones) to be directly comparable with established houses of the same size and construction. If the population saw them as perfect substitutes, enough new houses would be built to wipe out the prices pressure on established homes and return the prices of such houses to the levels that would prevail without the tax exemption (and related effects). If the population viewed newly built houses as very poor substitutes for established houses of the same size and construction, the amount of new building stimulated by the tax exemption would be smaller, and the continuing effect on the prices of established houses that much greater.

One could imagine a situation where a city's population viewed newly built houses in a very negative light: as being disadvantaged by distance from the city-centre and established social networks; as being ugly and lacking the 'charm' of older houses; as being on unattractive and small blocks of land if urban in-fill; and so on. Under those circumstances the market for newly built houses would be largely separate from the market for established houses, and might be expected to consist mainly of young families without the deposit and/or the borrowing capacity sufficient to buy into the established house market. The closer a city's housing market approached this type of dichotomised situation, the smaller would be the effect on the number of new houses built arising from the tax exemption for imputed rent (and related effects). The smaller also would therefore be the extent of the allocative inefficiency problem engendered. The portion of the inefficiency that did exist would manifest itself mainly through 'tasteful' additions and alterations to established houses in established suburbs being undertaken to an extent greater than would prevail in the absence of the tax exemption for imputed rent (and related effects).

From the discussion above, it should be clear that the question of whether Australia's taxation system *has* in fact led to over-investment in housing, is not susceptible to any quick and straightforward answer. A full analysis would need also to take into account the effective tax rates applying on the alternatives to housing investment, to which the nation's resources might have been re-allocated. And it should consider the various social benefits which it is sometimes claimed flow from a high level of home ownership.

The Industry Commission considered this issue in its December 1991 Report *Availability of Capital*. The main treatment forms a 28 page Appendix to that Report titled: 'Appendix C: Economy-wide effects of reducing tax disparities favouring home ownership'. The Commission's conclusion was:

> Investment in home ownership, stimulated by incentives in the taxation and social security systems, reduces the availability of domestic capital for business and distorts resource allocation towards the housing industry. There would be economic benefits to the Australian economy in removing the tax disparity in favour of housing. However, the Commission has concluded that taxing capital gains alone – as canvassed in the draft report – would not have a significant net effect, taking into account both economic and administrative considerations. (pp. xvi – xvii).

The phrase 'economic benefits' was used deliberately. The Commission made no claim to have addressed or assessed the 'social benefits' argument for promoting home-ownership. The Report indicated that further work on this and various other issues is required in order to allow for an: 'Estimation of the effects of practical tax policy options for reducing disparities between housing and non-housing investment' (p. C2).

Since publication of that Industry Commission Report, a number of new taxation concessions for business investment have been introduced, notably the accelerated depreciation allowance arrangements announced in the *One Nation* statement of February 1992. That type of measure has the effect of reducing the effective rate of taxation on investment in business plant and equipment relative to the effective rate on housing investment. Accelerated depreciation arrangements were 'wound-back' in September 1999, but with exceptions made for small businesses.

As a final word on the issue of housing, it should be remembered that Australia is by no means alone in the world in providing a tax treatment of the income from home ownership that deviates from the 'pure' income tax model. A 1990 OECD study (*The Personal Income Tax Base, A Comparative Survey*) found that even among those countries which *do* include imputed rent in taxable income (Belgium, Canada, Denmark, Finland, Germany, Greece, Italy, Netherlands, Norway, Spain and Sweden) it is typical for the rent thus imputed to be generously low, and the deductions allowed against it generously high. When the Industry Commission examined data for 22 OECD countries for the period 1976-1988, they found: 'Australia ranked 15th in the amount of total investment allocated to residential housing and 10th when housing investment is expressed as a percentage of gross domestic product'. (*Availability of Capital* p. C10).

Taxation and the debt-equity mix

Business ventures almost always require the commitment of funds, to initiate and sustain them, and to allow them to undertake planned growth. Sometimes those who manage and control the ventures are able to provide the required funds entirely from their own resources (including ploughed-back earnings). But much of the time those manager/controllers require outside funds also. Raising funds through debt instruments has the advantage to the manager/controllers that they part with little of their management and control prerogatives, while they also retain the right to all of the 'upside' of their ventures' profits, should things go well. It has the disadvantage of a contractual obligation to repay principal as well as interest according to an arranged schedule – and the retention by the manager/controllers of all the 'downside' of their ventures' profit performance, should things not go as well as expected.

Raising funds through outside injections of equity has the reverse characteristics. The funds providers take on a share of the risks of the venture's performance being poor, but have to be rewarded with a commensurate share of the profits if things go well. Equity providers also have to be provided with a share of the management and control rights that accompany 'ownership' – though they are often happy to be 'sleeping partners' (not exercising those rights) as long as they feel comfortable with the performance of the manager/controllers. The threat of the sleepers awaking can nevertheless make life less secure and attractive for the manager/controllers than they would ideally prefer.

The owner/controller of a small business enterprise who is seeking to expand that enterprise, who is highly confident of success, and who is willing to take on a high exposure to risk will have a strong preference for debt funding and will feel aggrieved if such funding is not available or is available only at interest rates incorporating a risk premium which he or she feels to be unwarranted. The owner/controller of an equivalent enterprise who is not quite so confident of the prospects of success and/or who is not so willing to take on risk exposure will have a preference for a mix of debt and equity – providing that equity partners can be found who will not 'interfere' too much in the running of things. The mix preferred will typically depend on the cost terms under which the two types of funding are available. For larger enterprises where ownership is typically already in the hands of outside shareholders rather than management, decisions on the preferred mix of new fund raising – as between debt and equity – are likely to be largely driven by cost factors.

That provides a brief outline of the demand side of the capital market, in terms of the fundamental factors influencing the preferred debt to equity instruments mix. On the supply side an equivalent picture can be painted, which has already been touched on in Chapter Three. Some individuals prefer to hold assets that provide the prospect of a share in some particular business venture's success, and possibly a say in its running. Other individuals would prefer to steer clear of the risks of loss and the monitoring costs involved in equity instruments and opt for the relatively more certain (and more passive) world of debt instruments.

Equity trusts (including property trusts) and investment companies provide a means for ultimate wealth holders to participate in the benefits of equity investment while obtaining a lower risk exposure through a mixed basket of underlying holdings, and delegating the monitoring costs to professional managers (who the unit holders then have to worry about monitoring). Equivalent unit trusts also exist which put unit-holders funds into a basket of interest-bearing assets, while passing a full flow-through of return (and risk) to unit holders.

Banks and other deposit taking institutions might appear to be the same as this at first sight. But in reality they differ significantly. The bank (or NBFI) promises the depositors that they can withdraw their principal according to agreed arrangements, and that they will receive a rate of return on that principal according to a predetermined arrangement. The bank (or NBFI) then uses these funds to make loans and acquire other interest bearing assets. If the return on the bank (or NBFI)'s loans exceeds the cost of servicing its deposits, the gap accrues to the bank's owners (i.e., the equity holders in the bank or non-bank deposit taking institution). If the return on the loans falls short of what is required to service the deposits, it is those equity holders who experience the pain. What happens if such a shortfall is sufficient to wipe out the equity held by equity holders in the bank (or NBFI) is something most depositors prefer not to think about. But the 1990s case of the Pyramid Building Society demonstrates that the unthinkable can happen. The relevant institutions are usually prepared to cooperate in prudential controls and oversight being imposed on them by a regulatory agency in order to reduce this type of risk, and thus improve depositor confidence.

The bottom line of all this is that for a given economy such as Australia, at a particular stage in its progress there is going to be some debt/equity mix of its financing arrangements which is *allocatively efficient* when judged against the economic fundamentals. The relevant fundamentals are the risk versus return preferences of fund providers and fund seekers; the balance of desires for ownership/control prerogatives versus the attractions of a more quiet life among the two sets of parties; the state of development of the economy's equity markets, and equity marshalling institutions; and the state of development of the economy's debt markets, and institutions of financial intermediation (banks and non-bank deposit taking institutions). If the various financial markets are operating on a competitive basis (that is without significant monopoly power positions), and in the absence of other systematic distortions, economists would expect free market mechanisms to press towards that position of allocative efficiency in the debt-equity mix. One possible distortion would be if the taxation system systematically advantaged the debt-financing channel vis-à-vis the equity financing channel, or vice versa.

The discussion in Chapter Three concluded that since the full implementation of the dividend imputation system in 1988, the Australian taxation arrangements provide for broadly equivalent rates of effective income taxation of equity and debt, *provided* that the rate of inflation is zero. When the inflation rate is significantly different from zero, the different manner in which the compensation for the inflation element in the return on the two classes of financial instrument is treated for taxation purposes has the potential to disrupt that equivalence of treatment (or *tax neutrality*). Whether that potential is turned into reality depends on the extent to which there is symmetry in the tax treatment of lenders and borrowers, and the extent to which market mechanisms move nominal interest rates to offset not just the rate of inflation *per se*, but to offset the tax effects of that inflation rate also.

It was pointed out in Chapter Three that in a debt market confined to business borrowers, and in which all borrowers and lenders had the same marginal income tax rates, one might expect – other things being equal – a competitive market to push the nominal interest rate to the level at which the real after tax position of both borrowers and lenders was the same as it would be under a zero rate of inflation. If that was all there was to the story, one could conclude that *tax neutrality* was not disturbed by the interaction of inflation and the tax system, and that allocative efficiency was therefore 'safe'.

Unfortunately the full story of our markets for debt instruments is more complex. Those borrowers who cannot claim interest costs as tax deductions, might be happy to pay nominal interest rates which incorporate compensation to the lender for the direct effect of the inflation rate on the value of money. But since they themselves gain nothing in tax advantages from their 'gearing', they will be unwilling to pay anything more than that in nominal interest to compensate the lenders for the latter's effective tax disadvantage from inflation. Debt markets dominated by this type of borrower can be expected to behave differently from debt markets dominated by 'tax-deductible' borrowers, therefore. But that different behaviour cannot involve the opening up of too great a nominal interest rate differential between two such markets, or the lenders will vote with their wallets and shift funds to the higher yielding market.

A second complication is that different lenders have different marginal tax rates, and different 'tax-deductible' borrowers have different marginal income tax rates. Sometimes this arises from special tax arrangements for particular entities. Sometimes it arises from the workings of the progressivity of the personal rate scale. What this means is that it is virtually impossible for the market nominal interest rate on a particular debt instrument to adjust for the tax effects of inflation in a way that preserves *tax neutrality* for *all* those participating in that market. In a single competitive market, all participants face the same rate. The rate that eventuates, in response to a particular inflation rate, is likely to produce an advantaged after-tax yield to lenders on low marginal tax rates; a disadvantaged after tax yield to lenders on high marginal tax rates;

an advantaged after-tax position for borrowers on high marginal tax rates (and with deductibility); and a disadvantaged after-tax position for borrowers on low marginal tax rates (and with deductibility).

These two complicating factors of non-deductibility for some borrowers, and the absence of true symmetry in the tax treatment of the two sides of debt markets, mean that one cannot be confident that nominal interest rates will be shifted through competitive market mechanisms to ensure the equivalence of effective tax treatment of debt investment vis-à-vis equity investment, in the presence of a positive inflation rate. But to estimate the dimensions of the allocative inefficiency engendered at various levels of the inflation rate would require a major research project. The writers are unaware of any such project under way.

Most professional economists would draw from the above the policy conclusion that the nation's inflation rate ought to be kept as close to zero as possible. As well as the allocative efficiency problems discussed above, inflation distorts economic decision-making in a number of other ways. Inflation distorts the operation of depreciation allowances calculated on the standard historical cost basis – in a way that disadvantages investment in longer-life assets vis-à-vis shorter-lived assets. Inflation erodes the value of carry-forward losses and hence acts to deter stand-alone investment projects which are expected to incur losses in the early years, but whose longer term prospects render them likely to be justified on economic fundamentals. Inflation disadvantages annuities by eroding the value of the undeducted purchase price. This list is far from exhaustive. It is sometimes argued that the income taxation system should be adjusted so that it systematically takes into account inflation and taxes only real income. The counter-argument is that that would be complex and disruptive, if attempted on a full and comprehensive basis, and would introduce new distortions if not full and comprehensive. It is also argued that in attempting to implement policies to help live with inflation, the resolve of the community to eliminate inflation might be diminished.

To form a verdict on these issues, it would be useful to have better information on the allocative inefficiency costs associated with various different inflation rates in today's Australian economic framework – and on the social costs associated with reducing the inflation rate by a given amount over a given period of time.

Compulsion

The SGC legislation requires employers to pay superannuation contributions on behalf of their employees, at rates not lower than a prescribed scale. The legislation also requires that the monies go into superannuation schemes which comply with the Superannuation Industry Supervision (SIS) legislation. If the employer fails to meet the SGC obligations, a sum of money equivalent to the required superannuation contributions plus an administrative charge must be forwarded to the Taxation Office (ATO) and that outlay is *not* tax deductible to the employer. Once the money is in the hands of the Taxation Office, efforts are made to get it out again – into an appropriate SIS complying superannuation fund and credited in the name(s) of the relevant employee(s).

The SGC legislation itself does *not* require the employer to pay SGC-mandated superannuation contributions into fund X rather than fund Y. Nor does it require any consultation between employer and employees that might provide the latter with individual choice in the matter, or a right to a single collective choice based on an employee ballot. The SGC legislation, read in isolation, appears to put fund choice entirely in the hands of the employer (subject to the choice being SIS complying). The fact that employers are often *not* in this position is the result of industrial award and industrial agreement requirements. Prior to the implementation of the SGC legislation in 1992, most Australian employees covered by the award system were in the position where their employers were required to pay 'productivity' superannuation contributions on their behalf (typically 3 per cent of wages or salary, but sometimes designated as flat rates) as a result of agreements or awards made in the Industrial Relations arena. Each such agreement or award typically specified the fund (or list of alternative funds) into which the 'productivity' super contributions should be paid. A common feature of these arrangements was that all employers in a given industry would be required to pay the super contributions into a single 'industry fund'. Employees changing employers but remaining in the same industry would then obtain the benefits of continuity of fund membership.

These arrangements which predated the SGC have continued to operate. In some cases the industrial awards and agreements have been updated to keep pace with the SGC-prescribed minimum contribution rates. In some cases the award/agreement required contribution rates have remained at 3 per cent, and the employers pay the rest of their SGC obligations into other superannuation schemes (as was the case with academic staff at Australian Universities until 2000 when the 3 per cent scheme and the "main" scheme were amalgamated into one). In other cases where award/agreement required rates have not been updated, the employers pay the full SGC contributions into the award/agreement specified schemes either for the sake of administrative convenience, or in the interests of harmonious industrial relations.

The bottom line, however, is that very few Australian employees have an effective choice as to which superannuation scheme their employer directs SGC-mandated contributions on their behalf into. And even those employees whose employers make contribution rates 'voluntarily' above the required minima are typically in the position that their employer makes the choice of fund, and their own choice is limited to take it or leave it (with the latter sometimes requiring leaving the job as well). Once the money is inside a superannuation scheme, it is the responsibility of the scheme's trustees to ensure that the funds are deployed and managed in such a way as to best serve the interests of the scheme's members. An increasing number of large superannuation schemes (the OPTUS scheme was an early example) allow members to indicate their preferred option from a menu of portfolio types available *within* the one scheme. It should be stressed though that the Australian Prudential Regulatory Authority (APRA) requires that such signalling of preference is *not* taken as releasing the trustees from their duties of trust.

It is sometimes argued that the absence of member choice of fund, and the absence of member choice over the portfolio pattern in which that member's superannuation assets are held, to the extent that these conditions prevail, generates economic inefficiencies. The claimed inefficiencies are of two types. Firstly there is the issue of *technical efficiency* in scheme administration and management. The trustees are responsible to members for ensuring that scheme administration and management functions are carried out cost-effectively and provide a quality of service that best serves the members' interests. Some commentators argue that the trustees would be under greater pressure to deliver the quality the members want, and on a cost-effective basis, if members were allowed to vote with their feet. This argument rests on standard microeconomic theory in which it is consumers' ability to choose among alternative suppliers, and the ability of new suppliers to establish themselves and enter the market, which drives the supply side of an industry towards *technical efficiency*. Where consumers do not have a choice among suppliers, and where 'new-entrant' suppliers are kept at bay by *barriers to entry*, standard theory maintains that consumers are likely to be charged prices which are higher than the economic fundamentals warrant. *Dynamic efficiency* might also be impaired, as the pressure on suppliers to keep abreast of technical improvements etc. is also reduced.

The second issue concerns *allocative efficiency*. In an idealised world of perfectly competitive microeconomic theory, one might imagine a whole range of superannuation vehicles to exist, offering their services to discerning well-informed citizens, with the latter enabled to exercise full freedom of choice. Some of the vehicles would offer underlying portfolios with one set of characteristics, some with completely different characteristics. Some would offer expert hands-on management and administration, or *Rolls-Royce* service. Others would be more stripped-down and austere – perhaps *Mini-Moke* service. The discerning well-informed citizens would self-assort themselves among the range of available vehicles. The funds would then pass-through into the pattern of equity and debt instruments across the economy as a whole that is as good as it gets in terms of *allocative efficiency*. To the 'true believer' in the merits of the competitive free-market system, that picture represents Nirvana, and any institutional constraints which appear to stand in the way of getting closer to it are seen as *distortions*, impeding the achievement of greater allocative efficiency.

Putting this in more tangible terms the absence of member-choice – it is argued – causes some superannuation fund members to have their wealth held in asset-mixes they would prefer *not* to hold. If the bias overall is towards too much fund investment being in equities and too little in debt instruments, this will lead to *too little* debt finance being available to the economy's would-be borrowers (and/or the terms being *too high*) – as compared with the notional benchmark of an allocatively efficient pattern of financing. Some have taken this argument a step further and claimed that compelling low and middle income Australian workers to save through superannuation schemes will divert funds which otherwise would have flowed to the nation's deposit-taking financial institutions, thus impairing the capacity of those institutions to provide the nation's would-be borrowers with an appropriate supply of debt-finance. Proponents of this view tend to focus on would-be borrowers who are small to medium-sized Australian business enterprises, rather than on individuals seeking to build a house-extension (or in-ground swimming pool) or seeking to borrow for an extended overseas holiday.

At the present state of research into these various issues, it would be foolhardy to draw any strong conclusions. Commentators who favour today's status quo argue that both fund-choice and member-choice within funds would increase costs of administration through increased duplication, and increased marketing costs. Fund-members faced with a barrage of conflicting advice and information, might opt for strategies which are too conservative to be allocatively efficient, or which encourage excessive short-termism in portfolio management, or which are prone to other types of fashion following or fashion-shift following. But can we be confident that trustees with 'captive' members will perform significantly better in their strategy choices? The more *responsive* trustees are to the wishes of their members, the less *responsible* they might be in terms of their long-term duties of trust to those members. What, for example, should be done where a scheme member (or members) is quite adamant they want their money put into lottery tickets (or the financial market equivalent)? Why should the answer be any different if the member's adamantly held personal preference was at the opposite pole of the risk spectrum and would severely damage the chance of the funds accumulating to a satisfactory retirement provision?

To the extent that compulsory superannuation *does* cause a rechannelling of funds away from deposit-taking institutions, this may *not* necessarily mean that funds are channelled away from being available for debt finance. Arrangements have already been put in place for some superannuation scheme monies to be made available for lending to home-buyers as first mortgage finance. In a speech in August 1995, the then executive director of the Association of Superannuation Funds of Australia (ASFA), Susan Ryan stated:

> A number of funds, together with National Mutual, have set up a housing trust which makes housing loans to fund-members at lower-than-bank interest rates and earns good returns for the funds which have invested in the trust. This model will shortly be applied to other areas; possibly lending to or investing in undercapitalised but successful export businesses; possibly establishing infrastructure vehicles.

Applying the model to areas such as pools of business loans appears to have been more difficult than ASFA envisaged in 1995. This is hardly surprising. First mortgage loans on owner-occupied houses are relatively easy to risk-assess, to performance-monitor etc., compared with business loans secured only on business plant and equipment, accounts receivable and the like. The bank which processes the business's day-to-day financial transactions would be likely to have a comparative advantage in such risk-assessment and performance monitoring over an entity having to gather and interpret all the information (and do so on an ongoing basis) from scratch. The end result might be more expensive terms of loan finance for small-to-medium business enterprises without good established track records, good collateral, or willing loan guarantors. That need not be allocatively inefficient or dynamically inefficient for the economy. But it might well be if the superannuation fund and mortgage originator channel were redirecting loan-monies away from the traditional intermediary channels only because of the special taxation arrangements accorded to super. Since the Wallis Inquiry into the Australian Financial System, the former segregation of Australian regulatory arrangements for financial enterprises/institutions by *category* has been diminished to some extent, allowing banking groups to be more flexible about participating in other areas of funds management activity (and vice-versa for specialists in the latter areas). This should serve to reduce the likelihood of allocative inefficiencies of this type being generated by Australia's compulsory superannuation saving system.

5 Policies on National Saving: Labour Market Considerations♦

Owen Covick

This chapter considers two questions: what are the effects of the SGC arrangements on labour costs and employment? And how is the capacity of governments to pursue unemployment reduction policies affected by assigning the instrument of fiscal policy to the national saving objective, and the instrument of monetary policy to the inflation containment objective?

Labour costs and employment

Ask a professional economist virtually any question under the sun, and the answer is likely to involve a diagram with a price concept on one axis and a quantity concept on the other. Into that diagram they will try to sketch what boils down to the boundary of the set of situations to which the aggregate of individual would-be suppliers of item x are willing to acquiesce voluntarily. A second line sketches what boils down to the boundary of the situations to which the aggregate of individual would-be users of item x are willing to acquiesce voluntarily. Note, in both cases, that the 'aggregate of individuals' approach that is used tries to see past any effects of collusion or of third-party intervention. Your economist will explain that under conditions of freedom of contract (and re-contract) with competitive bidding and good 'visibility', this *market* will tend to settle down at the intersection of the two lines – and that the point can usually be expected to go hand-in-hand with 'the greatest happiness for the greatest number'.

It takes but a small step for a person accultured to such modes of thought to conceive of this competitive market mechanism as being the 'natural' and general means by which human beings allocate scarce resources among competing uses – when individuals are *not* subject to coercion to behave otherwise. If the greatest happiness of the greatest number is failing to be achieved, the 'natural' place to look for culprits – in this way of thinking – is 'inflexibility' in markets. Is there some spanner (or spanners) in the works holding back the 'natural' propensities of individualistic competitive behaviour from pressing markets towards those happy intersections of economists' sketch diagrams?

When is a tax not a tax? To the sophist the answer is probably when you call it something else *and* get a reasonable proportion of your audience to accept your patter. On that basis, the almost universal unpopularity of payroll tax among the Australian community is probably attributable to the fact that it is actually called 'payroll tax'. Virtually no other government in the world has fallen into that trap. And consequently most Australians 'know' that our rate of payroll taxation is just about the highest in the

♦ The first part of this chapter (to p. 79) represents a condensed version of material previously published in Covick (1997).

world. If our payroll tax were renamed something along the lines of: 'compulsory contributions made by employers to a special government controlled trust fund to enable the government to provide important goodies to today's workers and their families in due course', the level of fear and loathing might be much lower. Australians could be assured that the level of such 'contributions' in Australia was the third lowest in the OECD as a proportion of GDP (see INDECS *State of Play 8*, p 199). Adverts might even be televised showing erstwhile payroll taxation monies being poured through watering cans by smiling employers onto seedlings being nurtured for the benefit of their equally satisfied-appearing employees.

The above might sound flippant, or even cynical. But the effects of payroll taxation cannot be properly appreciated if it is not recognised that the resources thus appropriated do *go* somewhere. And where they are perceived to be going, and to whose ultimate benefit, is of major importance in understanding how labour markets operate. The corollary is that any serious proposals to reduce payroll taxation are likely to need to be paired with proposals to increase alternative forms of taxation, or to cut back on government outlays programmes. *Who* bears the ultimate incidence of these attendant tax increases, or the ultimate costs of the attendant outlays cuts? And more importantly *who*, among the buyers and suppliers of labour, perceives themselves as affected by those attendant effects, and in what way(s)? The full picture needs to be taken into account. Otherwise the labour market analysis is likely to be defective.

In the economists' traditional depiction of the effects of a straightforward payroll tax, it is assumed that there is no direct nexus between the collection of the tax proceeds and the provision of benefits to either of the two sets of actors in the labour market - or at least no such direct nexus *perceived* by either of those two sets of actors. Those tax proceeds just disappear. Under these circumstances the supply and demand curve diagram must be redrawn to clarify the distinction between the gross-of-tax wage rate which the employer pays and the net-of-tax wage rate which the employee receives. The supply-demand equilibrium will typically[1] be at a quantity of employment strictly below the no payroll tax case, with the net-of-tax wage rate also strictly below that no payroll tax situation and the gross-of-tax wage rate higher than it.

But now imagine that the same payroll tax is administered a little differently. The government instructs each employer to keep a record of how much payroll tax is being collected on account of each employee, and to hand over special coupons to each employee at quantities strictly in proportion to the tax collected on each individual employee's account. The employee can present the coupons at a special government-administered agency and use them to 'purchase' units of a certain service: service m. To start the analysis, imagine that the government's supply price of service m in terms of coupons equates exactly to the dollar equivalent price private enterprise suppliers charge, and that every employee and potential employee was previously purchasing at least as much of service m as the new coupon regime allows them to obtain for 'free'.

How does this type of payroll tax affect labour market behaviour? Clearly the supply and demand curve diagram must be redrawn again. As well as clarifying the distinction

---

1 That is, assuming neither the supply curve nor the demand curve is a vertical (or horizontal) straight line.

in the eyes of the employer between the gross of tax wage rate and the net of tax wage rate actually handed to the employee, we must now also clarify the distinction in the eyes of the employee between the (net of tax) wage rate actually received and the gross-of-coupons consumption power that that wage represents. Under the scenario described, the two effects exactly offset one another. The supply-demand equilibrium is at exactly the same employment level as in the no payroll tax case, with the net-of-tax wage rate below the no payroll tax case by exactly the extent of the level of payroll tax on a unit of labour.

To make this story really interesting, one final frill is required. Let service m be one of those services which a government agency has particular advantages in supplying - perhaps insurance against the costs of involuntary unemployment, or insurance against the costs of one's children qualifying to become university students. Let the government's supply price of service m in terms of coupons therefore be strictly below the dollar equivalent price private enterprise suppliers need to charge for that service. Otherwise maintain the assumptions of the earlier scenario. Under these circumstances the supply-demand equilibrium *with* the payroll tax has a higher employment level than the *without* payroll tax case; the gross-of-tax wage rate paid by employers is below the no payroll tax case; while the gross-of-coupons consumption power earned through the supply of a unit of labour is higher than in the no payroll tax case. It is a win-win situation: one of those cases of Pareto improvement of which professional economists are so fond.

Two features are central to this welfare-improving payroll tax. First, there is a perceived direct nexus between the government's collection of the payroll tax and the government's provision to particular 'contributors' of services identified as financed through those tax collections. And second, the services thus provided from the tax's proceeds have peculiar features which mean that government intervention in their provision has advantages over *laissez-faire*. On the second count perception again needs to be stressed. It is the perception of the labour market players that counts in determining the labour market consequences. But if perceptions are later confounded by facts and experience, the situation is likely to be unstable. The same applies to whether 'contributors' are accruing 'entitlements' which will be honoured when they fall due (and whether non-contributors will be treated less attractively). The two features described can be present without the mechanics of an explicit coupon system. There may be contributory service records kept, as in European social security insurance administrations. Or it may be at the level of an 'implicit contract' between a government and its citizenry.

The nexus in the example described above has service m being provided to the employees identified as being those parties on whose 'behalf' the employer remits the payroll tax. It is possible to imagine a situation in which the nexus had the employing enterprise (or its proprietors) receiving coupons which they can convert into a service of direct value to them - perhaps rights to import components into the country outside otherwise-binding tariff quotas? The diagram would need to be redrawn, but the bottom line would be essentially unchanged: if the putative recipients of service m perceive a unit of it to be more attractive (at the appropriate margin) than the tax dollars required to 'purchase' that unit, the with-tax supply-demand equilibrium will be at a higher employment level than the without-tax equilibrium. As we shall see below, this principle is important to many more types of non-wage labour cost.

Focussing still on payroll tax, however, it is important at this point to note the *incidence* theorem. A tax law which places legal responsibility on the employer of labour to remit \$x per unit of labour employed per period will have exactly the same effects on the supply-demand intersection in the labour market diagram as a different tax law which placed legal responsibility on employees to remit labour income tax at \$x per unit of labour performed per period. Note that this result abstracts from any complications arising from interaction effects with other taxes. While an \$x per unit tax makes for ease of diagram drawing the same tax incidence theorem holds for the more common *ad valorem* case. This result can be extended further. Imagine that each worker spends 100 per cent of their labour income on private consumption each period, and faces a comprehensive *ad valorem* consumption tax on that expenditure. Whether the government chooses to collect a given aggregate of tax revenue from a proportionate payroll tax, from a proportionate tax on the labour income of employees, from a proportionate consumption tax on the expenditures of employees, or from *any* combination of the three will all produce the same supply-demand intersection in the labour market diagram - with the same employment level at that point, and the same effective tax incidence.

So next time you see someone trying to use a simple supply and demand diagram to 'prove' that cutting payroll tax would boost employment, I would suggest that two questions are in order: does the proposal involve the forgone revenue being made up by higher taxes on labour income and/or on the consumption spending of employees? Does the proposal involve cutting back on government service provision perceived by labour market players as a *quid pro quo* for their taxes, or higher direct charging for such services? If the proposal is for unfunded tax cuts you might want to discuss that on its merits. If the proposal involves replacing the forgone revenue from other sources, for example out of the income or consumption spending of rentiers, self-employed persons, and/or social security beneficiaries - that again may be worthy of discussion on its merits. But it all requires more than just one shift of one line in one supply-demand sketch diagram. And it needs to be remembered that the payroll tax has traditionally played an important role in the overall structure of the Australian taxation system by providing a higher overall effective tax rate on labour income than on capital income. That then serves to moderate the double-taxation of saving problem associated with a 'pure' income tax system.

There is an important caveat however. The discussion above has focussed on the point of intersection of a labour supply curve and a labour demand curve, each drawn to represent an aggregate of individual decision-makers' behaviour, with that behaviour assumed to be non collusive and not subject to restrictions imposed by third parties (other than requirements for fair dealing, the preclusion of fraudulent and reckless conduct etc). A payroll tax might alter the position of that intersection in the diagram, but *in and of itself* it does not affect the flexibility with which a labour market moves from a situation that is away from an intersection towards the relevant intersection. But now consider a state of affairs in which there is a downward rigidity in the wage as received by the employee, and that that downward rigidity is preventing the labour market from moving towards the intersection of the *underlying* demand and supply curves, as defined above. Under those circumstances reducing the payroll tax rate and covering the budgetary cost by other taxes on employees or by reductions in government services which employees perceive as the *quid pro quo* for the payroll tax *might* allow the labour market to move closer to the underlying supply-demand equilibrium. But 'might' is the operative word. It depends on the nature of the initial rigidity. If for example that rigidity was the result of collective behaviour on the part of labour suppliers to resist any cuts in their living standards, then it would seem likely that any move to cut the payroll tax rate in this way would simply trigger an upward movement in the targeted net-of-payroll-tax wage leaving the gross-of-payroll-tax wage unchanged - or even possibly raising it, if the provision of an efficiency-improving government service is diminished.

Workers' compensation

The incidence theorem of tax theory has a parallel in the area of the legal liability for costs associated with injuries. In a hypothetical society of full and costless information and zero transactions costs, it would make no difference to the substantive supply-demand equilibrium in a labour market whether individual employees were held to be responsible for bearing the costs to themselves of accidental work injuries (medical treatment and rehabilitation, forgone earnings etc.) or whether the employer was held to be responsible for paying appropriate compensation. With a perfect insurance market (which our hypothetical society would naturally have) the insurance costs for employment contract j would be the same whether the employer paid or the employee paid for the relevant cover, and those insurance premia would equate to the 'true' actuarial costs of the relevant risks. If the individual employees carried the legal responsibility for the risk, the supply-demand equilibrium wage would be inclusive of the value of that insurance premium. And no risk-averse worker would fail to insure. If the employer carried the legal liability, the supply-demand equilibrium wage would be lower by the exact value of the insurance premium. In both cases the supply-demand equilibrium employment level is the same.

We do not live in a world of full and costless information and zero transactions costs. Certain precautionary measures can reduce the risks of work accidents, or limit the extent of consequential damages. But information on the degree of cost-effectiveness of particular precautionary measures is resource consuming to obtain. It consumes further resources to obtain accurate information as to whether a particular precautionary measure is being implemented in a particular workplace and in what degree. Once an accident (or equivalent 'incident') has occurred, it is likely to consume resources to assess accurately the extent of the damage inflicted, and to put into pecuniary terms the costs to the injured party (or parties). It may consume further resources assessing whether particular injuries (and associated costs) are *fully* attributable to events in one defined employment engagement - and where this is found not to be the case, assessing the appropriate proportion. On top of all these informational costs there are costs of defining and recording the basis on which contracts have been struck, adjudicating disputes, prosecuting fraudulent misrepresentations etc.

It is usually argued that under these circumstances, it is reasonable for a government to compel that prescribed minimum standards of precautionary measures are maintained in all workplaces in its jurisdiction. That captures economies of scale in processing and disseminating the relevant information. It is also usually argued that informational advantages and transaction costs economies render it resource-efficient for the legal liability for costs of employee work injuries to rest with the employer in some well-defined way. Since the costs of an employer defaulting on any such obligations for compensation would be likely to fall in some significant degree on a nation's social security system - or on innocent widow(er)s and orphans - a government might reasonably make it compulsory that all employers have formal insurance cover with government approved insurers, or have special authorisation to self-insure. In examining any real world system for dealing with work injuries costs, it is useful to focus on these three defining features: what are the arrangements for the prescription of minimum precautionary standards? how well-defined are the employers' liability obligations? what regulatory arrangements surround the writing of employers' liability insurance contracts?

Imagine for a moment a system in which the minimum precautionary standards prescribed are within striking distance of being 'just right' in terms of the cost-efficiency of particular precautionary measures and the balance vis-à-vis the distribution and degree of risk aversion among suppliers of labour. Not only is this so, but it is *perceived* to be so by workers as a whole. Imagine also that full-cover employers' liability insurance is compulsory for all employers and is provided by a monopoly government-administered insurer which operates along lines (and at costs) compatible with insurance industry best practice, and which seeks to charge actuarially fair premiums on all contracts (i.e., no cross subsidies). This system has all the essential features of the case of a payroll tax levied to provide to workers, on a direct nexus basis, a service with special features that render the arrangements Pareto superior to individual procurement of that service by individual workers. The same would be true if we crossed out monopoly government-administered insurer and inserted instead private insurers (and authorised self-insurers) operating on the same basis and with no risk of default.

Under these circumstances, the responsible use of a supply-demand diagram to illustrate the effects of a proposal to reduce workers' compensation insurance premiums (or the costs of prescribed precautionary measures) should not proceed on the basis of shifting the demand curve *alone*, but should ask how the proposal is to be 'funded', and what effects that can be expected to have on the supply curve. The 'after-reform' supply-demand equilibrium could easily be at exactly the same employment level as the before-reform equilibrium - as would be the case if it were generally perceived as simply involving a cost-shifting. The 'after-reform' supply-demand equilibrium would be at a *reduced* level of employment, if it were perceived as involving a shifting of responsibilities towards parties who face higher resource costs in bearing them.

Some general rules for labour market analysis follow from this example, and from the discussion preceding:

- It needs to be appreciated that when an individual accepts hire into and works in a particular employment engagement, certain risks of injury to the person of that individual come into effect which would *not* otherwise be present.

- For decentralised decision-making to function, a society must have rules for determining who is to bear the legal responsibility for costs arising from any such injuries, how such costs are to be assessed (if that is required), how disputes in these areas are to be resolved, and how the costs of such dispute resolutions are to be allocated.
- The various sets of 'rules' can be left to the 'common law', and to evolve with test case interpretations of that law by the courts - or there can be legislated codification (or collectively bargained agreement) that stands in place of the common law (or defined parts thereof).
- Individual suppliers of labour need to form a view, in the light of the prevailing rules, as to how much expected cost is directly their liability in respect of each job engagement under their consideration. This expected cost needs to be lined up against the other non-wage advantages and disadvantages of each such job, and against the overall net advantages of alternative options (self-employment, engagement in production for in-home consumption, 'pure leisure' etc.) to allow each individual to deduce the lowest wage they are willing to work in that job for.
- Individual buyers of labour need to form a view, in the light of the prevailing rules, as to how much expected cost is directly their liability in respect of each additional worker hired onto their payroll. Note that the first employee hired is likely to trigger far higher expected costs than subsequent additional hirings. This expected cost needs to be factored into the employer's calculation of the overall cost of hiring an additional worker, and lined up against the expected contribution of that worker to enterprise revenues, in order to deduce the highest wage the employer will voluntarily employ that worker for.
- If the prevailing rules have a portion of the overall expected costs arising from work injuries chargeable to the public purse, it needs to be noted that those resources need to come from somewhere. If the funds are raised from taxes which affect the perceived rewards from working (or perceived rewards from the employing of labour) these effects also need to be taken into account in drawing the supply and demand curves in one's labour market diagram.
- Finally, the overall ex-ante work-injury-risks costs associated with a particular employment engagement are likely to consist of the sum of four parts: the portion representing the cost the employee expects to bear from their own pocket; the portion representing the cost the employer expects to bear and which is *not* covered by insurance; the cost to the employer of the relevant insurance premiums; and the cost picked up from the public purse. In terms of the *true* overall effects on supply-demand equilibrium in labour markets, it is the level of the *sum* of these four *combined* that is likely to be more important than the disposition of some given total as between the four components. Meaningful workers' compensation reform is about getting that *sum* of the four components down.

This discussion of workers' compensation has so far focussed on the point of intersection of a labour supply curve with a labour demand curve, each drawn to represent an aggregate of individual decision-makers' behaviour and abstracting from complications associated with collusive behaviour and/or restrictions imposed by third parties. The way we have talked about changes to arrangements for handling work-injury costs has conceived of such changes as possibly affecting the position of one (or both) of the two curves in our diagram, and hence the position of the intersection of the two lines in the diagram. In those terms we may have the position of supply-demand equilibrium altered, but we do not have results about the flexibility with which a labour market moves from a situation away from an intersection towards the relevant intersection.

The same caveat needs to be made here as was made in the context of payroll tax above. If a downward rigidity in the pecuniary wage received by the employee were present, at a level preventing the labour market from moving towards the intersection of the *underlying* demand and supply curves, a proposal to 'reform' workers' compensation that involved nothing more than cost-shifting towards the shoulders of the workers *might* allow the labour market to move closer to the underlying supply-demand equilibrium. But 'might' is again the operative word, and for exactly the same reasons as set out in the payroll tax context.

Superannuation

Whatever the moralists might seek to argue to the contrary, employer contributions to superannuation schemes for the benefit of their employees represent deferred pay for those employees. Money that the employer perceives quite correctly as an integral part of the cost of this week (or month)'s labour is not put into this week (or month)'s pay packets or salary cheques of the pertinent employees. Instead it is deployed towards the cost of 'tickets' which the employer does put in those pay packets (or 'salary advices'). Those 'tickets' are redeemable for cash under prescribed rules but are thus redeemable only at a time deferred into the future. The length of time between 'now' and redemption day will typically vary from employee to employee. Age is a major consideration, gender may be. Death is usually one means available for triggering redemption day. Other less 'terminal' means are sometimes available.

In the days when intervention in employer-superannuation contribution arrangements by government or by organised labour was a mere twinkle in Bill Kelty's great grandmother's eye, it was the individual employer's prerogative as to whether superannuation 'tickets' would be issued, and if so, on what terms. Today's professional economists postulate that such employers would have opted in such decision-making for strategies designed to further the individual employer's interest. Ticket-issue and vesting-provisions would, in this view, be set to favour those employees which the employer was most keen to lock-in to long-duration employment, and to then deter any such favoured employees from unilaterally quitting their jobs in favour of higher immediate-period wages elsewhere. Ticket issue would also be restricted to those employees for whom, in the employer's perception, it seemed likely that the expected implicit rate of return in the superannuation 'ticket' arrangements was at least as good as the recipient's average annual rate of subjective time discount over the period between 'now' and redemption. This latter would be over-ridden and 'ticket-issue' required of an employee in circumstances where a retired faithful and long-serving employee would, if otherwise without means of sustenance, be regarded by the broader community as having a legitimate claim for such sustenance on their erstwhile employer. This would have been particularly relevant where the employer was an entity in the public sector or an employer of domestic servants with a high profile locally for being 'socially responsible'.

The bottom line here is that in those hypothetically halcyon days of Bill Kelty's great grandmother, there is a clear basis for the proposition that employer-prerogative superannuation provision was labour-market-improving (assuming an absence of monopsony power). If the employer perceived it as being a benefit to the employer long-term interest to offer a particular package of remuneration arrangements which included super 'tickets', and if some employee(s) perceived that package as being more attractive than the alternatively available 'no-tickets' option, then that must involve a Pareto-improvement. Who could complain?

In today's Australia the payment of a portion of an employee's overall remuneration in the form of superannuation 'tickets' is more commonly characterised by access being provided to all of an employer's employees on a non-discriminatory basis, and with vesting provisions that have the effect of applying little if any penalties to those workers who choose to quit their jobs prior to 'normal' retirement age. It would seem obvious that under such circumstances much of the direct employer-interest angle on superannuation evaporates. The employer might fight a rearguard action defending the use of a defined benefit superannuation scheme which ties the benefit provided into a nexus with pecuniary salary in the final period of pre-retirement employment. That advantages the employee with a steeper-than-average promotion (or pay-rise) trajectory when employed - presumably the type of employee targeted for superannuation cover under the *halcyon-days* approach. It also quite obviously lends itself to manipulation at the employer's prerogative. But apart from effects associated with this type of rearguard action, what can be said of non-discriminatory, fully vested employer superannuation provision? Is it simply a matter of paying part of the employee's remuneration in the form of 'tickets' which have a cost to the employer and a value to the employee that are identical to one another?

A number of points need to be considered in responding to these questions.

- Remuneration through the vehicle of superannuation 'tickets' may be tax-advantaged, as compared with the alternative of direct pecuniary pay. That provides some 'fat' which can be shared between the employer and the employee. But where do the resources that provide that 'fat' come from? Does the burden fall on taxes which affect the real value of the rewards from working and/or on the real value of the rewards from employing labour? If so, there will be effects on the location of the demand and supply curves for labour, and those effects will need also to be incorporated into the analysis. Unless there is some third group of taxpayers bearing the burden (the self-employed, rentiers, etc.) the tax advantages for super may well operate like taking a box to stand on at a crowded sports event: when only a few spectators do so each of them gains an advantage, but when everyone is standing on a box, no-one gains.

- Superannuation 'tickets' may incorporate term life insurance cover and may exploit economies of scale in the administration costs of providing such cover. But the supposed cost savings associated with minimising adverse selection are likely to involve a simple cost shifting onto the shoulders of those who would prefer to 'adversely-select' themselves out of the cover.
- Superannuation 'tickets' may incorporate insurance cover against the risks of unanticipated longevity. Again this may allow the exploitation of economies of scale in administration costs and if so is likely to be labour market improving. But where cost reductions are simply the result of reduced adverse selection, this is likely to boil down to cost shifting.
- Superannuation 'tickets' may incorporate insurance cover against the risks of non-work-related accidents (or major illness) detracting from an individual worker's capacity to earn labour income over a 'full' working life. This cover is usually termed 'invalidity benefits'. Resource economies might be gained by the arrangement of this type of cover through the employer, rather than through individual employees making their own personal arrangements.
- In each of the preceding three areas of insurable risk, it may be that the individual worker whose individual choice is *against* obtaining the relevant cover is implicitly imposing an expected cost on the public purse, via the health budget or the social security safety net. It might be reasonable for a government therefore to view certain would-be self-insurers as being *de facto* cost shifters, and to seek to compel them to refrain from such free-riding. It should be noted however that the requirements of the superannuation guarantee charge (SGC) legislation in today's Australia involve no compulsion whatsoever regarding the first and third of these categories of insurable risk, and impose only a very crude form of requirement for the second type of cover (through the definition of 'preservation age' requirements).
- Deferred pay clearly represents a vehicle for personal saving. Some individuals appear to perceive advantage in arrangements which lock away their savings beyond immediate access and which oblige a regular programme of additions to such 'locked-away' savings. For such individuals the 'locking-away' and the policing of the ongoing obligation for new contributions represent services which are of positive value. Payment in the form of superannuation 'tickets' is to some extent then regarded as more valuable than the equivalent in dollar bills. This provides scope for employer superannuation provision to be labour market improving, if the employer can supply the 'locking-away' and policing services on a lower resource cost basis than under individual purchase of such services.
- There are, however, many individuals in the opposite position to that described in the preceding point. Life cycle factors are likely to cause some individuals at some stages in their lives to be *liquidity-constrained* in their consumption behaviour. For such individuals payment in the form of superannuation 'tickets' is almost certain to be perceived as *less* valuable than the equivalent in dollar bills. (The exceptions would be where associated insurance cover, or tax advantages were sufficient to tilt the scales).

Compulsory employer superannuation contributions under the SGC arrangements have been perceived by many Australian employers, particularly small to medium size employers and/or employers with significant numbers of casual (and other short-term) employees as simply an additional on-cost "imposed from outside". The knee-jerk response has been to point to the SGC as a destroyer of jobs. This chapter has attempted to point out that things are not as simple as that. Debate over labour 'on-costs' in Australia has been a regular feature of debate about Australia's labour markets since the early 1980s. But the nature of the 'on-costs' debate has shifted, and will continue to do so. In the days of centralised wage-fixing, and a Commonwealth government commitment to 'wages policy' the principal focus was on macro-economic issues. What were the various on-costs adding to the economy-wide average cost of labour? Were these components of labour costs growing so rapidly as to frustrate the effects of 'restraint' in direct wages? How did Australia's labour on-costs compare with the situation in the economies of our international competitors?[2]

Elements of that macroeconomic focus remain, but there has been a shift in the on-costs debate towards a microeconomic focus which has gone hand-in-hand with the shift in Australia's overall industrial relations system towards an enterprise-bargaining focus. The key questions now are: Does this particular on-cost serve a sensible economic purpose? Would the joint interests of the employees and proprietors of a particular enterprise be advantaged if on-cost arrangement x were modified in some way, or 'cashed-out', or some new on-cost arrangement z introduced? Is there a legitimate case for third-party intervention to *require* that some particular on-cost arrangement be maintained, or extended, or some new one introduced in a particular enterprise? These are the questions that need to be addressed when considering increasing the SGC-required minimum contribution rate beyond 9 per cent and/or introducing mandatory "employee" contributions (presumably to be collected and remitted by the ever-helpful employer under threat of legal penalties?).

Reducing unemployment while boosting national saving

Even today many students who take economics courses are left with the impression that the one and only *tool of policy* for reducing unemployment in a free-enterprise predominantly market-focussed economy is demand stimulus – meaning increased government sector spending on goods and services, and/or stimulating increased private sector spending by tax breaks, increased government transfer payments, easy credit/low interest rate policies etc. Clearly this type of *cure* for unemployment, as advocated by the macroeconomics textbooks of the 1950 and 1960s, would involve setting the stance of government fiscal and monetary policies on course for reductions in national saving rather than increases therein. As is discussed in Chapters Seven, Eight and Nine economic policy makers do *not* nowadays determine budgetary policy settings on the basis that the reader of 1950s and 1960s text books would expect, except in the special case of the troughs of major recessions.

---

2 See Owen Covick, 'Wages as a component of total remuneration', in John Niland (ed.) *Wage Fixation in Australia*, Allen and Unwin Australia, 1986 and *idem A Measure of Total Labour Costs*, Report prepared for the Advisory Committee on Prices and Incomes (ACPI), AGPS, Canberra 1987.

The consensus in the economics profession for some two decades now has been that demand stimulus is appropriate in the troughs of major recessions, but that *in and of itself* demand stimulus can only go a certain distance in driving down, on a sustainable basis, the unemployment rate of a given economy operating under a given microeconomic structure.

It is an economy's microeconomic structure that determines how the supply-side will respond to any increase in demand. Where monopoly privileges are prevalent in output and/or input markets; where there are barriers to the redeployment of economic resources from one use to another; where people and firms are unable or unwilling to acquire the skills and expertise the market requires, or unwilling/unable to adapt to the evolving demands of their customers (and potential customers); where there are barriers to a more intensive use of scarce plant and equipment inherited from the past; or of labour skills already acquired, an economy will experience a microeconomic malaise.

Such a microeconomic malaise will tend to manifest itself macroeconomically in two ways. An upsurge in internally-sourced demand, whether from public sector stimulus or from private sector 'confidence' effects, will - beyond some point - do more to stimulate an inflow of imports (net of exports) from outside the economy in question, than it does to generate sustainable jobs for that economy's own citizens. And secondly, an upsurge in demand, even if 'balanced' between internally-sourced and externally-sourced demand will - beyond some point - feed into an acceleration in domestic price and wage inflation, rather than generating sustainable jobs for the economy's unemployed.

Macroeconomic issues are usually discussed at a national level and the levers of macroeconomic policy regarded as a Commonwealth government responsibility in Australia. But the two points made in the previous paragraph apply at the State level (and the local or regional level) also. Consideration of whether a State government should use its own spending level, and/or changes in its own tax rates to stimulate State demand should pay careful heed to the first point - which boils down to the question: how much would the State government 'stimulus' initiative translate into increased indebtedness to parties outside the State? Consideration of whether a State's citizens and/or the State government should be lobbying the Commonwealth government to engage in nation-wide demand stimulus initiatives should pay careful heed to both points: would such action blow out Australia's current account deficit/external indebtedness position? would such action re-ignite inflation in Australia? Unless you were confident that neither of those speed-limits would bite, demand stimulus would seem to offer only a short-term respite in unemployment, not a sustainable improvement for the community. Coping with the costs incurred in achieving such a short-term respite might leave the situation worse than at the time of the respite's instigation.

The bottom line is that whenever one hears calls to improve the employment/ unemployment situation by techniques that amount to no more than demand stimulus, one has to ask the question: how is the supply-side of the economy likely to respond to such stimulus? Will we get sustainable additional employment in our economy, or will we hit these 'speed-limits' caused by problems within the micro-economic structure of our economy? Mainstream economic thinking about the supply side of the macroeconomy today gives prominence to a concept known by the acronym NAIRU. It is sometimes called the 'natural rate of unemployment' or 'equilibrium unemployment'. But that can be seriously misleading. As the London *Economist* stressed in 1994: 'some of these labels imply that the NAIRU is somehow preordained, beyond the reach of economic policy. That is wrong' (*The Economist*, February 19, 1994, p. 71). The acronym stands for the non-accelerating inflation rate of unemployment. It means the unemployment rate below which any pressure from aggregate demand feeds into boosting an economy's inflation rate. An economy's NAIRU in some particular period of time is determined by a number of factors, the most important of which seem to be the microeconomic structure of that economy at that time, the recent economic experience of that economy, and the external trading and investment environment it faces. The first and third are susceptible to economic policy initiatives. Some types of economic policy can be expected to act to reduce an economy's NAIRU. Other types of policy could be expected to have the opposite effect. Over time, good policy can gain additional leverage through the second of the three factors.

In the 1950s and 1960s, Australia's NAIRU was at levels which enabled Australians to enjoy 'full employment' in most years other than significant recession years, without accelerating inflation or a blowing out of the current account of the balance of payments. Since the early 1970s, Australia's NAIRU has been substantially higher. The pessimists believe Australia's NAIRU is at present only a smidgen below the figures we are currently experiencing (say around 6.5 per cent). Even optimists would be loath to bet with their own money that it is much below 5.5 per cent. Unless Australia's NAIRU can be reduced markedly, policies that focus on stimulating aggregate demand are doomed to run into the brick wall of accelerating inflation and/or a blowing out of external indebtedness. Demand management alone cannot achieve an acceptably low unemployment rate in the face of an unacceptably high NAIRU. That's the bad news. For the good news, let me quote from the London *Economist* of March 1997.

> *"...nobody any longer thinks that the NAIRU is fixed, which puts the spotlight back on policies that might reduce it".*[3]

How to reduce the NAIRU

Proposals for reducing an economy's NAIRU tend to fall into three broad major categories. There is the category which takes as its starting point, the proposition that where competing individual buyers of some good or service deal with competing individual sellers under conditions of freedom of contract (and re-contract), competitive bidding and 'good visibility', then this *market* will tend to move towards a supply/demand equilibrium, characterised by an absence of *either* frustrated buyers *or* frustrated sellers at the equilibrium 'price'. The question is then asked: What is stopping the market price of labour from adjusting flexibly in such a way as to reduce the number of frustrated sellers (i.e., the unemployed)? Where impediments to thus-

[3] *The Economist*, March 8, 1997, p. 98. Note that with monetary policy delegated to a Central Bank instructed to keep inflation under control, it becomes the Central Bank's perception of the NAIRU that is of more practical importance than whether the optimists' view is correct. Expansionary budgetary initiatives which the Central Bank perceived as inflationary would attract rapid-response monetary tightening.

defined labour market flexibility are identified, the internal logic of this approach calls for policy initiatives to remove, reduce or otherwise attenuate such impediments.

The second broad major category focuses on the issue of mismatch in an economy's labour market. Except for atypical cases, it is rare for any two alternative jobs to look exactly the same in the eyes of a worker - or for any two job-seekers to look like exact equivalents for one another in the eyes of a would-be employer. Mutually compatible job-seekers and employers-with-vacancies may fail to become aware of one-another, or may fail to recognise their mutual compatibility upon meeting. Better systems of information provision and possibly third-party intermediation by 'job-brokers' have the potential to reduce such *friction* in the system. A specialist third-party intermediary with a good feel for the market might be able to go further and advise a client when he/she is 'banging their head against a brick wall' in pursuing a particular type of job in some particular time and place at some particular required remuneration and conditions, and might suggest an alternative 'second best' (or 'third best') strategy that is preferable to continued frustration. This has its direct parallel in advice to the employer side.

The Commonwealth Employment Service (CES) was established to provide these types of service, and to do so on an almost-exclusively taxpayer-funded basis. The monopoly privileges conferred by the taxpayer-funding may have inhibited the development of a competitive market for such services and may have allowed the CES to fall behind best practice in the cost-efficient delivery of such services. The close identification, in public perceptions, of the CES with the nation's social security safety-net arrangements may also have impeded its capacity to perform effectively in the job-brokerage function. But announcing the abolition of the CES without first making *secure* appropriate provision for a smooth handover to effective successor arrangements was almost certainly unwise. The crisis in morale within the CES following the 1996 Commonwealth Budget was almost certainly of immediate detriment to Australia's NAIRU - even if the successor arrangements can be assessed to have eventually come out to be positive. It ought to have been possible for the Commonwealth government to handle the transition better – but that is now water under the bridge. Looking forward, the challenge is to improve the functioning of the new system further.

Also, within this second broad category of proposals for reducing an economy's NAIRU fall suggestions regarding the preparation-for-entry arrangements for persons about to enter, or re-enter, active job search in the economy in question. Persons completing compulsory full-time education form the biggest category. But there are other significant categories: immigrants; persons returning to the paid-labour market from child-rearing responsibilities; persons recovering from injuries; persons being released from detention; and so on. Focusing on persons completing full-time education, it is obvious that a risk is always present that the package of skills and training provided by the 'education supplier' does not harmonise with the package which putative employers feel they can reasonably state to be 'essential'. A teleological story about the development of compulsory taxpayer-funded school education would stress its role in delivering the skills and training packages required by that economy's employers. A well-trained economist would point out that the monopoly privileges conferred by the taxpayer-funding would inhibit the development of a competitive market for the delivery of such packages, and may have allowed the State-funded school system (and post-secondary system) to fall behind best practice in the cost-efficient delivery of such packages. The close identification, in public perceptions, of the State-funded school system, in preventing school-age 'children' from simply *roaming the streets* may also have impeded its capacity to perform effectively in its skills and training functions.

The third broad category of proposals for reducing an economy's NAIRU focuses on the statistical fact that the longer a person has been unemployed, the lower becomes that person's probability of succeeding in finding themself a job. Assessing the various studies of this phenomenon, Piggott and Chapman reported that the probability of obtaining employment over the next nine months is about 75 per cent for those who have been unemployed for less than nine months, but falls to about 25 per cent for those who have been unemployed longer than 18 months.[4] Outlining the factors causing this phenomenon, Chapman stated:

> As far as the individuals are concerned, it is likely that they reduce job search given a continued lack of success. Moreover, many in the group lose contact with the world of paid work, which means that they have less information about upcoming jobs. The evidence suggests strongly that having mainstream employment is a very important job search asset. Possibly more important is what potential employers believe about the labour-market skills of the long-term unemployed. It is rational for employers to use 'signals' as to the likely productivity of job applicants, with one of the negative signs being how long a person has been out of work.
>
> ... Over time, changes in the effectiveness of search, skill loss, and employers' use of unemployment duration as an indication of adverse characteristics combine to push the long-term unemployed to the back of the hiring queue.[5]

What this means is that as the level of demand in an economy starts to grow, employers are keener on competing with one another for the short-term unemployed, and/or bidding already-employed persons away from their existing employers, than in hiring from the pool of long-term unemployed. It is as if the long-term unemployed have ceased to be part of the *effective* supply of labour in the economy. Inflationary pressure emerges at a higher level of total unemployment than when the pool of long-term unemployed was smaller. By the simple fact of having experienced a period of sustained high unemployment, an economy's NAIRU is thus raised - even without a deterioration in its microeconomic structure, or in the external environment it faces.[6] This then provides the logic behind those proposals for reducing an economy's NAIRU which focus on the long-term unemployed (and/or those at risk of becoming long-term unemployed), and seek to assist such persons in reintegrating with the effective labour supply of the economy (that is, appearing to potential employers as equivalent to a

---

4 Cited in Bruce Chapman, (1997), 'Labour Market Programmes', in Industry Commission, *Changing Labour Markets: Prospects for Productivity Growth, Workshop Proceedings*, Industry Commission, Melbourne, p. 179.

5 *ibid*, p. 180.

6 The phenomenon of the NAIRU creeping up and down behind the actual unemployment rate is known as *hysteresis*. See pp. 80-86 of INDECS (1995), *State of Play 8*, Allen and Unwin Australia for more on this.

person who has recently been in work). One approach is to provide short-term wage subsidies to targeted persons, in effect buying them a period of work experience with a mainstream employer. A second approach is to create short-term jobs for targeted persons within the public sector (or quasi-public sector). For persons who mainstream employers are particularly resistant to hiring, the latter may be the only realistic alternative.

Of these three broad categories of proposals for reducing an economy's NAIRU, it is the second and third that are usually identified in the minds of the public with a compassionate approach to the plight of the unemployed - with the third in particular involving the community extending a tangible taxpayer-funded helping hand. The first category, in contrast, is often identified with a callous approach and hence carries a potential to stir community divisiveness between those favoured by good fortune in the market demand for their talents, and those not thus favoured.[7] These considerations will clearly affect the relative political acceptability to the community of the various proposals - something at least as important in a democratic society as the actual probability of the proposals in question succeeding in driving down the NAIRU. Political pragmatism carries the risk, however, that the politically most acceptable 'initiatives' for tackling the unemployment problem might have no probability of a beneficial effect on the NAIRU at all, or may even increase it. Such 'initiatives' satisfy only the requirement to be seen to be doing something. Explicit fatalism would be more honourable.

Stop, you're going the wrong way

Some of the so-called 'common-sense' remedies proposed for tackling today's unemployment problem actually serve to propel the NAIRU in the wrong direction (i.e., upwards). Freezing tariff-reduction programs bolsters the anti-competitive privileges of capital and labour already employed in the relevant industries. It also rewards the dedication of scarce Australian resources to the processes of political lobbying and favour-seeking. That acts as a signal for talented Australians to deploy their future energies thus, instead of into functions which have the potential to boost the welfare of the community as a whole. Giving artificial tax breaks (or specially-negotiated subsidy packages) to particular firms might create good photo opportunities and ribbon cutting footage. But it creates monopoly type privileges, rewards political lobbying and channels community talent into competing for government favours and away from furthering the genuine competitiveness of the economy's productive enterprises.

It might seem common sense that if State government agencies, State-owned enterprises or State-protected monopoly enterprises keep on their payrolls persons for whose services they no longer have a true functional need, that is good for the State's unemployment rate. In a short-term sense that is probably true. And if it were part of a humane process of helping the relevant individuals make the transition to alternative

---

7 Reserve Bank Governor, Ian Macfarlane, made an interesting point on this issue (*Financial Review*, 16 May, 1997, p. 12): *'... while income inequality may not seem fair, unemployment is not very fair either. Some of our labour market regulations, and many of our attitudes towards labour market outcomes, indeed some of our very ideas about fairness, stem from a time when the unemployment rate was 2-3 per cent'.*

employment, it might be good for the State's NAIRU. But pushing the State's NAIRU in the opposite direction is the cost of employing the relevant individuals. This has to be borne either by the user charges of the employing bodies, or by the State's tax-base. It will almost certainly increase the costs of other employers doing business (and providing employment) in the State - and/or increase the taxation wedge between the employer-cost of labour and the employee-reward from working. Those two things raise the NAIRU. In addition, unless the sheltered surplus workers have no possibility whatsoever of obtaining alternative employment, acting to keep them out of the labour markets serves to increase the NAIRU on those markets - because labour demand pressure will create upward pressure on inflation earlier than it would otherwise.

Mention of the taxation wedge between the employer-cost of labour and the employee-reward from working naturally leads to that old favourite of enthusiasts for a pain free anti-unemployment strategy: cutting payroll tax. Next time you hear someone advocating that approach, I would suggest you ask two questions. Does the proposal involve the forgone revenue being made up by higher taxes on labour income and/or the consumption spending of workers? Does the proposal involve cutting back on government service provision perceived by workers and/or employers as a *quid pro quo* for their taxes, or higher direct charging for such services? Under either of these two cases the taxation wedge *properly defined* is unchanged - so you need some other story as to why the NAIRU should be affected. If the proposed payroll tax cut is to be unfunded, it has to be assessed as just another demand stimulus tool.

Other common-sense sounding proposals for improving the unemployment situation which upon closer inspection turn out to be likely to drive the NAIRU in the wrong direction include: making it harder/more costly for an enterprise to dispense with the services of a newly hired employee whose performance proves unsatisfactory; compulsory early retirement for older workers who their employers would prefer to retain in employment; driving married women out of the paid workforce and back into the home; and compulsory reductions in the allowable weekly hours which employees may agree of their own free will to work. These issues were discussed further in Owen Covick, (1997), "The Australian Labour Market - September 1997", *Australian Bulletin of Labour*, Vol. 23, No. 3.

So what can be done about persistent high unemployment in Australia as a whole, and South Australia in particular? There are basically four possibilities:

- Press ahead more forcefully with microeconomic reform (or 'structural reform') initiatives, both to improve productivity and hence demand for labour, and to improve the functioning of the price mechanism in harmonising such demand with the supply of labour. This will encounter resistance from those who prefer to see our markets operate in the ways they have traditionally operated (particularly our wage determining and employment-conditions determining arrangements).
- Seek to improve the matching process between the skills employers want and the skills would-be employees offer. This will encounter resistance from those who prefer to see our employment services and our education system continue to operate in the traditional ways.

- Seek to equip the long-term unemployed with what is necessary to get them closer to the front of the hiring queue. This costs money - large sums of money. And the cost of delivering *true* help to the most disadvantaged is very high. This is likely to encounter resistance from tax payers.
- If resistance to one, two and three is insuperable, fall back on fatalism - or go through the motions of implementing *empty gesture* initiatives, while trying to select ones which do not actually make matters worse.

6 Demutualisation, Privatisation, and National Saving♦

Owen Covick

The last ten years or so have seen substantial changes in the ownership structure of major segments of Australian industry and commerce. Enterprises which had been owned by governments (Commonwealth and State), or had been operating as mutuals owned by their customers, have been - or are being - transformed into enterprises with ownership rights and responsibilities vested in shareholders able to trade those property rights for cash on easily-accessible and well-functioning markets. The process has perhaps gone furthest in the area of banks and bank-like financial intermediaries. The full privatisation of the Commonwealth Bank was completed in July 1996. No State government now owns a licensed bank. Almost all the still existing enterprises which were previously mutual building societies of significant size are now either stock-exchange listed companies (or components thereof) or unlisted companies with well functioning "over-the-counter" markets for their shares.[1]

Elsewhere within the arena of financial enterprises whereas once each State had its own wholly-owned insurance enterprise, Queensland is now the only State government to retain ownership rights over an insurer and it now shares those rights with private shareholders. The transformation of National Mutual from a fully mutual life office to a fully shareholder owned and stock exchange listed company was completed in 1995-96. In September 1996 the Colonial Group announced the details of how it proposed to transform itself from mutual to shareholder owned listed company by the end of the 1996-97 financial year. The nation's biggest life office, the AMP, demutualised in 1998. The operator of the nation's biggest general insurance enterprise, the NRMA (The National Roads and Motorists' Association of NSW), was well down the road to demutualisation in 1994 when its progress was stalled by a successful legal challenge. The NRMA's insurance enterprise (The NRMA Insurance Group, now called IAG), but *not* the NRMA itself, was then demutualised in 2000.

Outside the arena of financial enterprises, the same or similar processes of conversion of ownership structures are to be found in other sectors. While Paul Keating was prime minister, the Commonwealth government converted Qantas and CSL to fully private shareholder owned, stock exchange listed companies. Victoria did the same with its TAB, followed by NSW with its TAB. The Howard government in 1996-97 converted Telstra to a one-third private shareholder owned, two thirds Commonwealth-owned stock exchange listed company and in 1999 moved from this position to 49 per cent private/51 per cent Commonwealth. This list is not meant to be exhaustive. The basic

♦ A previous version of this chapter was published under the same title in *Economic Papers*, Vol. 15, December 1996.

1 The *Australian Financial Review* provides daily information on transactions in two unlisted building societies: The Illawarra Mutual (sic), and Pioneer. See the 'Unlisted Companies' section.

point is that property rights in the operation of a significant number of previously government owned enterprises have now become available for trade on the nation's capital markets. In addition, certain enterprises previously structured as farmers' co-operatives or retailers' co-operatives for conducting wholesaling functions have undergone (or are undergoing) demutualisation. The Australian Stock Exchange itself demutualised in 1998, and its shares are now traded through the facilities of itself. The Sydney Futures Exchange has also demutualised with its shares traded on the *Austock Exempt Market.*

Australia has thus clearly been going through a period of substantial change in the ownership structure of major segments of the nation's asset base and the direction of that change has been towards ownership rights which are more easily traded, or more "liquid" than had previously been the case. Under the newly emerging arrangements those with ultimate ownership of the relevant property rights and who wish to divest for a *quid pro quo* can more easily do so. Those seeking to acquire (or expand) ownership of the relevant property rights, and who are willing and able to provide an appropriate *quid pro quo* can also more easily do so. Of the 40 largest (by market capitalisation) Australian domiciled companies listed on the Australian Stock Exchange, 11 are there as a result of privatisations or demutualisations.

The purpose of this chapter is to examine the likely effects of these ownership structure changes on the level of Australian *national saving*. Can privatisation and demutualisation be expected to contribute to an increasing of Australia's rate of national saving, thus taking some pressure off the perceived need for tight budgetary policy and compulsory superannuation? Or is the likely effect in the opposite direction? In light of the stress placed by the Commonwealth government in successive Budgets during the 1990s on the perceived urgent requirement for a greater direct contribution from the public sector to increasing Australia's level of national saving, these would seem to be important questions.

The first section of this chapter outlines briefly the purely "national accounting" effects of instances of the demutualisation or the privatisation of an enterprise. The following two sections consider in more detail the consequences for national saving flowing from the principal behavioural effects that can be expected to be generated by demutualisation and privatisation initiatives. The chapter's findings are then summarised in the concluding comments section.

Stocks and flows

National saving is a flow variable. It represents the portion of the flow of national disposable income over a defined accounting period (usually a financial year, sometimes a quarter) which is *not* spent on current consumption purposes (either private consumption spending or public consumption spending) in that same accounting period. If Australia had an integrated national accounts system which included balance-sheet (or *stock*) data as well as *flow* data, there would be a clearly discernible relationship between the flow variable national saving and the stock variable national net wealth (which might perhaps be called "national savings" with an 's' on the end, to denote its distinction from the flow variable). National net wealth at the end of the defined accounting period would be equal to national net wealth at the beginning of the period *plus* national saving during the course of the period *plus* an adjustment for the net result of *revaluation* effects between the two balance sheet dates.

The view that Australia's level of national saving is too low, and that public policy action is needed to remedy that problem, is focussed firmly on the flow variable and in particular its relationship to two other flow variables: total new capital purpose spending within Australia (or *domestic investment spending*); and the current account deficit on Australia's balance of payments. The CAD is equal to the shortfall between national saving and total domestic investment spending as was explained in Chapter One. If the CAD is perceived as unacceptably high, it necessarily follows that any resolution to that problem must involve either national saving being increased or domestic investment spending being reduced, or some combination of the two. Note that if increases in national saving were accompanied by equal or greater increases in domestic investment spending that would *not* help achieve the purpose of reducing the CAD.

The demutualisation of an enterprise or the privatisation of an enterprise, *in and of itself* represents an act of balance sheet adjustment - possibly accompanied by revaluation effects. Thus *in and of itself*, some actual act of privatisation or of demutualisation has no immediate direct consequence for the flow variables of the economy. If the accounting system in use represents the receipt of privatisation proceeds by the vendor government as a 'flow' which boosts its recorded income and its recorded saving for the given accounting period, that same accounting system - to be consistent - should represent the payment of those proceeds as an 'outflow' from the purchasing sector, reducing its recorded saving by an equal and offsetting amount. If the purchasing sector is the domestic private sector there is clearly no overall impact on national saving. If the purchasing sector is the rest of the world, and provided one can feel confident that this is (on day one at least) purely a portfolio composition change in the mix of the net foreign capital inflow that would have occurred anyway, there is again no overall impact on national saving.[2]

This argument that acts of privatisation in and of themselves have direct effects on stock variables in the national balance sheet but no direct effects on flow variables such as national saving is well-known and widely-accepted. In the days when government Budgets in Australia were presented on a 'cash' accounting basis and not an 'accruals' basis, this led to the conclusion that asset sales proceeds should be excluded from the Budget bottom line before that bottom line could be analysed for year-to-year changes in the direct contribution of fiscal policy to the goal of an increased level of national saving. The emphasis given in the Commonwealth Budget papers to the 'underlying budget deficit' when discussing the 'cash' basis figures is evidence of Treasury acceptance of that argument. It should be noted though that certain peculiarities in the

[2] Note that if a particular act of privatisation caused the 'rest of the world' sector to alter its desired portfolio composition in the direction of increased overall net holdings of Australian liabilities (equity and debt combined) *cet. par*, then this could be expected to lead to a bidding up of the Australian dollar, a widening of the CAD, and a *reduction* in Australian national saving for the relevant period. The same effect could be triggered by an act of demutualisation as discussed later in the body of this paper.

'accruals' based accounting system means that some privatisation proceeds *are* included in the "accruals"-based bottom line (see Chapter Seven).

If that were the whole of the story about the effects of privatisation and demutualisation - that they alter the composition of balance sheets but have no impact on flow variables - it is hard to see why any economists would want to get enthusiastic about supporting such changes in ownership-structure arrangements. The changes themselves involve various costs of adjustment (legal costs, printing and distributing prospectuses, establishing share registry systems etc.). If the behaviour in flow terms of the relevant enterprises and of their ultimate owners is expected to be no different in future time periods under the new ownership-structure arrangements than would have occurred under unchanged arrangements, then why waste the resources consumed by those adjustment costs? If, on the other hand, future behaviour in flow terms is expected to be different in consequence of the ownership-structure changes, surely the effects of that behavioural change on future national saving should be taken into account as resulting from the triggering acts of privatisation or demutualisation?

In principle at least it is possible to separate the overall effects on future behaviour into two types. Firstly, effects concerning behaviour of the holders/erstwhile-holders of the ultimate property rights in a relevant enterprise, assuming that the enterprise itself behaves no differently after the privatisation or demutualisation than it would have done in the absence of such privatisation/demutualisation. That is: the enterprise is expected to continue producing the same flows of outputs , selling at the same prices, and using the same flows of inputs, incurring the same costs, as would have occurred anyway; its capital outlays are the same as would have occurred anyway; the mean expected present value of its projected future net income stream is unchanged, as is the degree of risk surrounding that mean expectation. Secondly, we consider effects concerning changes in the way the enterprise itself operates, and how these changes might cause "additional" changes in the behaviour of the holders/erstwhile-holders of property rights in the enterprise.

Liquidity effects

At the heart of the first of these two types of effect is the issue of liquidity. Imagine that two instruments (or "titles") existed, each of which entitled its owner or holder to an identical future stream of income receipts, identical rights of control over some defined economic entity, and an identical pattern of risk exposure. The two instruments would be of identical "net present value" as conventionally defined. But now let one of the instruments differ from the other in terms of the degree of costs associated with an assignment of the set of rights and obligations represented by it to a new holder (owner) in exchange for some mutually agreed *quid pro quo*. The more liquid instrument would clearly be of greater value to its holder than the less liquid. We would expect market prices to reflect that fact, assuming free markets. Differences in liquidity can of course arise from other sources such as ease of identification, divisibility, "depth" of market etc.[3] But for the moment focus on this particular source of liquidity difference. Moreover consider the extreme case where the relatively illiquid of the two otherwise-

3 The classic source on this issue is Karl Menger, 'On the Origin of Money' *Economic Journal*, Vol. 2 (1892), pp. 239-255.

identical instruments is subject to a complete legal prohibition on the assignment of the set of rights and obligations represented by it from one holder to a new holder in exchange for any *quid pro quo* which two such consenting parties might otherwise be happy to agree to. That essentially makes that instrument totally illiquid. There exists *no* market price at which its inherent 'value' can be *realised* by a current period holder.

In many 'mutual' organisations the property rights associated with membership are totally illiquid in this sense of the term.[4] A member might be legally permitted to divest at a price of zero (or at some non-market determined positive price labelled 'refund of member-share') by resignation. But the downside of that is that a current member's proportionate share in the total rights and obligations associated with the mutual's operations might be involuntarily expanded by the resignations of other members, or involuntarily diluted by the admission of new members at nominal (or in any event 'non-market') joining fees. A further complication arises if, as is the norm, the death of a member is treated in the same way as the voluntary resignation case above. An individual member with a life expectancy which is below that of the mutual organisation itself will then be holding 'title' to a stream of rights and obligations which is 'shorter' than a simple proportionate calculation of current members' shares would suggest.

When a government owns and operates a business enterprise, that government's 'stakeholders' (taxpayers and potential taxpayers, plus beneficiaries of unilaterally alterable transfer payments[5]) stand in a relationship to that particular business enterprise which has analogies with the situation of the mutual members outlined above. The major difference is that 'voluntary resignation of membership' typically requires a geographical relocation and full transfer of residency rights and obligations - as does 'joining' other than through birth. Individual South Australians could not walk out on the State Bank of South Australia as easily as individual Victorians could walk out on the Pyramid Building Society (pre-collapse).

Returning to the situation of a 'mutual' organisation which is initially in the situation described above, consider now the effects of a demutualisation. Remember that the enterprise activities previously conducted by the mutual are assumed to be expected to continue operating in the future exactly as if no demutualisation had taken place. Assume further, for simplicity, that each member's proportionate share in the present value of the income stream generated by the mutual's activities if it were not demutualised has been determined precisely, and that ordinary shares in the demutualised entity have been distributed for no pecuniary consideration[6], in proportion

---

4 Another example is the property rights to a person's own human capital in societies in which slavery is illegal.

5 Holders of a government's debt, concerned about possible default, form a separate category of stakeholder as they are typically free to sell their bonds. If some other government (perhaps the Commonwealth?) has guaranteed that government's bondholders, the circle of 'stakeholders' as defined here is widened to include *that* government's taxpayers, potential taxpayers, and transfer payment beneficiaries.

6 The success of the legal challenge to the originally proposed NRMA demutualisation seems to have turned largely on the fact that 'for no pecuniary consideration' was represented in the various documents sent to members by the word 'free'. Economists who subscribe to the aphorism 'there is no such thing as a free lunch' will no doubt have applauded the court's finding on that challenge.

to these 'share-entitlements', to the membership base of the erstwhile mutual. The new shares are assumed to be fully transferable from the earliest convenient date after the completion of the various formalities and paperwork. The shares are assumed to be listed at a recognised and easily accessible stock exchange from that date.

Under these circumstances the balance sheet adjustments associated with the restructuring of the stock of pre-existing property rights will almost certainly be accompanied by major revaluation effects. Prior to the restructuring, the mutual's members would have valued their membership rights in their personal (notional) balance sheets at a significant discount from a conventionally calculated present value basis, because of their extreme illiquidity. Many of the mutual's members may have entered (notionally) a value of zero against those rights. Listing day will see that set of discounts for illiquidity eliminated. The new shares can be valued in their holders' (notional) balance sheets at a readily discernible market price, adjusted now only for brokerage and other such anticipatable costs (stamp duty, postage etc.). If we assume that the various mutual members were in a situation of equilibrium prior to the demutualisation, in terms of their desired balance between their stock of net wealth and their flow of income, they *must* now be in a state of disequilibrium. Each can be expected to act to restore equilibrium by increasing their flow of consumption expenditure. Some will finance this directly by selling demutualisation shares, others by running down other asset holdings, and still others (possibly the majority) by simply easing back on the pace at which they accumulate other assets or seek to discharge debts. In the extreme case of the liquidity constrained, they can be expected to sell their demutualisation shares as soon as possible and immediately outlay the entire proceeds on current consumption.

To summarise, when we set aside the enterprise-behaviour effects of a demutualisation and concentrate our attention on the liquidity effects alone, we have a situation that amounts to a one-off windfall gain effect under either a permanent income or a life-cycle income type model of consumption behaviour. All affected households will respond by saving less and consuming more. For those who are not liquidity constrained and who have a planning horizon which is long, the effect will be relatively slight but lasting. For those nearing the end of their life expectancy and not desirous of leaving bequests, and for the liquidity constrained, the effect will be time-concentrated and marked. Note that all affected are better off. Society has moved to a Pareto superior state. But national saving is definitely reduced by this part of the demutualisation effect. The extent to which that reduction is concentrated into the period immediately following the share listing day will depend on the proportion of the mutual's members (weighted by the extent to which they benefit) who are either liquidity constrained or elderly.[7]

It should be noted that in some demutualisations the process is accompanied by a new capital raising to which members are invited to subscribe funds, and with non-subscribing members effectively shut out from the distribution of highly liquid 'shares' in replacement of the pre-existing and highly illiquid membership property rights.

---

[7] Note that some of the reduced saving effect can occur prior to listing day through anticipation of the 'windfall'. By definition, however, such anticipation effects are ruled out for the liquidity constrained.

There is often a significant time-lag between the point at which the member must hand over additional funds and the point at which the member becomes free to realise their restructured titles *in full* for cash on the capital market. This time-lag can be accomplished by setting a date in the future at which a bonus issue of 'loyalty shares' will be made to those who have continuously held the new capital raising instruments over the full period up to that date. This type of arrangement clearly has distributional implications across the mutual's membership base. Essentially it will serve to preclude the liquidity constrained from participating in the liquidity effect upward-revaluations of the items in their personal (notional) balance sheets representing their membership rights in the mutual. All of the liquidity effects will be experienced by members who are not liquidity constrained.[8] All can be expected to respond by saving less and consuming more, but the overall effect on national saving will be less 'front-loaded', more smoothed and more lasting than under the 'free' share distribution arrangement discussed earlier.

Turning now to privatisations, but continuing to keep enterprise behaviour effects out of the analysis until the next section, three types of case need to be distinguished. In case one the vendor government distributes shares in the relevant enterprise to all or some of its citizens at zero pecuniary consideration. In case two the vendor government goes to great pains to forecast accurately the post-listing market price of the shares, (*cet. par.*) does that job accurately, and sells the shares to its citizens at exactly that price. In case three the vendor government sells the shares to its citizens, subject to some sort of rationing arrangement, at a price somewhere between zero and the case two price.

Case one is directly analogous to the demutualisation arrangement with 'free' shares. If it were possible to distribute the 'free' shares exactly in accordance with the pre-existing pattern of underlying 'stakeholder' property rights in the enterprise, the revaluation effects on personal balance sheets generated by the liquidity effect would all be positive. National saving would be reduced. The extent to which that national saving reduction was 'frontloaded' would depend on the proportion of the shares going to persons who are liquidity constrained or have short planning horizons. If the share distribution is *not* in accordance with the pre-existing pattern of underlying 'stakeholder' rights, a further factor needs to be considered. The future income stream of the now-privatised enterprise will accrue to its shareholders, not to the government. The government will therefore need to raise additional future taxes or reduce future transfer payment flows, assuming it seeks to maintain a level of government saving unchanged from under the no privatisation case. If citizens factor those additional future taxes and/or reduced transfer payments into their personal financial planning, the non-liquidity constrained who get significantly less than their 'fair share' of the 'free' privatisation shares will tend to save more and consume less as a consequence of the privatisation.

---

8 Some members who are not liquidity constrained will fail to participate, either because they have neglected to do their arithmetic properly, or because they are suspicious of financial complexity. They, together with the liquidity constrained, will see their previously existing property rights in the mutual stripped from them. If they had previously valued those rights at zero in their personal (notional) balance sheets, this will have no effect on their consumption/saving behaviour.

Case two is completely different from anything discussed earlier under the demutualisation heading. The float is assumed to be priced in such a way that all of the revaluation effects generated by the liquidity effect are captured by the vendor government. If we assume that governments have infinite time horizons and never have to consider facing liquidity problems, the value of the pre-privatised enterprise in the government's balance sheet should not have been subject to any discount for illiquidity, and should therefore have been exactly equal to the proceeds from the 'fully-priced' privatisation appearing in the 'post-privatisation' balance sheet (assuming away transactions costs etc., incurred in connection with the float). Under these circumstances there is no change in the level of national saving. Case three is clearly a 'half-way-house' between cases one and two. The closer the float price is to the case two price the smaller will be the national saving effects. Such national saving effects as are present from the liquidity effect will almost certainly be in the direction of reduced national saving.[9]

Enterprise behaviour effects

A change in the ownership structure of an enterprise from mutual to a listed shareholder owned company may cause changes in the enterprise's behaviour. As a mutual, the enterprise's managers might have faced conflicting messages from the members as to the desired objectives of the enterprise. The members may have starved the enterprise of capital, or may themselves have been starved of appropriate distributions from its operating surplus. A managerial elite may have seized effective control of the enterprise and opted for a growing staff pyramid, a comfortable work-life and enhanced managerial 'perks', rather than pursuing maximum technical efficiency in production and strategies to put (and keep) the enterprise on an optimal path for dealing with emerging changes in technologies, markets and client requirements. The existence of a market on which voting rights can be bought and sold, and on which price changes provide a visible indicator of enterprise performance, may stimulate management to improve technical and dynamic efficiency. Providing management with stock options may help overcome principal-agent problems. And once listed, organising new capital raisings (and the reverse) - where these are justified on cost-return grounds - should be easier for the enterprise.[10] Essentially the same story can be valid for a change in the ownership structure of an enterprise from government owned to listed private shareholder owned company. Indeed it is where these types of argument are considered to be valid that economists have enthusiastically advocated particular privatisations, (and demutualisations) - provided these are not outweighed by other factors present tilting the scales in favour of continued government (or mutual) ownership. These matters are discussed in detail in Vickers and Yarrow (1988). It is the enterprise behaviour effects which most professional economists see as the prime issue in assessing whether a particular act of privatisation (or demutualisation) should be supported or opposed.

---

9 When the float price is below the 'full' price as defined in this paragraph, the government will need to raise additional future taxes, or prune transfer payments to maintain an unchanged policy stance. In order for national saving to rise it would be necessary for 'Ricardian equivalence' effects stemming from this to overwhelm the direct windfall gain effects of the float under-pricing.

10 See Thomson (1995), and the references cited therein for a full discussion of these effects.

Consider the case of an enterprise at present with a mutual ownership structure which, upon demutualisation, can be confidently expected to operate with improved technical efficiency and perhaps also improved dynamic efficiency. Any resources displaced from employment by the enterprise across various future time periods are assumed to obtain alternative employment at no disadvantage to their suppliers. We assume that either there are no losers from the ending of cross-subsidies among the enterprise's outputs, or that any such losers are somehow fully compensated. Under these circumstances the demutualisation causes the future net income stream accruing to the enterprise to increase in present value. And that boost to the enterprise's future income is simultaneously a boost to the community's aggregate future income stream.[11]

Focussing on this effect (and leaving aside now the liquidity effects associated with demutualisation), how does it impact on those members of the mutual whose membership rights in the mutual are replaced by shares in the 'successor' company? Each such company share now provides title to a greater future net income stream than did the equivalent 'share' of membership property rights on the eve of demutualisation. The present value of that enhancement to the future net income stream can be expected to be built into the market price of the shares upon listing - at least to the extent of the 'market's' best guess of the size of that enhancement.

As far as the consumption/saving decision as conventionally modelled is concerned, the key point to notice is that the enhanced future income stream permits the relevant shareholder to enjoy an exactly matching enhanced consumption stream, conduct exactly the same saving behaviour program as originally planned, *and* have something left over when they die (assuming the enterprise and its enhanced behaviour outlasts their lifetime.) Unless the individual shareholder has a time horizon which is effectively infinite (as frequently assumed in formal models of the permanent income hypothesis), he or she can be expected to seek to consume that otherwise 'left-over' element during their own lifetime. That means lifting current and future period consumption levels by more than the extent of the income enhancement.[12] In short, each saves less than would have occurred in the absence of the enterprise behaviour effects triggered by demutualisation. For the liquidity constrained the story is much simpler, each sells their shares as soon as they can, spends the proceeds on current period consumption, and then reverts to the time path of behaviour they would have followed in the absence of the demutualisation. Overall the story is essentially the same as in the liquidity effects case: the demutualisation will cause national saving to be reduced, with that reduction the more "front loaded" the greater the proportion of the demutualisation shares flowing to the liquidity constrained or to those with relatively short planning horizons.

The above analysis assumes that the enhancements to the community's income are all captured by those mutual members participating in the initial float. In practice

---

11 Note that if the one and only source of the enterprise's enhanced future profits was a more thorough exploitation of monopoly (or monopsony) powers, the community's aggregate future income would be reduced.

12 If the enhancement to the income stream were heavily 'front-loaded', it would be possible for 'smoothing' of the increased consumption effect to allow a temporary positive effect on saving. It would be unusual, however, for the income enhancement effect to be expected to be heavily 'front-loaded' in that way.

government(s) will receive some of that additional income, under unchanged tax rates and transfer payment means-testing arrangements. If government(s) save every additional dollar thus accruing to them, the extent of the national saving reduction as described in the paragraph above will be mitigated. But the bottom line will remain : a reduction in national saving.

Turning to privatisations, let us replicate the above assumptions for the enterprise behaviour effects of some hypothetical conversion of a previously government owned enterprise to a listed fully private shareholder-owned company. Once again consider three cases. In case one the vendor government prices the float so as to allow the whole of the enhanced income stream benefits of privatisation to be captured by the subscribers to the float. In case two the vendor government prices the float so that it captures the whole of the enhanced income effects. It then "banks" the entire proceeds, making no changes to the taxation and transfer payments policies that would have prevailed in the absence of the privatisation. In case three the vendor government sells the shares to its citizens at a price somewhere between the case one and case two prices. Again it 'banks' the entire proceeds.

Case one is clearly directly analogous to the demutualisation equivalent which we have already analysed. Public sector saving is unaffected. Private sector saving is reduced, with the reduction more "frontloaded" the greater the number of short-term horizon individuals among the fortunate float subscribers. National saving is unambiguously reduced.

Case two is now more complex. Successful subscribers to shares in the privatisation have altered the composition of their personal portfolios, but their net wealth and their future expected income streams are unchanged. Private sector saving could therefore be expected to remain unchanged. Public sector saving, meanwhile is clearly increased. Hence overall national saving is increased. Some individuals may refuse to believe that the government will continue to save the entire proceeds of the enterprise behaviour effects through to infinity. That might trigger some additional private consumption spending and reduced private saving. But unless one takes an extreme view of such 'Ricardian equivalence' effects, the bottom line remains an increase in national saving.

Case three is of course the most interesting. It is also the one which gives us an ambiguous result for national saving. The portion of the enterprise behaviour effect on future national income that is captured by the government is, by assumption, fully saved - every last dollar. The portion that accrues to the private sector[13] is, on the analysis presented here, more than fully consumed. Private sector saving is unambiguously reduced. But whether national saving goes up or goes down depends on the relative strengths of the two effects. If the private sector effect is heavily frontloaded and large, the upshot might be that overall national saving is reduced in the immediate wake of the privatisation (as compared with a no privatisation counter-factual) but then a crossover to an enduring boost to the flow of national saving would follow.

---

13 Note that some of the enterprise behaviour effect on future national income might accrue to persons other than those directly participating in the initial float. There might be externalities from the enterprise behaviour changes. Or the market might take time to build into the share price a full allowance for the internalisable gains.

There is a further, and separate point to be made on enterprise behaviour effects. If a previously capital-starved enterprise is demutualised or privatised one might expect that to cause total domestic investment spending in the economy to move to a higher level than would otherwise have been the case. If national saving simultaneously falls, remains unchanged, or rises only a little, the overall impact will be to widen the current account deficit. That may not be a bad thing. Whether it is, or is not, depends essentially on whether the additional investment spending generates revenues sufficient to service the additional net foreign liabilities incurred in financing it. This chapter does not attempt to expand further on that issue. But it is perhaps worth noting that if a vendor government in case three above opts against banking its *entire* proceeds from the enhanced income effects, and opts instead to outlay some portion on new domestic investment spending, that could easily lead to the overall result of the policy being a *widening* of the CAD, even where the overall impact on national saving is positive.

Concluding comments

A transfer of ownership of an already existing asset, *immediately and directly in itself* has no effect on a country's GDP or any of the flow variables into which GDP can be decomposed. That is well known. Insofar as there has been professional comment on the impact on national saving of demutualisation and privatisation initiatives in Australia, it has usually been to stress this point, and to warn of accounting systems which might suggest otherwise.

But the *full* effects of demutualisation and privatisation initiatives include the behavioural changes which the changes in ownership structure trigger. This chapter has sought to trace through the effects of such behavioural changes on national saving. The results are at variance with what might be described as the 'traditional' view: that a demutualisation will have no effect on national saving; and that a privatisation will have no effect on national saving, providing the vendor government 'banks' the entire privatisation proceeds.

The results of this chapter can be summarised as follows:

- a demutualisation will cause national saving to be lower than it would otherwise have been.
- that effect will be to some extent 'frontloaded' into the period(s) immediately following the act of demutualisation.
- where the demutualisation consists of distributing shares which are immediately transferable (without penalty) the proportion of such shares going to liquidity constrained individuals and elderly individuals will largely determine the extent of that 'frontloading' effect.
- these demutualisation results hold irrespective of whether there are beneficial enterprise behaviour effects, or only liquidity effects from the process.
- where a privatisation has liquidity effects only, it will cause national saving to be lower than it otherwise would have been *unless* the government captures and 'banks' the whole of the revaluation-effects proceeds arising

from such liquidity effects (including the full 'banking' of the future 'interest' accruing thereon).

- where a privatisation has beneficial enterprise behaviour effects, and the vendor government prices the float to capture in full, and then 'bank', the entire present value of the additional national income arising from such effects (including all future 'interest' thereon), national saving can be guaranteed to rise.
- but if the benefits of the enterprise behaviour effects are divided between the vendor government and the private sector, this will cause public sector saving to rise but private sector saving to fall. The net effect on national saving then depends on the relative strengths of these two effects.
- if a privatisation is priced in such a way that the private sector's share of the effects is low enough for national saving to be unchanged (or to rise) this might still see the current account deficit expand if the government uses some of the proceeds (or 'interest' thereon) to boost domestic investment spending (by an extent greater than the national saving increase).

7 The Commonwealth Budgets 1996-2000

Owen Covick

This chapter provides lightly edited versions of the analyses which were originally published in SACES *Economic Briefing Reports*, and distributed to the corporate members of SACES a few weeks after the relevant Commonwealth Budget day of each year 1996 to 2000. The editing process has *not* been used to make any corrections based on 'the wisdom of hindsight'. The role of the SACES analyses is not to describe the *detail* of a Budget in the way expected of same day (or next day) commentary. The intention has been to 'place' the Budget in the broader economic context of its time. That has meant a strong focus on national saving.

7.1 The 1996 Commonwealth Budget

To understand the economic thinking behind the 1996 Commonwealth Budget, you need first to appreciate that its principal focus is *not* on managing aggregate demand within the Australian economy. Teachers of introductory economics mislead if they represent budgetary policy in terms of its effect on aggregate demand *alone*. That may have made sense before the mid nineteen-seventies. But since then, with occasional exceptions (as in 1992), the source of macroeconomic malaise in the Australian economy - as indeed in most comparable economies - has been perceived to be on the supply side. Macroeconomic policy, as a whole, has needed to focus on the supply-side accordingly - apart from in the exceptional years. And budgetary policy has needed to be judged in terms of its role in that supply-side focus.

Modern economic thinking about the supply-side of the macroeconomy gives prominence to a concept known by the acronym NAIRU. Some economic commentators who try to shield their audiences from technical jargon typically substitute for NAIRU the phrase 'natural rate of unemployment'. But that can be seriously misleading. The NAIRU is not something ordained by nature, which one simply has to put up with - like the weather or the passage of time. It is something which certain types of economic policy can be expected to reduce, and which other types of policy can be expected to increase. The acronym stands for the non-accelerating inflation rate of unemployment. It means the unemployment rate below which any pressure from aggregate demand feeds into boosting the economy's inflation rate. In Australia's case it is closely associated with the point at which additional demand pressure starts to blow out the current account deficit (CAD), on our balance of payments to unsustainable levels. (The NAIRU is discussed in more detail in Chapter Five, above).

In the 1950s and 1960s, Australia's NAIRU was at levels which enabled Australians to enjoy 'full employment' without accelerating inflation or a blowing out of the CAD. Since the early 1970s Australia's NAIRU has been substantially higher. Unless it can be reduced markedly, policies that focus on stimulating aggregate demand are doomed to run into the brick wall of accelerating domestic inflation and/or a blowing out of the CAD. Demand management alone cannot achieve an acceptably low unemployment rate, in the face of an unacceptably high NAIRU. Hence, to judge budgetary policy in terms solely of its effects of aggregate demand is now an anachronism - except in years where the actual unemployment rate is clearly so far above the economy's NAIRU that demand stimulus is clearly the *sine qua non* - as in 1992.

March 1996 saw a new Commonwealth government take office with markedly different views from its predecessor's as to how best to reduce Australia's NAIRU. A directly parallel event occurred in March 1983. In 1983 the new government viewed centralised wages determination based on the Accord agreement with the trade union movement as its principal focus for reducing Australia's NAIRU. Certain government budget outlays programmes were viewed as playing significant roles in securing trade union agreement to wages restraint and thus being *supporting mechanisms* to that principal focus on wage policy. These programmes came to be known as the 'social wage' -with Medicare being the most prominent. What the Hawke government budgeted to spend on these programmes (and later on tax cuts for middle income earners) needed to be adjudged and evaluated in terms of their leverage through wages policy on the NAIRU, and not simply on their demand management effects. With Keating as Prime Minister, the focus shifted. The *Working Nation* statement of 1994 sought to reduce Australia's NAIRU by outlaying funds on programmes intended to re-integrate the long-term unemployed into the nation's *effective* labour supply.[1] But once again the budgetary message from Canberra was the same: don't just focus on what this does to the pressure of aggregate demand - ask what it does to Australia's NAIRU.

In the August 1996 Budget the incoming Commonwealth government throws down the same gauntlet to economists, but with a reversal of the arithmetic signs. Whereas in 1983 the proposal was that Australia's NAIRU would be driven down via consent from organised labour supplemented by increases in government outlays programmes, the 1996 agenda is for the NAIRU to be driven down via the greater exposure of labour markets to the pressures of wage and work practices bargaining at an enterprise level - supplemented by a paring back of certain government outlays programmes. The new government has targeted the *Working Nation* labour market programmes for particularly heavy cost-cutting. Implicit is the view that that spending was not cost-effective in terms of reducing Australia's NAIRU. The central role of labour market initiatives in the new government's macroeconomic strategy is spelt out in pages 39 to 47 of Budget Statement Number 2. The core elements are summarised: 'The changes proposed by the Government to Australia's industrial relations system seek to reduce some of the major structural impediments to faster employment growth... In addition, reforms to the provision of labour market assistance and activity tests for unemployment benefits will address incentives for job search...' (p. 43).

Having addressed what role the 1996 Budget does *not* attempt to play in the macroeconomic strategy of the Howard-Costello government (demand management), the

---

[1] *Working Nation* also increased budget outlays by modifying the means testing arrangements imposed when the spouse of an unemployed person obtained paid employment. This should also operate to reduce the economy's NAIRU.

question naturally arises: what *is* its apportioned role? Again the answer is set out quite explicitly in Budget Statement Number 2: 'The focus of this Budget is on the need to repair the past structural deterioration in public saving' (p. 31). 'The [fiscal strategy's] guiding objective is that the Commonwealth budget should remain broadly in underlying balance, on average, over the business cycle: that is, neither adding to, nor detracting from, national net lending, on average, over the cycle' (p. 39). This *guiding objective* has clear parallels with the Reserve Bank's inflation target. The target variable is defined in 'underlying' as distinct from 'headline' terms. The target is defined over the course of the business cycle. There is thus some scope for disagreement as to how well the objective is being fulfilled, through time. But it is nevertheless, a far firmer performance benchmark for Commonwealth fiscal policy than has existed since the time of Bob Hawke's 'trilogy' commitment.

So how well does the 1996 Commonwealth Budget stack up in terms of its proclaimed objective of repairing 'the past structural deterioration in public saving'?

On Budget night, much of the focus was on the impact of the new government's fiscal policy decisions on the projected Commonwealth budget deficit - using the Government's own statistics for the deficit corrected for 'abnormal' items: i.e., the *underlying budget deficit.* On that basis, fiscal policy decisions announced by the Howard-Costello government either in the Budget or between the election and the Budget had reduced the Commonwealth deficit by $3.9 billion for 1996-97, and by $7.2 billion for 1997-98.[2] Combined with Mr Costello's claim that he had stuck by his 'no new taxes', and 'no increases in tax rates' pledges, the message most Australians would have received was of a government taking a mighty axe to its outlays programmes. The government's critics rose to the bait with rhetoric of a 'slash and burn' budget.

Individuals heavily affected by some of the measures comprising the Budget may well feel themselves to have been 'slashed' or 'burnt'. But the figures in Tables 7.1.1 and 7.1.2 tell a somewhat different story overall. Personal benefit payments are the largest single category of Commonwealth outlays (35.6 per cent of total current outlays in 1995-96), and probably the most visible to the ordinary citizen. Social security pensions and benefits, family assistance payments, AUSTUDY, Medicare payments for the costs of visits to doctors, and pharmaceutical benefit payments are the principal components. From Table 7.1.1 it can be seen that the dollar value of Commonwealth personal benefit payments is projected to continue rising over the next four years in the 1996 Budget. Table 7.1.2 indicates that that represents real growth in each of those years. The second biggest single category of Commonwealth outlays is current purpose grants to State, Territory and local governments (24.3 per cent of total current outlays in 1995-96). From Table 7.1.1, it can be seen that that item too is projected to continue rising in dollar terms over each of the next four years. Although, lower down in the table, one can see

---

2 The government's definition of the *underlying budget deficit* corrects the bottom line for those 'abnormal' items which fall within the definition of 'net advances'. Some abnormal items are not covered by that definition, however. Examples include the one-off running down of $302 million of cash balances held by Statutory Bodies in 1996-97; the proposed refinancing of the DASFLEET vehicles (essentially a sale-and-leaseback); and the shift to off-Budget funding arrangements for the construction of the Melbourne Law Courts Building.

Table 7.1.1
Budget Outlays By Economic Type ($ Million)

	1995-96	1996-97	1997-98	1998-99	1999-00
	Actual	Budget	Forward Estimates		
Final Consumption Expenditure					
Defence	9,947	9,999	10,340	10,581	10,840
Non-Defence	11,550	12,359	11,858	11,801	11,954
Current Transfer Payments					
Personal Benefit Payments	45,541	47,317	48,644	51,278	54,429
Grants to Non-Profit Institutions	3,031	2,736	2,743	2,808	2,862
Grants to Non-Budget Sector	13,549	13,775	14,838	15,442	16,426
Grants to State & Local Govt.	31,137	32,260	32,281	33,467	35,055
Subsidies, Grants Overseas & Other	4,103	4,259	4,152	4,246	4,221
Interest	9,219	9,884	9,922	9,875	9,287
Total Current Outlays	**128,076**	**132,589**	**134,776**	**139,497**	**145,074**
Capital Outlays & Goods & Land	625	339	151	639	210
Capital Grants to Non-Budget Sector	304	344	304	309	315
Capital Grants to State & Local Govt.	2,807	2,437	2,332	2,294	2,247
Capital Grants to Other Sector	166	158	105	84	64
Total Capital Outlays (excluding advances)	**3,902**	**3,278**	**2,892**	**3,326**	**2,835**
Contingency Reserve	0	-57	943	1,542	2,149
Total Underlying Outlays	**131,978**	**135,810**	**138,611**	**144,365**	**150,058**
Net Advances	-5,273	-6,123	-8,186	-2,518	-72

Source: 1996 Commonwealth Budget Paper Number 1.

that those other two tiers of Australian government are to be squeezed in terms of capital grants.

Overall the picture presented by Tables 7.1.1 and 7.1.2 is quite different from the rhetoric that has surrounded the Budget. The running costs of the Commonwealth public service (part of final consumption expenditure), grants to non-profit institutions, and capital outlays in general are marked down for significant real cuts over the four year period to 1999-00, it is true. But overall total underlying outlays will be greater in real terms in 1998-99 than in 1995-96, and are projected to grow further in the following year. That stands in stark contrast to the period when Peter Walsh was Finance Minister. Page 1.24 of the 1996 Budget Paper No. 1 indicates that total underlying Commonwealth Budget outlays were cut in real terms by 0.8 per cent in 1987-88, and then by a further 4.4 per cent in 1988-89. In 1989-90 there was real growth of 0.9 per cent, but total underlying outlays remained a full one per cent lower than four years earlier (1985-86) in real terms. Mr Costello's projection for 1999-00 has total underlying outlays about one and a half percentage points higher, in real terms, than four years earlier (1995-96).

Why then has the 1996 Budget been perceived by so many to be harsher in overall spending terms than was actually the case? Firstly there is the fact that real growth in total Commonwealth Budget sector underlying outlays has not been lower than 3.5 per cent in any of the years since Peter Walsh ceased being Finance Minister in 1990. The threshold of perception of fiscal discomfort may have been lowered. Secondly there is the conspiracy-theorists' view that those economic commentators who complained about the fiscal laxity of the previous government loudly and continually from 1983 to 1996 (including during 1986 to 1989) simply opted to be nice to Mr Costello.

Thirdly, there is a view which the present writer would like to put forward. The budgetary-policy re-alignments of the Howard-Costello government are not entirely a matter of hair-shirts, and hair-shirts alone. On the outlays side, delivery on the Coalition's election commitments (plus other new spending but excluding the Firearms programme) is costed in the Budget Papers at just over one billion dollars in 1996-97 and then about two billion dollars per year thereafter. On top of that there are new tax expenditures costed at over one third of a billion dollars in 1996-97 rising to above one billion dollars per year in 1998-99 and beyond. In order to cover the costs of these 'goodies', the 1996 Budget has needed to be that much harsher in other areas in order to achieve a given bottom line. To some extent the winners from these new tax expenditure and personal transfers programmes are the same people who are paying for them through changes resulting from other Budget policy decisions.

Table 7.1.2
1996 Commonwealth Budget
Annual Percentage Change in Budget Outlays (Constant Price Basis)

	1995-96	1996-97	1997-98	1998-99	1999-00
	Actual	Budget	Forward Estimates		
Final Consumption Expenditure	2.3	1.1	-3.2	-2.1	-1.1
Personal Benefit Payments	4.6	1.0	0.2	2.3	3.0
Total Current Transfer Payments	4.5	0.5	-0.4	1.0	1.4
Total Current Outlays	4.1	0.6	-0.9	0.5	1.0
Capital Grants	-6.4	-12.9	-9.1	-4.9	-5.1
Total Underlying Outlays	3.9	0.1	-0.7	1.2	1.0

Source: 1996 Commonwealth Budget Paper Number 1.

But in other cases one person's (or family's) advantage is funded by another's hair shirt. For thirteen years in Australia the continuity of ALP in federal government provided some significant degree of 'confidence' in how people could expect to stand in terms of being contributors/beneficiaries in the Commonwealth government's tax and transfer apparatus. The new Commonwealth Government has different views. Those who are net beneficiaries of those new views might be expected to make their gratitude known *sotto voce* (if at all). Those who are in the opposite position might be expected to be more immediate in going public and seeking to draw public attention to the equity-issues concerning their plight - particularly if they see this Budget as 'the thin end of the wedge'.

There is a fourth possibility - related to the campaign for an introduction of VAT type taxation on consumption spending in Australia. Consider Table 7.1.3. It tells two stories. The decline in projected non-taxation revenue relates to the process of privatisation. It means that some appropriate proportion of diminishing projected Commonwealth interest outlays should be corrected for in assessing the 'true' growth in underlying outlays. But more importantly, the story in the first row of the table is that the total tax revenues of the Commonwealth government over the next four years, are not projected to grow much more rapidly than real GDP. That is despite the fact that the Budget contained new revenue raising measures projected to add between $2.5 and $3 billion to Commonwealth tax-revenues in each of the years beyond 1996-97, and $1.3 billion (including the gun levy) in 1996-97. The days appear to have gone when the Commonwealth could simply sit back and watch moderate economic growth line the tax coffers at unchanged tax rates on already existing taxes. The Australian income tax system is again beginning to look frayed, or like a bucket with too many holes. As in 1985, there needs to be either major reform of the income tax system, or the creation of a big new tax revenue raising machine, or perhaps both. If the community were to begin feeling there are only two choices – 'slash and burn' outlays policies; or the introduction of a new consumption tax of the value-added type - that could be a plus for advocates of the latter.

So where does all this leave South Australia? Lesson one is that if the Howard-Costello government is serious about its new target for Commonwealth budgetary policy, there will need to be further significant rounds of fiscal tightening. Ed Shann argued the same point in his article 'Budget Pain is Far From Over', (*Business Review Weekly*, 21 October, 1996, p. 58). It is hard to see Commonwealth personal benefit payments and the tax system being quarantined in such further tightening.

Table 7.1.3
1996 Commonwealth Budget
Annual Percentage Change In Budget Revenues (Constant Price Basis)

	1995-96	**1996-97**	**1997-98**	**1998-99**	**1999-00**
	Actual	**Budget**	**Forward Estimates**		
Total Tax Revenue	7.2	4.5	3.4	3.3	4.3
Non-Tax Revenue	8.8	-5.9	-19.3	-7.3	-0.6
Total	**7.3**	**4.0**	**2.5**	**3.0**	**4.1**

Source: 1996 Commonwealth Budget Overview and Economic Outlook (p. 1).

That leads immediately to lesson two. It is the States with the poorest-performing economies which stand to feel the most pain when Commonwealth transfer payment programmes are pruned. Essentially the Commonwealth's progressive personal income tax system and nationally uniform means-tested system of transfer payments to the household sector acts as a national Robin Hood: robbing the rich parts of the country to pay the poor. From Table 7.1.4 it can be seen that across the nation as a whole the household sector receives 16.8 per cent of its total pre-tax income directly from government transfers, and pays back 15.5 per cent in personal income tax. That 'gap' of 1.3 percentage points is a much smaller gap in NSW and WA, and is a substantial gap in the opposite direction in the prosperous ACT (or the 'was-prosperous' ACT of 1994-95 -

the year for which the most up to date figures are currently available). It will be no surprise that the transfers-minus-tax gap is widest for Tasmania. But South Australia is a fairly close second. Clearly any moves to make the Commonwealth taxation system 'flatter' (or 'less progressive') and any moves to prune back nationally on spending on Commonwealth transfer payments programmes are likely to have a more marked downward impact on household disposable income in South Australia and Tasmania than in other parts of Australia - other things being equal.

Table 7.1.4
Household Income, Australia and States/Territories, 1994-95

	Government Transfers* (%)	Income Tax Paid** (%)	Household Income Per Capita ($)
New South Wales	16.4	16.1	20,667
Victoria	16.4	15.3	19,976
Queensland	18.3	15.0	17,794
South Australia	19.2	14.2	18,194
Western Australia	16.2	15.7	19,292
Tasmania	20.9	15.2	16,765
Northern Territory	14.8	15.2	19,227
ACT	10.7	17.6	26,331
Australia	16.8	15.5	19,620

Note: * This component of household income is the sum of two parts: personal benefit payments to residents; and current grants to non-profit institutions. Of the Australia-wide total, 88.6 per cent is paid directly by the Commonwealth government (96.7 per cent of personal benefit payments and 33 per cent of current grants to non-profit institutions).
** 'Personal' income tax only (i.e., excludes company tax, tax on the income of superannuation funds and life offices, FBT etc.).

Source: ABS, *Australian National Accounts* (5204.0) and *Australian National Accounts: State Accounts* (5220.0).

The focus of national macroeconomic policy on the NAIRU means monetary policy is not relaxed until the tighter labour markets of the country are considered capable of bearing additional demand pressure without re-igniting inflationary pressure. Meanwhile, South Australian labour markets are left to mark time. The focus of Commonwealth budgetary policy on national saving means that household incomes in the high unemployment states are likely to be squeezed proportionately harder than in the low unemployment parts of Australia. The effects on the strength of consumer demand across different parts of the country could easily prove perverse to the objective of reducing the nation-wide NAIRU. These issues of regional economics will need to be pressed home in Canberra.

7.2 The 1997 Commonwealth Budget

Treasurer Costello regards his second Budget as targeted at the goal of jobs. The concluding sentence of his May 13, 1997 Budget Speech stressed the role of his budget strategy in securing the creation of job opportunities in Australia. But the Budget does not seek to do this in the style of a 1950s or 1960s macroeconomics textbook - by using increased government spending or reduced taxes to stimulate aggregate domestic spending on goods and services. Rather, the Costello approach focuses on trying to do something about those 'speed limits' on growth in economic activity in Australia which have required that each employment expansion phase of the last two decades be brought to a halt before achieving an unemployment rate low enough to be regarded as satisfactory. If the 'speed limits' are *not* addressed, according to this view, an attempt to boost aggregate domestic spending by fiscal stimulus would at best buy only a short period of jobs growth - and that at the price of further major economic disruption when remedial measures had to be implemented. If, on the other hand, the 'speed limits' *are* tackled effectively and raised, in Mr Costello's thinking, the natural buoyancy of a competitive free enterprise system can be given its head to create additional jobs - which can be sustained.

The Commonwealth Treasurer is not unique in thinking this way. The last three Budgets of the previous government were framed on the basis of broadly the same approach to the role of fiscal policy in Australia. Indeed, the 1992 Commonwealth Budget (and the immediately preceding *One Nation* economic statement) was the exception in Australian budgetary policy-making since at least the very early Accord period, in the way it emphasised demand management. As was pointed out in the SACES review of the 1996 Commonwealth Budget (see above): 'Teachers of introductory economics mislead if they represent budgetary policy in terms of its effect on aggregate demand *alone*'. The same clearly applies to economic commentators, and to interest-group lobbyists.

What are the 'speed limits' that stand between the present state of the Australian economy and the attainment (on a sustainable basis) of levels of unemployment that are *significantly less unacceptable*? One is the domestic 'inflation' rate. The other is the state of the current account of our balance of payments vis-à-vis the rest of the world. When the first is considered, it is usually in the context of the economy's NAIRU (or non-accelerating inflation rate of unemployment). If Australia's NAIRU can be reduced, that particular speed limit on employment growth is relaxed. When the current account deficit is considered, it is usually in the context of Australia's national saving performance. If Australia's national saving rate can be increased, then other things being equal, the balance of payments speed limit on our employment growth is relaxed.

These are the same two speed limits that were the focus of attention to achieve sustained reductions in unemployment during the period from 1993 up to Mr Howard's election victory. But the Coalition has different views on how best to tackle them as compared with the Keating Government. Under Keating, Australia's NAIRU was to be driven down by a focus on additional government spending on training and job experience programmes, and a 'softly-softly' approach to improved labour market flexibility negotiated cooperatively with Australia's trade unions. Under Howard there is a *less* 'softly-softly' approach to improved labour market flexibility and a smaller carrot/bigger stick approach on the training and job experience front. Under Keating, compulsory superannuation and a medium-term budget deficit reduction strategy formed a two prong strategy to boost national saving. Under Howard the same two prongs are there, but with less weight on compulsory super, and greater declared urgency in shifting the Commonwealth Budget into (underlying) surplus.

The present Commonwealth Government thus sees the macroeconomic goals of budgetary policy as:

- shift the Commonwealth Budget into underlying surplus, so as to boost Australia's national saving rate;
- by achieving this, raise the speed limit on employment growth in Australia; and
- establish a framework in which the underlying Commonwealth Budget bottom line is in balance on average over the course of the economic cycle - with deficits in the low growth years being offset by surpluses in the high growth years.

To quote from the 1997 year's Budget Statement No. 1:

> The overriding aim of the Government's economic strategy is to achieve the maximum sustainable rate of reduction in unemployment by lifting the pace at which economic growth can be maintained without running into inflationary and external pressures...
>
> A central plank of the Government's economic strategy is to put in place policies to lift national saving. Of particular importance is the need to correct the structural weakness in the Commonwealth's fiscal position evident in the past twenty years which has underpinned the structural deterioration in the current account deficit.[3]

Data on the Commonwealth's fiscal position since 1960-61 are presented in Figure 7.2.1. The outlays figures are the 'underlying outlays' as published in the Budget papers. These figures take the traditionally published Budget outlays and subtract 'net advances' made by the Commonwealth Budget sector. The typical advance would be a loan made by the Commonwealth to a State government (or to a Commonwealth off-budget agency), or an injection of additional equity funds into a Commonwealth off-budget entity. Repayment of such loans, or sales of equity by the Commonwealth Budget sector are negative advances. By excluding 'net advances', a clearer picture of the Commonwealth's fiscal position is obtained. In the 1960s, substantial positive advances by the Commonwealth to the States made the traditionally published budget bottom line look 'weaker' than is depicted in Figure 7.2.1. In some more recent years, repayment of State debts to the Commonwealth, and Commonwealth major asset sales[4] have made the traditionally published bottom line look 'stronger'.

---

3 Commonwealth of Australia, (1997), *Budget Strategy and Outlook 1997-98*, Budget Paper No. 1, Canberra, pp. 1-8. Note that the word 'structural' in this context should be interpreted to mean *on average over the course of economic cycles*.

4 It should be noted that the Budget Paper's methodology 'corrects' for transactions in *some* but not *all* 'major' assets. A sale of existing buildings, plant or equipment which does *not* involve the sale of equity in a corporate entity owning those assets will not be adjusted for. Transactions in land are *not* adjusted for. The 1997-98 *underlying* Commonwealth Budget bottom line benefits from an unusually high $662 million in net sales of land. This was discussed by Brian Frith in *The Australian* (15 May 1997), p. 28.

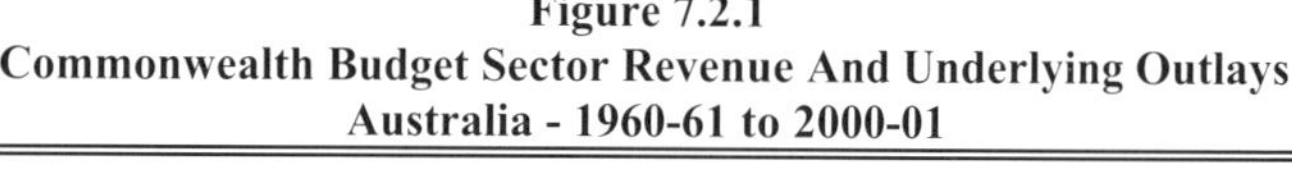

Figure 7.2.1
Commonwealth Budget Sector Revenue And Underlying Outlays
Australia - 1960-61 to 2000-01

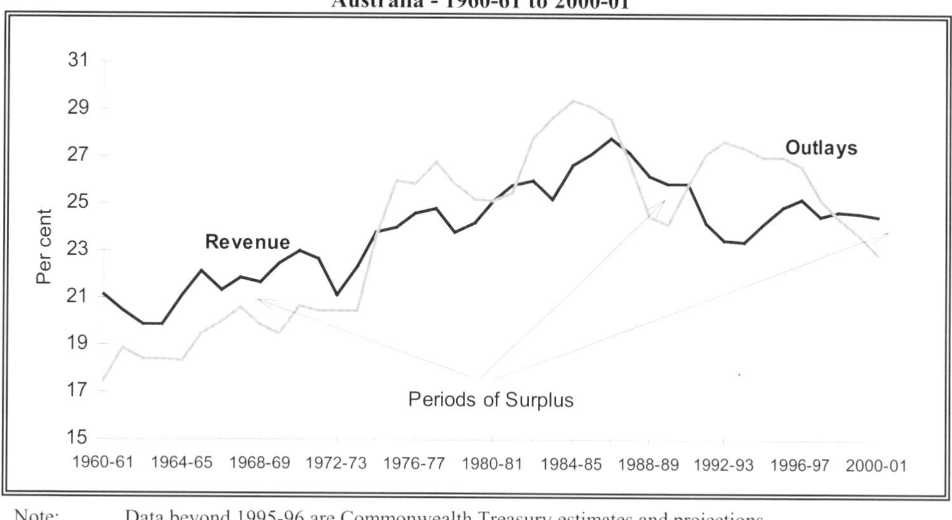

Note: Data beyond 1995-96 are Commonwealth Treasury estimates and projections.
Source: *Commonwealth Budget Paper No. 1,* 1997.

The message that a decline in Australia's national saving performance has been central to the upsurge in our average annual current account deficit, over the period since 1973-74 is not new. Nor is the message that it has been the public sector's contribution to national saving that has been predominantly responsible for Australia's reduced national saving over the past two decades. The FitzGgerald Inquiry into national saving in 1992 stressed those points. In 1990, Chapter 11 of INDECS *State of Play 6* had spelt out the same basic arguments. Earlier still those propositions formed part of the now-discredited 'twin-deficits' view of Australia's balance of payments problem.

What *is* new in the picture painted by the figures in Figure 7.2.1 (which were first published in the August 1996 Budget Papers, in essentially the same form) is the way the finger is now pointed at the Commonwealth government, as distinct from the State/local tier, to take responsibility for rectifying the situation. During the late 1980s Paul Keating seemed to claim monopoly rights in the provision of fiscal responsibility. The fact that Peter Walsh was not such an aggressive salesman has meant that Keating continues to bask in the glow of the Commonwealth Budget surpluses recorded for the period preceding the 'recession we had to have'.

Keating's views on the fiscal responsibility exhibited by Australia's State government tier are well known. A key part of his campaign in overthrowing Hawke rested on this precise issue. Believers in the Keating rhetoric would have expected the FitzGerald Report to have nailed the true culprits - the spendthrift and taxation-lax State premiers. When FitzGerald did *not* do so, true believers perhaps thought there had been something wrong with the economic statistics supplied to the Inquiry, or that Dr Vince had misinterpreted those figures. Why wasn't he pointing the finger at the States?

Ironically an early fruit of Bob Hawke's new 'co-operative' federalism which Keating had sought to derail in 1991 was agreement by the States to publish Budget data using agreed uniform conventions. The agreement extends to cooperation between Commonwealth and State Treasuries to produce consolidated data on the budgetary position and *fiscal outlook* for the State/local tier of Australia's public sector. To overcome the issue of differences in the dividing line between budget sectors and off-budget agencies, these data are compiled for the *general government sector* - a concept which seeks to cover all public sector entities except those operating commercially in the marketplace as trading or financial (business) enterprises. These data are published annually in the *National Fiscal Outlook* statement. Updates are presented in Statement No. 7 of 1997 Commonwealth Budget Paper No. 1.

The new series have been published only for years since 1983-84, so there is still scope for argument about the degree of State government fiscal profligacy during the mid-to-late 70s and early 80s. But for the period since the mid 80s the Keating rhetoric can be judged against the facts. The rhetoric does not look crash hot. From 1984-85 to 1986-87 the underlying deficit of Australia's State/local general government sector remained fairly static as a proportion of GDP at 2.1 to 2.2 per cent. It then started to move down, reaching 0.4 per cent of GDP in 1992-93 and crossing into the black the following year. It has remained in the black each year since, and is projected to remain that way in each of the forward estimates years out to 2000-01 as shown in Figure 7.2.2. For more details, see page 7.26 of 1997 Commonwealth Budget Paper No. 1. A peculiarity of the data just described is that they do not take full account of the losses accrued by certain State government in respect of State governments financial enterprises in the late 1980s. Equity injections and equity write-offs are not part of "underlying outlays", while any dividends actually paid by the relevant enterprises *are* recorded as general government sector revenue. But that does not affect the picture for the more recent years, or (one hopes) the forward estimates years.

The bottom line then is that when one compares the mid 1990s with the 1960s and sees the opening up of a structural imbalance in Australia's overall saving-investment position which seems largely attributable to a downward shift in public sector saving between the two periods, the responsibility for that downward shift appears to rest firmly with the Commonwealth tier of government. It would seem logical that responsibility for rectifying the imbalance should therefore also rest with the Commonwealth tier of government. The commentary in this year's Commonwealth Budget papers accepts that responsibility (see the passages at page 1.8 of 1997 Budget Paper No. 1, quoted above).

Having spelt out the Budgetary policy task that the Commonwealth Government has set itself, it remains to ask the question: how well does the 1997 Budget deliver in terms of performance in that task?

To answer this question, it is not sufficient simply to point to the figures in Figure 7.2.1 and cite the further cut in the underlying deficit in 1997-98, and the move into surplus in the forward estimates years as evidence of exemplary achievement. The continuation of economic recovery which has been factored into those budget estimates and projections creates of itself revenue growth and containment of social security outlays. And many of the budget policy decisions announced in Mr Costello's 1996 Budget were structured so as to build-up in their impact between 1996-97 and 1997-98, and into the out-years.

Looking at Figure 7.2.1 alone does not tell us whether the net impact of the spending and taxing measures announced on May 13, 1997 was to accelerate the process of Commonwealth fiscal consolidation, decelerate it, or leave it unchanged.

Figure 7.2.2
Underlying Deficit by Level of Government
Australia - 1984-85 to 2000-01

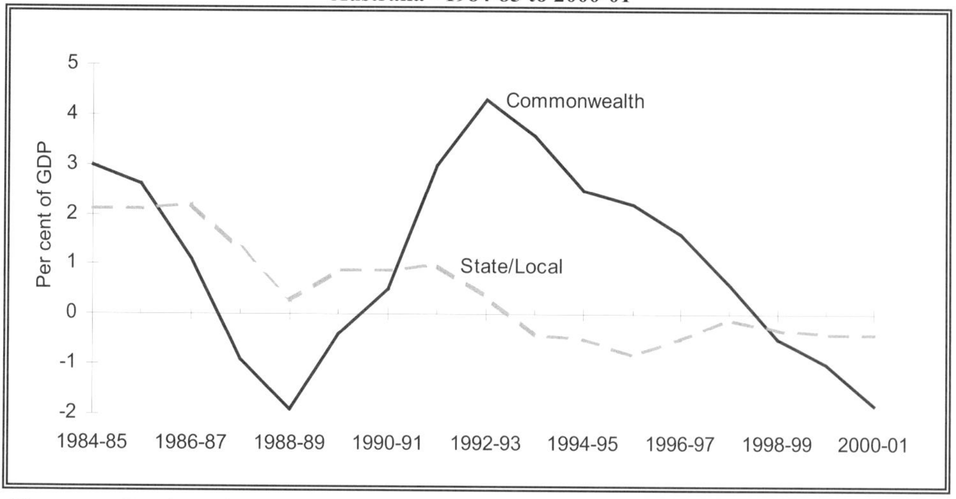

Note: Data beyond 1995-96 are Commonwealth Treasury estimates and projections.
Source: *Commonwealth Budget Paper No. 1, 1997.*

Table 7.2.1
Reconciliation of 1996-97 Budget and 1997-98 Budget Estimates

	1996-97 $ Million	**1997-98 $ Million**	**1998-99 $ Million**	**1999-00 $ Million**
1996-97 Budget underlying balance estimate	-5,649	-1,548	957	6,571
1997-98 Budget underlying balance estimate	-6,856	-3,853	1,597	5,383
Effect of reclassifications	-33	-45	-40	-39
Effect of Parameter variations etc.	119	3,008	997	1,958
Effect of pre-budget policy decisions	1,062	-306	344	379
Effect of budget policy decisions:				
Underlying outlays	57	-313	-1,749	-3,193
Revenue	0	39	192	-1,182
Total	57	-352	-1,941	-2,011

Note: * Note that 'the parameter and other variations' row has been adjusted to recognize that the cost of adjusting pensions to meet the 25% of AWE benchmark and of allocating the Telstra money for Environmental projects had already been factored into the 1996 forward estimates. These 1997 'policy decisions' did not (not underlined) therefore have any true (true underlined) effect on the bottom line.
Source: 1997 Commonwealth Budget Paper No. 1, p.1.5.

The best place to find the answer to that question is the Reconciliation Table which the Commonwealth Department of Finance prepares each year, and which was published in the 1997 Budget Paper No. 1 at page 1.5. Table 7.2.1 is a simplified version of that

Table. The table explains the *sources* of the changes in the underlying budget balance estimates for 1996-97 to 1999-00 between those published in last year's Budget and those published in this year's. Three types of source are distinguished: changes in the accounting conventions ('classification' changes); changes arising from the expected state of the economy ('parameter' changes); and changes arising from policy decisions (including Senate amendments or rejections of previously announced government proposals). The sign convention is that positive numbers are changes that add to the underlying deficit, while negative numbers are changes which reduce the underlying deficit (or add to the surplus), for all the entries except revenue (which have the opposite interpretation).

The message from Table 7.2.1 is that although policy decisions announced in the 1997 Budget make only a modest additional contribution to fiscal consolidation in respect of the 1997-98 financial year ($352 million), the effect in the following two years is $2 billion per year. Indeed, in the absence of these policy decisions, the Commonwealth would still be expecting to be in underlying deficit in 1998-99. So to the extent that media commentators wrote-off the 1997 Commonwealth Budget as a macroeconomic "non-event", that was misleading. In all the hoopla over the conversion of the projected superannuation co-contribution scheme to the savings rebate scheme - whether the latter would actually induce any net additional private thrift, whether Mr Howard could evade the obligation to receive the rebate and so on - it seemed to escape many commentators' attention that the budget bottom line was a clear winner from the conversion. If the outlays savings from abandoning the co-contributions scheme (page 148 of Budget Paper No. 2) are compared with the revenue costs of the new savings rebate (page 186 of Budget Paper No. 2), it becomes clear that the net effect on the budget bottom line is +$729 million in 1998-99; +$1.0 billion in 1999-000; and +$1.9 billion in 2000-01. Delivering in *full* the second tranche of Mr Keating's L.A.W. tax cuts was clearly another 'non-core' promise in Mr Howard's 1996 election campaign. The partial retraction of that commitment was the major item in the additional fiscal consolidation delivered in this year's Budget.

Mr Costello claims that the fiscal consolidation task has been concentrated on the outlay side of the Budget. But as was pointed out in Section 7.1 above the rhetoric of a 'slash and burn' approach to fiscal policy needs to be tested against the facts. Page 2.63 of the 1997 Budget Paper No. 1 does show real budget outlays (in underlying terms) falling by 1.4 per cent in 1997-98. But that comes after a rise of 1.1 per cent in 1996-97. And at the end of the forward estimates period real Budget outlays (in underlying terms) will be no lower than when the Coalition won government. That stands in marked contrast to the period when Peter Walsh was Minister for Finance, when real underlying outlays were cut by an overall 5.2 per cent in the course of two consecutive years. And that is not the end of the story. The Howard government is displaying a predilection for using tax expenditure programs rather than new outlays programs to deliver its fiscal 'goodies'. Page 2.56 of the 1997 Budget Paper No. 1 shows aggregate tax expenditures rising rapidly in proportion to budget outlays from 1995-96 through to 2000-01. This is despite the reduction of some tax expenditures (in R&D, and through the superannuation surcharge, for example), and a passage in Budget Paper No. 2 extolling the virtues of converting tax expenditure programmes into more 'transparent' outlays programmes (p. 169).

Although aggregate Commonwealth tax revenues are projected to remain around 24 per cent of GDP through the forward estimates period, a greater and greater portion of the revenue raising task is falling on personal income tax gross of the various new rebates. As more and more Australians find themselves in the high *marginal* tax rate bands, this will create increasing tensions in the system, which the effects of the various new rebates on average personal tax rates will do little to alleviate. This is the time-bomb that is ticking away in the Budget Papers.

7.3 The 1998 Commonwealth Budget

In the Paul Keating era, there came to be an expectation that Commonwealth Budget night would see the Treasurer pull a metaphorical rabbit out of a top hat, thus reaffirming his credentials as a magician of matters fiscal. Peter Costello, though not without certain similarities to the former maestro, adopts a distinctively different approach to his Budget night performances. And yet by the time he sat down on the evening of 12 May 1998, there was something looking remarkably like a rabbit peering from his Budget into his audience.

- the 1997-98 Budget Deficit which he had forecast twelve months earlier would be $3,853 million in underlying terms, was now set to come in at $1,155 million;
- the 1998-99 Budget bottom line which he had projected twelve months earlier would be an underlying surplus of $1,597 million, was now set to be over a billion dollars further into the black at $2,688 million;
- the various outlays and revenue measures announced seemed to contain few major 'nasties' of the type Australia's citizens have been repeatedly warned to expect from this 'slash and burn' Treasurer; and
- all this with a *Charter of Budget Honesty* seal of approval to assure us the figuring is sound, notwithstanding the disturbed financial market circumstances to our near north (the area Ms Hanson's disciples probably still refer to as the far east).

For Mr Costello's 1998 Commonwealth Budget to achieve those four things simultaneously was a remarkable feat. How was it done?

As far as the first three legs of this remarkable rabbit are concerned, the answer is to be found in the *Reconciliation Tables* published in the Budget papers. Given the importance of the information contained in these tables, it is amazing how little coverage they receive in the media reportage on Commonwealth Budgets. In 1998 the principal reconciliation table appeared in Budget Statement 1 (at page 1.5 of 1998 Budget Paper No. 1), with two supplementary tables providing additional detail on outlays and revenues respectively in Budget Statement 2 (see page 2.32 and page 2.36 of 1998 Budget Paper No. 1). The publication of reconciliation tables in Budget Papers predated Mr Howard's Charter of Budget Honesty. It commenced when Mr Hawke was Prime Minister.

Table 7.3.1 represents a condensed and simplified version of the principal reconciliation tables from this year's Commonwealth Budget. The figuring is in terms of the *underlying* budget bottom line, which is the 'traditional' budget bottom line adjusted to exclude proceeds from equity sales such as Telstra, and other 'net advances' such as repayments of State government loans etc.. The first line of the Table gives the set of figures as presented in Mr Costello's 1997 Budget, the final line presents this year's Budget figures. And the body of the table tells us what factors were responsible for the movement between the first-line figures and the final line figures. The arithmetic signs in the middle part of the table need to be interpreted with due care. A positive sign indicates an effect which has added to the magnitude of the deficit, or *reduced* the magnitude of a surplus (see the note to Table 7.3.1 for a fuller explanation).

What does Table 7.3.1 tell us? It tells us three things:

- first, that the improvements to the underlying budget balance estimates between May 1997 and May 1998 are not the consequence of changes to accounting conventions (the 'reclassifications' effects do improve the underlying budget balance in the first two columns, but only in a relatively modest way);
- second, that government policy decisions during the year up to and including Budget night 1998 are not responsible for the improvements to the underlying budget balance estimates over that period. Indeed the net effect of government policy decisions in *both* the first half *and* the second half of that period has been to push the underlying balance significantly in the opposite direction; and
- third, 'parameter' variations have been very kind to us. It is these effects which have allowed us to both have our cake (looser budgetary policy) and eat it too (improved budgetary bottom lines).

The fact that movements in various factors and variables outside direct government policy control (i.e., 'parameters') were exerting a marked and benign effect on the Commonwealth's fiscal position had been known at the time of the Mid Year Economic and Fiscal Outlook Statement (MYEFO). By the time of that statement, despite the policy loosening recorded in row 4 of Table 7.3.1, the 1997-98 forecast underlying Budget deficit had been revised down by over $1 billion (to $2,746 million) and the 1998-99 underlying surplus revised up by almost one billion dollars (to $2,458 million). Further benign parameter movements in the months immediately preceding the May 1998 Budget provided for a further substantial reduction to the 1997-98 underlying surplus, and also 'paid' for significant further budgetary belt-loosening by Mr Costello for the 1998-99 budgetary year *without* altering the 1998-99 underlying surplus estimate significantly from the MYEFO figure.

To quote from the 1998 Budget papers:

> In net terms, policy decisions since the MYEFO detract from the starting point underlying surpluses. Net outlays policy measures… amounting to around $1.4 billion in 1998-99 and rising to $1.5 billion in 1999-2000 and

$1.9 billion in 2000-01 have been announced since the MYEFO. (pp. 1.5-1.6)

In total, net outlays measures since the 1997-98 Budget increase underlying outlays by $2.0 billion in 1998-99, $2.3 billion in 1999-2000, $3.1 billion in 2000-01, and $2.6 billion in 2001-02. (p. 2.33)

Table 7.3.1
Reconciliation of May 1998 Budget With May 1997 Budget

	1997-98 ($m)	1998-99 ($m)	1999-00 ($m)	2000-01 ($m)
May 1997 Budget underlying balance	-3,853	1,597	5,383	10,692
Effect of reclassifications *	-26	-69	5	5
Effect of parameters variations etc. *	-3,215	-2,939	-1,682	-1,593
Effect of policy decisions: *				
• up to mid-year review	392	639	846	1,486
• since mid-year review and in May 1998 Budget	152	1,279	1,481	2,180
May 1998 Budget underlying balance	-1,155	2,688	4,733	8,614

Note: * These 'effects' figures are presented such that a negative figure improves the budget balance, and a positive figure detracts from the budget balance. This is the sign convention adopted in the Budget Papers. It seems to represent a hangover from the period when we were normally discussing the various effects on a *deficit* bottom line, with 'positive' effect figures increasing that deficit and negative effect figures reducing that deficit.

Source: Commonwealth of Australia, *Budget Strategy and Outlook 1998-99*, Budget Paper No. 1, page 1.5.

So if you had got the impression that during the last year or so Mr Costello has been less 'hair-shirt', (or less 'slash and burn') in his fiscal actions than during his first year and a quarter as Treasurer, the figures would seem to bear that out. The 1998 Budget did not see a tightening of the stance of Commonwealth fiscal policy. *Nor* was it a do-nothing Budget in terms of the stance of fiscal policy. It represented a marked softening in the stance of Commonwealth fiscal policy.

That takes us back to the fourth of the four dot points listed at the beginning of this section. To be blunt, how come Commonwealth Treasury seem to be so happy with a Budget that represents a marked softening in the stance of Commonwealth fiscal policy? Having waged a virtually unbroken quarter-century long campaign in favour of tighter fiscal policy in Australia, Commonwealth Treasury gives every appearance of being perfectly happy with the current stance of Commonwealth fiscal policy - the past year's softenings notwithstanding. Statement 3 in the 1998 Budget Paper No. 1 bears every stamp of being a Treasury document. And it sets out quite deliberately to argue and to persuade that the worsening of Australia's current account deficit that is in prospect for 1998-99 should *not* be taken as evidence that the present stance of Commonwealth fiscal policy is too soft or loose.

There are a number of possible hypotheses that might explain the Treasury support:

- the fiscal tightening in Mr Costello's earlier Budgets has been sufficient to rectify Australia's *structural* fiscal imbalance. As far as the budget aggregates are concerned, the outlook is now okay.
- the (hopefully) shorter-term disturbances to the Australian economy emanating from the Asian financial market upheavals render the present time a period when the public sector's contribution to domestic aggregate demand in Australia should *not* be markedly reduced.
- you should never expect much fiscal 'courage' of a government about to face its electorate. Turn a blind eye to this Budget, and try harder for 'hair-shirts' after the election.
- if it has to be a choice between endorsing a moderate softening of the stance of fiscal policy *with* the assured introduction of an Australian value added tax, or holding a hard line fiscally and waving goodbye to the VAT again, take the former.

Statement 3, together with the other Treasury-sourced parts of the Budget documentation provide little that would support any of the above hypotheses apart from the first. The need for taxation reform is stressed in several places, notably at the very end of Statement 3 where the call for structural improvements in public sector saving to be 'sustained' is paired with: 'It will also be important to proceed along the path of further microeconomic and regulatory reform, including taxation reform' (page 3.18).

In the context of the *Charter for Budget Honesty*, which itself is stressed a number of times in the Budget Papers, it would be difficult for the Commonwealth Treasury to come out immediately after the forthcoming federal election arguing the pressing need for further substantial structural improvements in the Commonwealth Budget's direct contribution to Australian national saving.

It would be *difficult* for Treasury to be seen to do that. But did Mr Costello's first two Budgets really work such profound wonders to the Commonwealth's finances? There are a number of grounds for hesitation on this. Consider Table 7.3.2. This reproduces data presented in Table VIII of Statement No. 4 in 1998 Budget Paper No. 1 (a Department of Finance document). The bottom line shows total Budget underlying outlays falling in real terms by 0.9 per cent in 1997-98, after a modest real rise of 0.5 per cent the preceding year. That looks impressive compared with the figures for the years 1990-91 to 1994-95 (all between 3.8 per cent and 5.4 per cent). But compared with the figures for the last four years Peter Walsh was Finance Minister (0.4, -1.3, -4.7, 0.8), Peter Costello's achievement looks somewhat less impressive. For the full historical picture see pages 2.70-2.71 of 1998 Budget Paper No. 1.

Table 7.3.2 also makes it clear that the negative figure for real outlays growth in 1997-98 is driven by a massive reduction in capital outlays. Total current outlays recorded growth of 0.7 per cent. In 1988-89, when total underlying budget outlays fell 4.7 per cent in real terms, the total *current* outlays component fell 4.2 per cent. It is true that Mr Costello's projected total current outlays go down in real terms in the budget out-years.

But that is heavily influenced by the public debt interest component (see row 7 of Table 7.3.2). And that in turn is a reflection of major asset sales effects, which if the sale of the remainder of Telstra does *not* proceed, will have to be taken out of those figures.

There is also another factor that needs to be borne in mind, concerning the apparent restraint in budget outlays recorded in Table 7.3.2. A number of the Howard government's policy initiatives towards a loosening of the stance of fiscal policy have taken the form of *taxation expenditures* rather than explicit government outlays programmes. Appendix C to Statement 2 in 1998 Budget Paper No. 1 presents estimates of the projected growth in total identified Commonwealth tax expenditures. As a proportion of total Budget underlying outlays the 1998-99 figure (14.5 per cent) is set to be markedly higher than 1997-98 (13.8 per cent). And this growth is projected to continue through the out-years: 15.5 per cent in 1999-00; 16.0 per cent in 2000-01; 16.7 per cent in 2001-02. By 'tucking-away' new government spending initiatives in tax expenditure programmes, a government is able to make its projected outlays growth look more modest, while simultaneously appearing to be restrained in the total taxation revenue it is intending to raise.

Bearing in mind these various factors, it does seem rather hard to believe that the Commonwealth Treasury will *not* be arguing for further structural tightening to the stance of budgetary policy when normal Cabinet processes resume after the federal election. Perhaps Statement 3 in the May 1998 Budget papers should be regarded as primarily for overseas and financial market consumption. It reads rather like a letter to one's creditors arguing why *you* are not at all like the other debtors in your neighbourhood, why *you* should not be subject to withdrawal of credit, and why your creditors will soon be very very happy that they put their funds with you. In such letters it is *de rigueur* to 'embroider' somewhat on the truth.

Looking at the Budget from a South Australian perspective, we should probably applaud the easing in the stance of fiscal policy while it lasts. The fact that Mr Costello targeted older Australians for many of his increased Commonwealth spending initiatives is a bonus for a State with a larger than the national average representation of older citizens. Any across-the-board moves to reduce Commonwealth spending on health and welfare would tend to take more spending power out of the South Australian economy as compared with the other States and Territories.

One final point deserves mention. Since the 1998 Budget Paper No. 1 repeatedly emphasises the benefits of the Charter of Budget Honesty, it was unfortunate to find an obvious and outright lie at the fifteenth page of Statement 1:

> The Government's Commitment to no new taxes or increases in existing taxes over the life of this Parliament has been met.

I thought the charade of the superannuation surcharge being compatible with that commitment had long ago been dropped. Budget Statement 1 has traditionally had much greater input from the Treasurer's office than the remainder of Budget Paper No. 1. But I would be surprised if Ted Evans had not made some effort to remonstrate about such an outright 'porkie' being printed in the Commonwealth Budget Papers. If the

Table 7.3.2
Commonwealth Budget Underlying Outlays By Economic Type
Annual Percentage Change (89-90 prices) [(a)]

	1994-95	1995-96	1996-97	1997-98	1998-99	1999-00	2000-01	2001-02
Current Outlays								
Final Consumption Expenditure	1.0	2.3	-1.1	6.3	4.4	-3.5	-0.4	-2.4
Defence Salaries	-5.3	0.3	0.8	-1.1	-3.1	-5.4	-4.3	2.0
Non-Salaries	0.9	0.6	-3.6	3.8	5.2	-0.5	0.7	-1.3
Non-Defence Salaries	-3.9	-1.6	-3.3	-7.1	1.3	-11.6	-1.7	-1.8
Non-Salaries	8.2	7.6	1.5	19.3	8.0	-1.5	0.7	-4.8
Total Current Transfer Payments	5.3	4.4	0.7	-0.4	-0.8	0.6	0.2	0.2
Interest	22.0	10.7	1.2	-13.1	-8.4	-11.8	-14.1	-26.8
Subsidies	-0.6	3.9	3.3	-2.6	-5.7	-3.5	-7.3	2.6
Personal Benefit Payments	2.1	4.5	2.8	-0.1	0.5	1.4	0.9	1.5
Grants to Non-Profit Institutions	21.5	23.5	-9.4	-10.7	3.0	1.7	1.6	2.1
Grants to Non-Budget Sector	9.8	3.0	-2.2	6.4	0.1	2.3	1.7	3.2
Grants to State Governments	3.0	2.1	0.1	0.6	-0.3	3.0	0.9	2.0
Grants through State Govt.	8.4	2.3	3.8	8.1	1.1	1.4	2.1	0.2
Grants Direct to Local Govt.	5.9	2.9	-4.5	-5.3	5.7	3.4	4.4	4.8
Grants to Multi Jurisdictional Sect.	8.3	0.3	-2.5	-1.2	-9.3	-6.1	-3.6	-1.8
Grants Overseas	2.1	-2.0	-14.5	2.5	-1.8	0.4	-1.2	1.4
Other Transfers	-49.3	5.4	-9.9	-31.7	n.a.	-12.4	-1.9	-0.9
Total Current Outlays	**4.6**	**4.0**	**0.4**	**0.7**	**0.1**	**-0.2**	**-0.2**	**-0.2**

Table 7.3.2 (Continued)
Commonwealth Budget Underlying Outlays By Economic Type
Annual Percentage Change (89-90 prices) [a]

	1994-95	1995-96	1996-97	1997-98	1998-99	1999-00	2000-01	2001-02
Capital Outlays								
Capital Outlays on Goods	-16.3	20.0	-27.9	-180.5	-140.2	198.7	31.6	18.7
Capital Outlays on Land	-57.6	-57.1	-155.4	n.a.	-146.3	-28.8	22.2	-22.6
Total Capital Transfer Payments	-17.1	-5.3	8.6	-27.0	-0.5	-7.1	-2.7	-5.0
Grants to Non-Budget Sector	96.8	-3.02	103.5	-53.0	0.2	-8.3	6.9	-22.6
Grants to State Governments	-21.4	-1.2	-0.1	-22.9	-0.5	-4.9	-3.0	-2.6
Grants through State Govt.	-10.5	0.7	-13.7	1.0	-10.1	-10.3	-12.5	-1.2
Grants Direct to Local Govt.	-89.5	n.a.	-78.4	-10.1	31.1	-29.7	-35.8	-52.1
Grants to Multi Jurisdictional Sect.	-67.2	-18.7	0.7	-9.7	-1.4	-0.7	-0.9	-0.7
Grants to Other Sectors	-13.0	-16.7	3.9	-16.5	4.1	-33.7	-13.0	-1.9
Total Capital Outlays	**-15.2**	**-0.6**	**3.9**	**-49.6**	**37.9**	**3.6**	**3.2**	**-0.6**
Contingency Reserve	n.a.	n.a.	n.a.	n.a.	238.6	n.a.	98.3	52.1
Total Underlying Outlays	**3.8**	**3.9**	**0.5**	**-0.9**	**0.6**	**1.0**	**0.8**	**0.8**

Note: [a] The non-farm GDP (NFGDP) deflator is used as a general measure of price change.

Treasurer's office were so keen for that sentence to be uttered, why didn't they put it in the Budget Speech and leave Budget Paper No. 1 'honest'?

7.4 The 1999 Commonwealth Budget

It might seem paradoxical that in the midst of implementing fiscal policy initiatives so sweeping that the tag 'once-per-generation' is probably an understatement, Treasurer Costello was able to bring down a Commonwealth Budget that caused little more than a chorus of yawns across Australia on the evening of May 11th, 1999.

It is also unusual in our type of political system for the first budget put before parliament following a general election to produce a mix of yawns and smiles among the watching and listening general public. Traditionally, post-election Budgets are 'Mother Hubbard' time. The Treasurer announces a series of plausible reasons for the stance of fiscal policy to need to be much tighter than had been envisaged by his (or her) party during the election campaign (i.e., 'the cupboard is bare'). The 'Sir Humphreys' of Treasury and the Department of Finance tend to assume that cabinet's propensity for 'courageous decisions' is generally at its peak when the expected time to the next general election is also at its peak.

Some might feel tempted to believe that it *was* a 'Mother Hubbard' budget but in cunning disguise (perhaps a 'Red Riding Hood'?). That is *not* a viable interpretation.

On the evening of May 11th, 1999 Treasurer Costello announced a series of revenue measures with a combined net effect of plus $27.7 million to revenue in 1999-2000; $21.9 million in 2000-01; $16.6 million in 2001-02 and $25.9 million in 2002-03 (these figures together with a breakdown by the measures that give rise to them are detailed at page 3 of *Budget Paper No. 2: Budget Measures 1999-2000*). On that same evening he announced a series of outlays measures with a combined net effect of plus $861 million on Commonwealth outlays (now called 'expenses') in 1999-2000; $1020.9 million in 2000-01; $722.3 million in 2001-02 and $383.4 million in 2002-03 (see p. 29 *ibid*). The trained eye will note the rapid tail-off in the net cost of the outlays initiatives in the out-years. That gets nods of approval from Treasury and Department of Finance bureaucrats, whether still on the payrolls of those august establishments, or out-to-pasture on the payrolls of financial enterprises.

In the Treasurer's Budget speech the various 'goodies' are usually presented in terms of their four year additive cost. Presentationally that has two obvious benefits. First, it makes the numbers sound more impressive to the *non cognoscenti*. At the same time it avoids alerting them to the fact that the 'generosity' of the package is time limited. Interestingly enough, it seems to be quite rare for the Budget speech to represent tax increase measures in terms of their four year additive effect on the bottom line. Perhaps there are some things the *non cognoscenti* are best left not knowing?

So, Treasurer Costello's role on Budget night was not so much Mother Hubbard but that of a very restrained, perhaps even parsimonious, Santa Claus - but a distributor of new presents (in net terms) nevertheless. Subtracting the $27.7 million positive revenue measures for 1999-2000 from the $861 million in net outlays (or 'expenses') increases still leaves $833 million of goodies. For 2000-01 the equivalent figure is almost $1 billion, then phasing back to about one-third that level in 2002-03.

At the same time as distributing the goodies, Treasurer Costello was able to announce a stronger budget surplus for 1999-2000 than had hitherto been officially acknowledged. Of course, the new accounting rules of the accruals framework mean that we should not actually say 'budget surplus'. The bottom line of this year's budget is called the 'fiscal balance'. It differs from the previous focus of attention, 'the underlying cash balance', in a number of respects, all described in exquisite detail in Appendix A to *Budget Statement 1*, in *Budget Paper No. 1: Budget Strategy and Outlook 1999-2000.*

One feature of the differences, however, that has received little attention is that the *new* bottom line refers to a broader range of Commonwealth Government activity than the *old* one: the entire 'general government' sector rather than the previous 'budget sector'. This means non-commercial Commonwealth authorities such as the CSIRO and the ABC which were previously *excluded* are now included. The word 'excluded' is in italics because those agencies' appropriations from the Budget always were there in the figures. But now we have what they actually spend, and any 'borrowing' (or the opposite) which they undertake brought into the figures.

The cynic who might expect every change in budgetary accounting procedures implemented by a government to produce presentational improvements in the figures should look carefully at the Table on page 1.12 of 1999 *Budget Paper No. 1.* The new accounting framework does add half a billion dollars to the bottom line surplus for financial year 1998-99 it is true. But for the budget year itself, 1999-2000, the new framework sent the bottom line a little over $1 billion backwards. For 2000-01 there is a substantial presentational improvement effect (almost $5 billion), but for 2001-02 the contrary (by almost $1.4 billion). It is thus difficult to sustain the cynical position. The new accounting framework is clearly superior to the old one, and a step forward for the transparency of public finances in Australia. The presentation of the transition could have been better, and the treatment of the proposed additional share sales in Telstra does have certain peculiarities however (see below).

The question nevertheless remains: how was Treasurer Costello able to play Santa Claus on May 11th, 1999 to the net value of $833 million for the 1999-2000 financial year, while still closing the evening with his 'sack' fuller than when he had risen to his feet at 7.30 p.m. (i.e., a bigger fiscal surplus for 1999-2000)? To answer this type of question one has to turn to the reconciliation table in the Budget Papers. The absence of reconciliation tables and forward years' estimates from the Budget papers published during Mr Howard's time as Treasurer in the Fraser government marred Australia's public finances during that period. At the same time as we give the present Commonwealth Government proper credit for its initiatives in the field of 'Budget Honesty', one should give the Hawke government due credit for the incorporation of forward estimates and reconciliation tables into published Commonwealth Budget documentation.

This year's reconciliation table is more difficult to read than previous years' because of the shift to the accruals accounting framework. The first half year of the table is presented on the *old* accounting system and reconciles the Commonwealth fiscal position at the time of the *Mid-Year Economic and Fiscal Outlook* (MYEFO) Statement with the 1998 Budget figuring. The mid-year figures are then converted to the new accounting basis, with the changes of dimensions as discussed already. The second half-year of the table is then presented in terms of the new accounting system and reconciles the Commonwealth's fiscal position as set out in this year's Budget with the MYEFO figuring.

The 1998 Budget's forward estimates projected that the budget bottom line would be $4,830 million in the black for the year 1999-2000. By the time of the MYEFO, that figure was down to $2,686 million on the old accounting system and $1,624 million on the new accounting system. The reconciliation table tells us that of that diminution in the expected surplus, only $365 million was attributable to variations in economic parameters and the like. The remaining $1,779 million was the result of policy decisions announced by the Commonwealth government during the relevant period - with the ANTS (*A New Taxation System*) package announced in August 1998 accounting for the lion's share of that.

Between the MYEFO and Budget night (May 11th, 1999), the Commonwealth had announced further policy initiatives with projected impact on the 1999-2000 fiscal balance of minus $151.3 million in revenue and plus $103.5 million in outlays (see pages 4 and 31 of *Budget Paper No. 2*). Thus when Treasurer Costello rose to his feet in Parliament on May 11th 1999, his 'starting point' was a projected fiscal surplus of $1,369 million. By the time he sat down again that surplus had increased to $5,426 million, despite the $833 million net cost of the new policy initiatives announced in the Budget. The great bulk of the almost $5 billion required to square the story came from the effects of revisions to Treasury's economic parameters etc., on forecast Commonwealth revenue for 1999-2000 (up by $4459 million).

The major economic parameter forecasts underlying Treasury's new estimates of 1999-2000 Commonwealth revenue are published at page 6.4 of the *1999 Budget Paper No. 1*. They are: growth in nominal GDP of 4.75 per cent; average earnings growth of 3.75 per cent; growth in wage and salary earner employment of 1.5 per cent; an increase in nominal consumer spending of 5.75 per cent and growth in 1998-99 company income of around 4.5 per cent (*loc cit*). Note that the lags in the company tax collection arrangements mean that it is Treasury's estimate of 1998-99 company income that is pertinent for projecting company tax collections in 1999-2000. Every economic forecaster will tell you it is easier to forecast something that has already happened than something yet to happen.

To quote from the *1999 Budget Statement 6*:

> Total revenue is expected to increase by 6.2 per cent with the ratio of revenue to GDP increasing slightly to 26.3 per cent from 25.9 per cent in 1998-99. The growth in taxation revenue in 1999-2000 reflects ongoing expansion of economic activity... Particularly strong growth is expected in: company tax, reflecting income growth through 1998-99; petroleum resource rent tax, as a result of the resumption of production in Victoria; and other excise, due to reform of tobacco taxation announced in ANTS.

It should be pointed out that the forward estimate information published in the Commonwealth Budget papers in respect to revenue is extremely rudimentary when compared with the equivalent information regarding Commonwealth outlays. Publication of forward estimates information for outlays in Commonwealth Budget papers commenced in the early period of the Hawke government. But Commonwealth Treasury successfully resisted the publication of *any* equivalent revenue side information until John Dawkins' time as Treasurer. Even then, forward estimates for tax revenue were published only for total tax revenue and two or three very broad sub-categories. That remains the position today (see page 6.14 of *1999 Budget Paper No. 1*).

It is practically impossible to see from the 1999 Budget papers *how* that $4.5 billion of additional revenue for 1999-2000 was generated by *which* revisions in *which* economic parameters working through *which* taxes. Surely 'Budget Honesty' should require as much transparency on this side of the Budget as Australians have already enjoyed for many years in respect of the outlays side? Commonwealth Treasury's arguments against the publication of more detailed revenue forward estimates smack of sophistry. If the 'unknowability' argument is to be believed, why are Treasury happy to provide such detailed out-year forecasts of the effects of *changes* to tax revenue from individual revenue policy announcements? If any of the 'spending' departments of the Commonwealth sought to suppress publication of forward estimates of the fiscal impact of their programs, and thus obtain a diminution in their public accountability re the conduct of those programs, would not Commonwealth Treasury be among the first to object?

Interestingly the various revisions to Commonwealth Treasury parameters which boosted forecast revenue for 1999-2000 by $4.5 billion had effects in the opposite direction for the next two financial years - *reducing* previously projected revenue in 2000-01 by $642 million and in 2001-02 by $546 million. A betting person might care to speculate that when Treasurer Costello announces the government's business tax reform measures arising from the Review of Business Taxation (or Ralph Inquiry) process, if that package of measures is revenue-reducing its announcement might be paired with that of revised Treasury economic parameters for 2000-01 and 2001-02. Alternatively that rabbit might remain inside the Treasurer's hat until Budget night 2000.

We turn now to the broader context of Commonwealth government fiscal policy decision-making, and decision-implementation. The days when a government could announce all of a year's significant fiscal policy initiatives on one day probably never did exist. Even if they did they are long gone now. The main action of 1999 fiscal policy-making was forced into the role of 'supporting player' on Budget night. One set of crucially important taxation, social security and payments to States initiatives had been announced to the public before the 1998 federal election, debated during that election campaign, voted through the House of Representatives, and subjected to investigation by Senate Committees all before Budget night. On Budget night itself, it was still unclear to anyone what (if any) modifications to that set of initiatives would be necessary to secure its passage through the Senate.

At the same time a second set of crucially important taxation initiatives were going through a gestation process the government called the *RBT* (Review of Business Taxation) and everyone else called 'the Ralph Inquiry'. At the time of writing, the RBT Final Report to the government is imminent. It is not clear how long Federal Cabinet will require before there is an announcement by the government of the business tax package that it proposes to implement, in the wake of the final report. Even after such an announcement has been made, there is still likely to be a period of uncertainty pending clarification of whether the proposed package is likely to have the 'numbers' to go through the Senate without significant amendments.

There is a third big-picture issue for Australia's fiscal situation which *was* on the stage on 1999 Budget night, but in a fairly peculiar way, namely the further sales of shares in Telstra. The arithmetic in the Budget papers is based on the announced intention of the Howard cabinet to sell *all* of the Commonwealth government's remaining shares in Telstra, and receive all the sales proceeds, by the end of financial year 2002-03. From the figures in the 'cash-flows' statement published at page 4.9 of *Budget Paper No. 1* it is clear that the Telstra proceeds are expected to come into the Commonwealth Budget in three separate financial years: 1999-2000; 2001-02 and 2002-03. On Budget night, it would have been a brave punter who would have put any money on the Senate approving more than the sale of 16.6 per cent of Telstra shares by the Commonwealth. To factor into the Budget Papers the proceeds from the remaining 50 per cent in those two out-years thus required a degree of 'optimism'. It could be argued that Budget arithmetic *must* be based on the government's stated intentions rather than on a realistic assessment of what might or might not obtain passage through the Senate. But for the Treasurer's Budget Speech to infer from this that: 'We now have the prospect of completely eliminating Commonwealth net debt' (p. 11), does seem to have been *stretching* the facts.

This criticism could be taken further. A definition of what the Commonwealth Budget Papers actually *mean* by net debt can be found at page 1.10 of *1999 Budget Paper No. 1*. It reads:

> Net debt…comprises selected financial liabilities (deposits held, advances received and borrowing) less selected financial assets (cash and deposits, advances paid and investments).

The balance-sheet data in *Budget Statement 4* indicate that at 30 June 1999 the Commonwealth's estimated superannuation liabilities to its employees and ex-employees exceed $69 billion and are expected to grow to $72.4 billion by June 30, 2003 (see p. 4.15). These sums are *not* included in Treasurer Costello's definition of Commonwealth net debt, although most Australians would probably view this as something the Commonwealth 'owes' and therefore a 'debt'. The same applies to the long-service leave entitlements etc., of Commonwealth employees where the June 30, 2003 expected Commonwealth liability is $3.3 billion *(loc cit)*.

More importantly though, the shift to an accruals accounting framework is lauded by most economists and economic commentators, on the basis that it removes the illusion that sales or purchases of assets by a government can be viewed as having the same effects on a government's *bottom line* as current revenues or current outlays. Where cash is received from the sale of an asset, the impact should be considered as an alteration in the *composition* of the balance sheet, rather than recorded as 'income'. If one tries to focus the attention of the gullible on a subset of the balance sheet, as Mr Costello is attempting to do with his particular definition of 'net debt', then one risks recreating a similar type of 'illusion' to the one we had hoped we had banished.

This danger of creating 'illusions' even under an accrual accounting approach is further illustrated by the following hypothetical example. Imagine a government selling a major asset for $2 billion, frittering $1 billion away on low priority current outlays programs in marginal seats (perhaps worked out on a big white-board) and using the other $1 billion to retire debt. On the old accounting system one could focus the attention of the gullible on the $1 billion 'improvement ' in the deficit/surplus. If the new accounting system simply sees the gullibles attention refocused on the $1 billion 'improvement' in the government's net debt, little is achieved.

And unfortunately it gets worse. At page 1.20 of *1999 Budget Paper No. 1*, it is stated:

> Telstra is currently recorded in the Commonwealth's balance sheet at book value, which is significantly below its expected market value. That is, the estimate of the Government's current net asset position is, in fact, distorted by this valuation issue. As Telstra is sold, however, this under-valuation is undone, contributing to the significant improvement in the measure of net assets.

It would seem incompatible with 'Budget Honesty' for a government to claim kudos for a significant improvement in its reported balance sheet position when in fact that improvement was more a matter of the removal of a 'distortion' rather than a *true* improvement of composition.

In the SACES Economic Briefing Report on the 1998 Commonwealth Budget (see Section 7.3 above), it was noted that there had been a pronounced softening in the stance of Commonwealth Budgeting Policy over the year to May 1998. From what has been said already, it will be clear that there has been a further pronounced softening during the last twelve months or so. Policy decisions announced during the second half of calendar year 1998 pushed the stance of fiscal policy in the expansionary direction to the extent of $1.8 billion for 1999-2000, $5.2 billion for 2000-01, and $5.5 billion for 2002-03. The aggregate of the ANTS initiatives account for the lion's share of that loosening. The 1999 Budget itself saw a further but more modest shift in its direction of loosening, with a peak effect of about $1 billion in 2000-01 (see above). The measures announced by the Treasurer in the weeks following Budget night, associated with ensuring passage of the principal ANTS initiatives (and the 16.6 per cent tranche of Telstra) through the Senate have seen the fiscal lever edged further in that same direction by another notch or two.

Those who like to see fiscal policy loosening should recognise that this is probably as good as it gets. Apart from some sweeteners to render the impending business tax reform package palatable to the business community and acceptable to the Senate, it is hard to see any more major Santa Claus performances from the Commonwealth Treasurer, or the Minister for Finance, over the immediate future.

7.5 The 2000 Commonwealth Budget

Paul Keating once described his concept of beauty (in human-created works) in terms of 'classical lines' - the idea of graceful orderly symmetry permeating a work as a whole, with no unnecessary ornamentation or the complexity-for-complexity's-sake that distracts the eye (or ear) from appreciation of the elegant totality of the whole construct.

On that concept of beauty, Treasurer Costello's May 2000 Commonwealth Budget was a most abysmal failure. Yet on a more philistine conception of what constitutes a Budget that is worthy of admiration, namely the economist's calculus of what its consequences are for the material living standards of the Australian community, Treasurer Costello's fifth Commonwealth Budget deserves congratulation as a 'beautiful set of numbers'.

Those who believed that the adoption of the disciplines of accruals accounting would improve the transparency of Budget documentation must have been wringing their hands in grief on 9th May, 2000. In this new 'accruals' world the 'bottom line' of the Budget is termed the *Budget fiscal balance*. On the very first page of Budget Statement No. 1 we are told that 'the fiscal balance is expected to be in surplus by $5.4 billion or 0.8 per cent of GDP in 2000-01'. But when we look at the details of the revenue side of the Budget in Statement No. 5 and of the expenses side in Statement No. 6 we find that the numbers do not articulate with the key Table in Statement No. 1 which explains the genesis of that $5.4 billion 'bottom line'. Table 1 of Statement No. 5 tells us total revenue in 2000-01 is estimated to be $158.7 billion, whereas Table 3 of Statement No. 1 had reported $153.5 billion. To get from total revenue to the fiscal balance in Statement No. 1 we need to subtract two aggregates: total expenses of an 'operating' (or 'current purpose') nature; and net capital investment. Statement No. 6 tells us that total expenses in 2000-01 are estimated to be $153.7 billion, whereas Statement No. 1 had reported $150.3 billion. Statement No. 6 (p. 6.10) tells us net capital investment in 2000-01 is estimated to be $0.2 billion (positive), whereas Statement No. 1 had reported (minus) $2.2 billion. The explanation is that two different accounting standards have been used to prepare the accruals figuring in the Budget papers, one being Australian Accounting Standard 31 *Financial Reporting by Governments* (AAS31), the other based on the *Government Finance Statistics* (GFS) framework. All the details of the two sides of the Budget in Statements 4, 5 and 6 is reported on the AAS31 basis. But the overview of the Budget in Statement No. 1 is on the GFS basis and the reconciliation tables between the two types of figures that are provided are presented on only a highly aggregated basis.

But there's more, as the man in the steak knives advert says with such enthusiasm. As stated above, the very first page of 2000 Budget Statement No. 1 reported that the budgeted fiscal balance for 2000-01 is $5.4 billion. But that page gives equal prominence to the old pre-accruals days accounting concept of *underlying cash balance*. 'In cash terms', we are told, 'an underlying surplus of $2.8 billion or 0.4 per cent of GDP is expected in 2000-01, an improvement of $2.3 billion on the corresponding estimate at the time of the MYEFO' *(Mid Year Economic and Fiscal Outlook 1999-2000)*.

In Mr Costello's Budget Speech it was this latter concept of the budget bottom-line that was the *only* one he cited. 'The Budget I present tonight is in surplus for the fourth year in a row, a cash surplus of $2.8 billion' (p. 1). Perhaps he was too modest to mention a surplus figure almost twice as big? Perhaps the fact that on that concept this would be the third rather than fourth surplus in a row weighed against it in the rhetoric stakes? Who knows how the mind of the writer of a Budget Speech works? But the glossy blue A4 document titled *Budget Overview* is produced by the Commonwealth Treasury, and that also gives top of first page prominence to the $2.8 billion figure. The question naturally arises: if both Treasurer and Treasury are so keen on the cash based concept of the budget bottom line, why present all the supporting detail of the government's incomings and outgoings on a completely different basis (well to be accurate *two* completely different *bases*) and with virtually no hope, for a reader, of tracking down *why* the cash surplus as estimated in the May Budget was $2.3 billion bigger than the corresponding estimate at the time of the MYEFO?

Having burst onto the scene so spectacularly in the *Budget Overview* and on the first page of Budget Statement No. 1, the old underlying cash balance concept scarcely gets a mention in the Budget Papers until page 35 of Budget Statement No. 8. Here at last we have a column of numbers telling us how the $2.8 billion figure was arrived at. But trying to reconcile numbers in that column with the figuring in the body of the Budget Papers is not easy. Total cash receipts from taxes is reported on page 8.35 to be budgeted at $163.0 billion in 2000-01. In Budget Statement No. 4 cash receipts from taxes in 2000-01 was given as $139.6 billion (p. 4.10). The discrepancy cannot be wholly attributed to GST revenues being excluded from the latter figure. GST revenues for 2000-01 are estimated to be $24.053 billion in cash receipts terms in Statement No. 4 (p. 4.20) and total Commonwealth cash receipts from all taxes including those collected 'on behalf of' the States and Territories $164.2 billion. Discussion of the matter of where GST receipts ought to be reported is resumed later in this section.

It might be thought that now we have entered the new world of accruals accounting, it would make no sense to clutter up the Budget Papers with figures based on the old and seemingly discredited cash accounting basis. But it would appear that it was that old basis which led to the government's announcement last year that there *would* be an East Timor Levy, and to the government's announcement in this May's Budget that that levy *would not* in fact be implemented. To quote from Budget Statement No. 1 (p. 1.9):

> On the basis of the budget estimates when the levy was announced last November, the unanticipated costs of Australia's East Timor deployment would have pushed the Budget into deficit in underlying cash terms in 2000-01. The improved budget position since then means that the costs of the East Timor deployment in 2000-01 can be absorbed without a levy while still achieving a substantial surplus.

Treasurer Costello's Budget Speech (p. 2) portrayed the nexus between the cash concept of the Budget bottom line and the East Timor levy in stronger terms:

> Since the Levy was announced as a measure to keep the Budget in surplus and the Budget will now be in surplus without it, it would not be right to proceed with the levy.

If a Commonwealth government decision worth $900 million in 2000-01 was driven by the state of the old concept of the budget bottom line and not by either of the two new concepts which jostle with one another throughout the budget documentation, shouldn't the principle of Budget transparency (and Budget Honesty) require that a more detailed account be provided of the mechanics driving the cash concept of the bottom line? Or could it be that the truth of the matter is that the nexus between the East Timor levy and the cash surplus was cosmetic (or 'presentational') rather than real?

In the SACES *Economic Briefing Report* on the 1999 Commonwealth Budget (see Section 7.4 above) we confirmed that Treasurer Costello had performed a remarkable feat in his May 1999 Budget. He had played Santa Claus to the extent of distributing new presents to the net value of $0.8 billion for the 1999-2000 financial year, while still closing the evening with his 'sack' fuller than when he had risen to his feet at 7.30 p.m. (i.e., a bigger fiscal surplus for 1999-2000). We advised that that was:

> probably as good as its gets. Apart from some sweeteners to render the impending business tax reform package palatable to the business community and acceptable to the Senate, it is hard to see any more major Santa Claus performances from the Commonwealth Treasurer or the Minister for Finance, over the immediate future (p. 89).

We were wrong. The evening of 9 May 2000 saw a repeat performance by Treasurer Costello of the remarkable feat of announcing the distribution of valuable new 'goodies' (in net terms) to the community, while still being able to declare his 'sack' to be growing fatter rather than being diminished by the exercise. Policy decisions announced on Budget night (together with some announced earlier but no earlier than the MYEFO) were budgeted to have a combined net effect of depressing revenues by $1,390 million in 2000-01; $427 million in 2001-02; $392 million in 2002-03; and $325 million in 2003-04 while increasing expenses by $872 million in 2000-01; $832 million in 2001-02; $728 million in 2002-03 and $589 million in 2003-04.

Against this, consider the following. The Budget fiscal balance projected for 2000-01 at the time of the MYEFO had been $4,392 million. Budget night closed with that figure raised to $5,436 million - although the outyear figures went in the opposite direction: the year 2001-02 projection down from $2,941 million to $1,072 million; and 2002-03 down from $10,056 million to $7,610 million.

So how do you add $872 million to your expenses, take $1,390 million off your revenues and still come out with a bottom line for 2000-01 that is $1,044 million healthier? To put the answer in a nutshell, you need to obtain $3,306 million from 'somewhere completely different'. To find out where Mr Costello got that $3.3 billion, the standard procedure requires one to consult the Reconciliation tables presented in Budget Paper No. 1 (p. 1.7, p. 5.4, p. 6.7, and p. 6.11). But because the last three of those tables are on a different accruals accounting basis to that used for the first, it is far more difficult to find the answer than when asking the same question of previous Commonwealth Budgets.

It seems clear however that only about $0.5 billion of the $3.3 billion is attributable to the types of economic parameter variations (including stronger than previously expected tax revenue growth) that one usually expects to be the answer to this type of question. The lion's share of the figure, namely $2.8 billion:

> mainly reflects an upward revision to the expected proceeds from the sale of non-financial assets, principally telecommunications spectrum licenses. In the calculation of net capital investment, proceeds from the sale of non-financial assets are subtracted from purchases of non-financial assets. Consequently, an increase in the proceeds from the sale of non-financial assets reduces net capital investment and increases the fiscal balance. (2000 Budget Statement No. 1, p. 1.10).

So it's as simple as that! Santa's sack got bigger on the night of 9 May, 2000 because one of the assets the government had already earmarked for sale had its expected sales proceeds revalued upwards substantially. Isn't accruals accounting wonderful? I bet Mr Keating is wishing the Treasury and Finance bureaucrats had told him about it years ago! Perhaps this explains why Mr Costello was keen in his Budget Speech to stress the more modest budget bottom line figure generated by the old-fashioned (and seemingly discredited?) underlying cash balance approach? But if that was his (highly commendable) motive, why not do the logical next step and require Treasury to publish a reconciliation table explaining how the underlying cash surplus got from $0.5 billion at the time of the MYEFO to $2.8 billion by the time the Treasurer sat down on the evening of 9 May - his Santa Claus measures on taxation and outlays notwithstanding?

To repeat what was said in Section 7.4 above: the days when a government could announce all of a year's significant fiscal policy initiatives on one day probably never did exist. And even if they did, they have long gone now. Between the May 1999 Budget and the starting point for the May 2000 Budget discussed above, there were three major Commonwealth fiscal policy statements and a number of minor ones. It is useful to recap on how the overall stance of Commonwealth government fiscal policy had shifted over that period.

The first major fiscal policy 'event' following the May 1999 Budget was the announcement of the deal agreed between the Commonwealth government and the Democrats over the Tax System (ANTS) package. The impact of those changes on the Commonwealth's projected revenues and receipts is summarised in Table 7.5.1 below.

It might seem strange that the Democrats' amendments are reported in the Budget Papers as *boosting* Commonwealth revenues when the single biggest item in the deal was the removal of a range of food items from the GST base. That is because the Budget Papers are presented on a basis that denies that the GST is a Commonwealth Tax. More of that matter in a moment, but what isn't yours you obviously don't miss when it is taken away from you, so the revenue figures in Table 7.5.1 are dominated by the decision to reduce personal income tax cuts for income earners above $50,000 p.a.. Hence the positive signs.

The Commonwealth's claim that the GST is not a Commonwealth tax goes hand in hand with its contention that the disbursal of the proceeds (net of collection costs) to the States does not represent an 'expense' to the Commonwealth. Hence there were no major cuts to expenses recorded in the Budget papers as emerging from the Democrats amendments. The big ticket items underlying row two of Table 7.5.1 were the Commonwealth's resuming continuing responsibility for making Financial Assistance Grants (FAGs) to Local Governments plus identified Local Road Grants; increased GST compensation payments to pensioners and beneficiaries; and increased grants to States and Territories to guarantee 'no detriment' from the GST package. These latter figures should not be construed as indicating the quantum of GST raisings forgone as a result of the Democrats amendments. The revised timetable for the phasing out of certain State financial taxes plus the decision on FAGs to Local Government and Road Grants make the equation more complicated than that. The bottom line is that the government's deal with the Democrats had the effect of pushing the stance of fiscal policy (at both the Commonwealth and the nation-wide level) in the expansionary direction to the extent of $1.5 billion for 2000-01, tailing off down to about a quarter of that level by 2003-04.

Table 7.5.1
Effect of Democrats' Amendments to ANTS ($ Million)

	2000-01	2001-02	2002-03	2003-04
Revenue	1569.1	1682.0	1896.0	2138.0
Expenses	3115.9	2222.5	2691.0	2510.3
'Bottom Line'	-1546.8	-540.5	-795.0	-372.3

Source: 2000 Commonwealth Budget Paper No. 2, pages 3 and 43.

The second and third major fiscal policy 'events' of the period since the May 1999 Budget were the announcement of the Business Tax System changes resulting from the Ralph Inquiry, and the announcement of the measures associated with East Timor peace enforcement and peace keeping. The impact of these together with other policy decisions made before the MYEFO on the Commonwealth's projected revenues and receipts is summarised in Table 7.5.2. The decision to impose an East Timor surcharge on the personal income tax scale for a one year period served to render the overall impact of these measures on the stance of fiscal policy broadly neutral for the year 2000-01, but significantly expansionary in 2001-02 (to the extent of $1.9 billion) thereafter tailing off rapidly to a mild expansionary effect in 2003-04.

Putting the two tables together it is clear that the stance of Commonwealth fiscal policy had already been shifted in the expansionary direction for both 2000-01 and 2001-02 between Treasurer Costello's Santa Claus performance in May 1999 and his re-run of that role in May of this year. The two questions that naturally arise are: how do those shifts fit into the government's overall medium-term fiscal strategy? And are they compatible with a *prudent* fiscal policy?

The Commonwealth government's medium-term fiscal strategy is explained in Part iv of Budget Statement No. 1. It is described as consisting of one primary objective and three supplementary objectives:

> The primary objective of the strategy is to achieve fiscal balance on average over the course of the economic cycle. With the budget now in surplus, the supplementary objectives of the strategy are:

- maintaining fiscal surpluses over the forward estimates period while economic growth prospects remain sound;
- no increase in the overall tax burden from its 1996-97 level; and
- improving the Commonwealth net assets position over the medium to longer term.

(*2000 Commonwealth Budget Paper No. 1*, p. 1-23).

How the government's fiscal policy strategy fits into its overall economic policy strategy is explained in Budget Statement No. 3:

> Fiscal and monetary policies are directed at keeping economic growth at a strong but sustainable rate, with a stable environment for saving and investing. Structural reform policies are directed at raising the economy's growth capacity over time and reducing the rate of unemployment that can be achieved without threatening inflation. (p. 3.21)

Table 7.5.2
Effects of Other Policy Decisions Prior to the MYEFO ($ Million)

	2000-01	**2001-02**	**2002-03**	**2003-04**
Revenue	1481.5	-459.9	491.9	709.7
Expenses	1143.3	1310.3	972.2	891.4
Net capital investment	254.9	109.9	25.9	26.7
'Bottom Line'	83.3	-1880.1	-506.2	-208.4

Source: 2000 Commonwealth Budget Paper No. 2, pages 3 and 43.

The last few words there go about as close as one can get to using the economics term known by the acronym NAIRU (non-accelerating inflation rate of unemployment) - the economics concept that apparently the government dares not speak its name. As has been stressed in previous sections of this chapter, the consensus in the economics profession for some two decades now has been that demand stimulus is appropriate in the troughs of major recessions, but that *in and of itself* demand stimulus can only go a certain distance in driving down, on a sustainable basis, the unemployment rate of a given economy operating under a given microeconomic structure. Once your economy's unemployment rate has fallen to the vicinity of that 'certain level' (called by economists the NAIRU), the task of driving the unemployment rate down further becomes a matter of driving down the NAIRU, and this means improving the microeconomic structure of the economy.

The term NAIRU is obviously clumsy-sounding and apparently a turn-off to the *non-cognoscenti*. But those economists who seek to describe the concept in terms they view as less displeasing to the ear: *the natural rate of unemployment*, or the *equilibrium rate of unemployment* risk seriously confusing their soothed listeners, I suspect.

The terms 'natural' or 'equilibrium' connote to most non-economists, I suspect, the idea of the best you can get, or the best *we think* you can get. If you were a professional economist working in a country already operating with a microeconomic structure that you viewed as being as 'good' as you could realistically expect to be achievable, you might feel comfortable about your words of wisdom being interpreted in that light. Perhaps that is why those American-sourced textbooks, which our long-suffering economics students are presented with as 'required reading', are so blasé about using those various terms interchangeably?

But there is nothing 'natural' (in the everyday sense of the word) in Germany's NAIRU being substantially higher than Australia's, Australia's being substantially higher than that of the United States, or that of the United States being substantially higher than that of Hong Kong's. It is to a very large extent a matter of community choice. Do you want the attractive consequences of a microeconomic structure that is 'smoothly efficient' in the sense well understood since the time of Adam Smith (if not before)? Or do you regard the social advantages of features of your society which 'hold you back' from that 'economic efficiency' as yielding social benefits which more than compensate for the higher NAIRU that is the necessarily inevitable accompaniment? Different members of a given community are likely to have different views on that question - although it seems unlikely that most citizens have ever had available to them such of the potentially available information as would allow for a rational indication of their views.

The types of change to microeconomic structure that produce significant reductions in a society's NAIRU must, in all probability, generate both direct winners and direct losers on a significant scale. Assuming that the 'direct losers' have a voice over the affairs of the community, and focusing on changes where the volume of the direct winners' gains exceeds the volume of the direct losers' losses, the political problem in implementing policies designed to reduce a society's NAIRU becomes one of assuring those members of a community who would otherwise stand to be the unequivocal direct losers from the process that the overall social benefits from that process are to be distributed in a manner that provides all with appropriate compensation in some way or another. There are, of course, situations where those who are 'direct losers' from a microeconomic reform initiative are regarded by the community as not deserving of full compensation for the consequences. Here the issue often becomes a matter of assessing how much damage those (potential) direct losers can inflict upon the community as a whole if they are not pacified, as compared with the overall social gains from powering through and imposing without consent the proposed effect. The Howard government opted to play tough with the waterside workers, but has shifted tack to a quite different approach towards the medical fraternity.

The discussion in the above paragraphs has been necessary because it is crucial to understand three points: (a) that it is possible to reduce a society's NAIRU, (b) that it is possible to do so on a basis that advances a community's overall social welfare; and (c) that it is unlikely to be an easy or rapid process to do (a) and (b).

Treasurer Costello's argument that his May 2000 Budget is compatible with the primary objective of his government's medium term fiscal strategy is entirely dependant on his argument that Australia's NAIRU has been successfully driven down to lower levels now (and prospectively) than was the experience during the overall course of Australia's most recent two major economic cycles. If the latter were not true, if Australia's NAIRU was no different now than it was in the late 1980s, it would not have been prudent for the Budget arithmetic to have been based on continuing real GDP growth of 3.5 per cent plus for the next four years. It would have been necessary to factor in the anticipation that 2000-01 represents a very advanced stage in the present major economic cycle in Australia. The proposition that the fiscal surplus budgeted for 2000-01 is compatible with 'fiscal balance on average over the course of the economic cycle' would on that basis be highly questionable.

Since you can never know accurately at what point you are in the economic cycle until you have the luxury of several years wisdom of hindsight, a conclusive verdict on whether Treasurer Costello is performing up to the primary objective of his government's medium-term fiscal strategy will have to wait. But the case put forward by Treasury in Budget Paper No 1 that Australia's NAIRU has now been successfully driven down by the series of waves of microeconomic (or 'structural') reform that Australia has 'enjoyed' over the past decade-or-so is very persuasive.

> Structural reform … is likely to have reduced the unemployment rate at which inflationary pressures emerge. This should allow a lower average unemployment rate to be achieved over future cycles compared with that achieved in the past twenty years. In turn, a lower average unemployment rate in the future would mean that a lower budget balance is required to achieve a structurally balanced budget….These factors suggest that consideration of the surplus levels needed to adhere to the medium-term strategy should not be based on the experience of recent cycles….Part of the fiscal dividend from this structural improvement can be allocated to tax reductions and carefully targeted new spending, while still maintaining a sound budget position (pp. 1.27 - 1.29).

So there you have it: the engine that is driving Santa's Sleigh is a declining NAIRU, powered by the fruits of microeconomic reform. I can't understand why Treasurer Costello didn't put it that way in his Budget speech.

Stripped back to its core essentials the May 2000 Commonwealth Budget was therefore a fiscally responsible one, with some modest dollops of good news for the beneficiaries of the government's 'carefully targeted new spending'. In that sense it replicated its May 1999 predecessor. On the core essentials then: 'a beautiful set of numbers' for practitioners of the dismal science.

It was a pity therefore about the rather tasteless 'window dressing' of the Budget. The gaudiness of the non-matching accounting systems has already been mentioned. Other examples include:

- The phrase 'the largest income tax cuts ever' when page 5.32 of Budget Paper No. 1 reveals that in 2000-01 total collections of income tax from individuals are budgeted to be almost exactly the same percentage of GDP as they were in 1992-93; and page 5.20 projects that by 2003-04 that figure will be back above its level of 1995-96. As Terry McCrann has repeatedly pointed out in the pages of *The Australian*, the whopping-great personal income tax cuts are essentially giving us back what fiscal drag has taken away from us since the last round of whopping-great personal income tax cuts (in November 1993).

- The repeated assertion that the GST is not a Commonwealth tax, and the exclusion of estimates of its proceeds from all tables of Commonwealth revenues except those on pages 8.29 and 4.20. If all the State (and Territory) premiers and all the State parliaments were unanimous in desiring some amendment to the GST legislation (perhaps to close off some future-discovered legal loophole or a like 'unintended consequence') nothing would happen unless the measure obtained majority support in both chambers of the federal parliament. Conversely, if all the State premiers and all the State parliaments were opposed to some amendment to the GST legislation (perhaps a 'rollback' provision), that would not prevent the legislation being thus amended were the measure to obtain majority support in both chambers of federal parliament. The paragraphs of the Budget Papers in which Treasury denigrates the Australian Bureau of Statistics for recognising those facts (see pages 8.4 and 8.26) are not persuasive.
- The mysterious case of the Commonwealth's one-year interest-free loans to the States, with the Commonwealth promising the States exactly matching grants in 2001-02 so as to allow the 'indebtedness' to be discharged. The details of this $1.7 billion worth of transactions appears in Budget Paper No 3. The wonders of accruals accounting mean that handing over $1.7 billion as interest-free loans represents the acquisition of financial assets to the value of $1.7 billion. It therefore does not appear as a Budget expense as, for example, $1.7 billion of grants would. So the back-to-back loan(s) plus promised grant(s) next year to-discharge-the-same shifts $1.7 billion directly out of the accruals Budget bottom line of one year and into the adjacent year's. If you reflect upon it for a second you can see that with appropriate creativity you could make any one year's accruals Budget bottom line into any number you cared to pluck from the air. Perhaps that is why the Commonwealth Deputy Auditor-General Mr Ian MacPhee told the Senate Estimates hearing on 24 May that this matter is 'under scrutiny' (see *Australian Financial Review*, Friday, 26 May 2000, page 4).
- The phrase 'Eliminating Net Debt' used as the headline for page 14 of the *Budget Overview* document and accompanied by a bar chart showing Commonwealth general government net debt projected to shrink away to less than nothing in 2003-04. The same chart appears at page 1.11 of Budget Paper No 1. To obtain the result indicated by this bar chart it is necessary for the Commonwealth government to obtain cash proceeds from asset sales of $9.8 billion in 2001-02, $16.6 billion in 2002-03 and $6.8 billion in 2003-04 (Budget Paper No 1, page 4.10). That requires the sale of the Commonwealth's remaining shareholding in Telstra - a fact that is admitted to on page 14 of the *Budget Overview* document, but not until the fourth sentence from the bottom of the page and definitely not directly next to the bar chart (as in Budget Paper No. 1) where it might spoil a casual reader's pleasure. At page 4.31 of Budget Paper No 1, in a discussion of the various risk factors that might jeopardise the Budget Paper arithmetic actually coming about, we find: '*The Government has committed to retaining its shareholding in Telstra unless and until the independent telecommunications service inquiry certifies that service levels are adequate*'. The thought crossed my mind: if the government made a commitment not to sell

> Tasmania unless and until some particular condition was met, would it be reasonable to factor the potential proceeds into the Budget figuring for a particular three-year period and publish bar charts based on that figuring? More importantly of course is the fact that any major asset sale is likely to be more a matter of altering the composition of one's balance sheet, than of improving one's overall net asset position - at least when focusing on the impact effect over just a handful of years. But that was a matter which was covered at some length in Section 7.4 above.

Readers who dislike the 'window dressing' metaphor might care to think of it another way. Why take a perfectly okay First Empire clock and cover it with ugly rococo 'embroidery'?

8 The South Australian Budgets 1998 and 1999

Cliff Walsh

This chapter provides a lightly edited version of the analyses which were originally published in SACES *Economic Briefing Reports*, and distributed to the corporate members of SACES a few weeks after the relevant State Budget days of 1998 and 1999. The editing process has *not* been used to make any corrections based on 'the wisdom of hindsight'. The role of the SACES analyses is not to describe the *detail* of a Budget in the way expected of same day (or next day) commentary. The intention has been to 'place' the Budget in the broader economic context of its time. That has meant a strong focus on national saving.

8.1 The 1998 South Australian Budget

In 1998 for the first time the State Budget has presented public sector financial data on an accruals basis. In the past, the estimates have been presented in cash terms, although in recent years the cash treatment has been modified somewhat to bring the cash results closer to the accruals concept. Related to the introduction of accruals accounting, the Budget has moved to an output basis of budgeting.

These are reforms to South Australia's methods of presenting its public sector accounting, and to its system of providing information for promoting better management of non-commercial sector agencies, that were strongly recommended by the 1994 Report of the Audit Commission. Their introduction in the 1998-99 Budget context honours the commitment made by the Government in its response to the Report. The data presented in the 1998 Budget Papers are somewhat tentative and experimental, but mark the beginning of a major improvement in the quality of Budget information as a basis for evaluating public sector performance overall, and by agency.

The introduction of accruals accounting is a valuable step from several points of view.

From a whole of government point of view, and as stated in the Budget Papers, accrual budgeting has a benefit in that '... it is easier to see whether the budget strategy is funded in a sustainable manner - that we are living within our means ...'

Benefits should emerge at the agency level as well, once agencies become familiar with the accruals data. Accruals data should be a more useful form of management accounts than cash based data, as arbitrary timing effects are eliminated from the decision making process. Service planning can be improved as a result. Agencies will plan on the basis of an accruals cost of service which more accurately reflects resource costs.

The shift to an output based budgeting approach is supported by the introduction of accruals data. The output based approach looks at the Government as a purchaser of goods and services from government agencies (or, potentially, other providers) on behalf of the community. The output based model will be extended further in the 1999 State Budget.

From an analyst's point of view, the change is also helpful. There is a move toward accrual accounting across the States, and the introduction of accrual accounting should enable better comparisons of the financial positions of the State Governments.

Diagram 8.1.1 shows the adjustments which are required to convert from a cash set of accounts to accruals based (the diagram is taken from the 1998 South Australian Budget Papers).
The accrual budget presentation differs from the cash presentation in two essential respects.

Firstly, it includes a depreciation charge to reflect consumption of capital by government in the services that it provides. Government capital expenditures involve the funding of long lived assets which then deliver services over a period of years. Cash payments are made up front and the assets are then used later. The costs of the services in subsequent years are:

- the financing cost of the asset (e.g., the interest cost of holding it); and
- the degree to which the asset is used up - i.e., depreciated.

Interest costs are a cash payment, and are thus recorded in cash and accruals accounts. However, cash accounts do not include a charge for depreciation. Department of Treasury and Finance's practice in recent years has been to include 'social capital' spending in the underlying deficit calculation. 'Social capital' is defined as capital spending in the non-commercial sector of government, which is not recovered from users on a commercial basis via user charges. Social capital spending has thus acted as a surrogate for a depreciation expense.

A true estimate of depreciation will be more meaningful than a surrogate such as social capital spending. Social capital is more 'lumpy' than underlying depreciation costs. Over a longer term these lumps will tend to iron out, but they can give a misleading short term picture.

Secondly, the accruals framework includes a range of timing adjustments relating to the fact that cash transactions may not occur in the same year that liabilities and entitlements are incurred.

The most important such adjustment relates to accruing employee entitlements - superannuation, leave entitlements, etc. In recent years Treasury and Finance has funded accruing superannuation liabilities in respect of current service, and included these costs in the underlying deficit measure.

The operating result reported in the Budget is based on accruals accounting standards. Although the accruals method represents an improvement over cash based budgeting, it is still inadequate in one important respect. Ideally budget statements would report a bottom line in terms of 'change in wealth', and the accrual operating result does not do that.

Diagram 8.1.1
Converting Cash Estimates to Accrual Estimates

CASH PAYMENTS
+
DEPRECIATION
The allocation of the cost of a physical asset over its life +
EMPLOYEE ENTITLEMENTS
Costs incurred for increases to staff entitlements such as long service leave, where the leave has been earned but won't be taken until a future year +
PURCHASES ON CREDIT
Expenses incurred in the budget year but where payment falls due in a subsequent year —
PREVIOUS ACCRUALS PAID
Amounts paid in the budget year but where the expense has been recognised in a previous year —
PREPAYMENTS IN THE BUDGET YEAR
Amounts relating to a future year but paid in the budget year, i.e., payments made in advance +
PREPAYMENTS IN PRIOR YEARS
Amounts relating to the budget year but paid in a prior year =
ACCRUAL COST
Outputs purchased by Government will reflect the full cost of their delivery under accrual budgeting. In a cash budgeting regime, a budget decision can result in some costs not being visible until a subsequent budget year

Accruals based budgeting goes a significant way toward the change in wealth concept, with its inclusion of a consumption of capital component and inclusion of accrued benefits and liabilities which have not been settled in a cash sense. However, the accruals method does not generally include a revaluation factor to reflect the upward influence on asset values of general price inflation.

This is quite inconsistent with the treatment of interest payments in the budget. Interest payments include an inflation component, which is effectively an amortisation of capital, and this is treated as an expense.

By way of illustration, an investor in a rental property might find that interest payments actually exceed rental payments. The accrual treatment employed in the State budget would report a deficit on the accrual operating result.

This does not mean that the investment is a loss making proposition. The investor needs to take into account increases in the value of the asset - i.e., capital gains. Other things equal, an asset's value (before consumption of capital) could be expected to rise in line with inflation. The net wealth of the investor may in fact be increasing, but the accrual operating result gives a contrary impression.

However, an analysis based purely on the operating result would conclude that the investor was going backward with the property investment.

The analogy in the public sector is that public sector holdings of physical assets (whether directly or via equity stakes in trading enterprises) will generally be subject to upward valuation effects which are not brought into the operating result unless crystallised via a sale process.[1]

The current budget presentation is thus still less than ideal in that it fails to capture the totality of changes in net wealth.[2] This means that it is not possible to draw robust conclusions about whether we are 'living within our means' from the operating result. It would be useful if future budgets produced some additional information regarding asset revaluation and change in net wealth - perhaps in a format like that illustrated in Diagram 8.1.2.

Diagram 8.1.2
Change in Net Wealth

OPERATING RESULT
+
ASSET REVALUATIONS (NOT INCLUDED IN OPERATING RESULT
=
CHANGE IN NET WEALTH

The item 'change in net wealth' would then be equal to the change in net assets in the Statement of Financial Position.

This is not to say that accrual accounting is a backward step from the cash approach - it is not - but rather to say that the accrual operating result is a still less than ideal indicator of changes in the net worth of the public sector. Impacts on the accrual operating result are still likely to give unrealistic impressions of the financial implications of asset sales, for instance.

Figure 8.1.1 shows trends in South Australia's budget result on two bases - the accruals concept (the operating result) and the cash based concept - ABS *Government Finance Statistics* (GFS) result.

1 By way of example, an asset such as ETSA, with a valuation in the vicinity of $5 billion, could be expected to appreciate by about $100 million per annum in a 2 per cent inflation environment.

2 The arbitrary quality of the operating result is highlighted by the fact that (consistent with accounting standards) some asset writedowns flow through the operating result, some are absorbed into an asset revaluation reserve, and upward revaluations flow into the revaluation reserve. Each has an impact on equity, but only some appear in the operating result.

Figure 8.1.1
Measures of Budget Surplus
South Australia - Budget Estimates and Forecasts
1997-98 to 2001-02

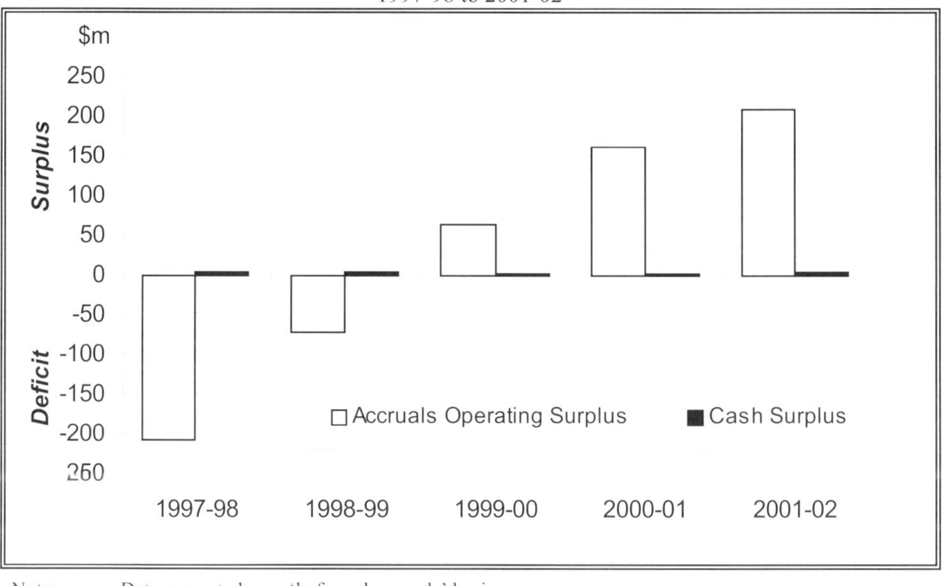

Note: Data presented on a 'before abnormals' basis.
Source: SA Budget Papers 1998-99.

There is a clear contrast between the two measures. On the GFS measure, the budget is marginally in surplus and is projected to stay marginally in surplus over the coming four years. However, on an accruals basis, the budget is still significantly in deficit but will improve rapidly and move into a period of significant and growing surpluses from 1999-2000 onward. The improvement in the operating result amounts to over $280 million per annum between 1998-99 and 2001-02.

Table 8.1.1 (based on the 1998 South Australian Budget papers) shows the adjustments that take us from the cash result to the accrual result. The primary reason for the different trends over the four years to 2000-01 is that employee entitlements cease to increase and actually start to fall. Liabilities for employee entitlements are included in the accruals result but not in the cash measure.

The improvement in 'change in liability for employee entitlements' is mainly attributable to trends in superannuation liabilities. The Government's decision to fund backlog super is projected to see a peak in the unfunded superannuation liability during the forward estimates period.

In terms of its own components, the improvement in the accruals operating result reflects a fall in revenue in real terms, accompanied by a (larger) fall in real outlays.

Although total revenue falls in real terms, taxation revenue rises significantly in real terms. Most of the tax increase (8.8 per cent in nominal terms) takes place in 1998-99. Between 1998-99 and 2000-01, taxation rises a further 7.6 per cent.

Table 8.1.1
Reconciliation of Cash Result to Operating Result ($m)

	1997-98 Estimated Result	1998-99 Estimate	1999-2000 Estimate	2000-01 Estimate	2001-02 Estimate
GFS result	**4**	**4**	**2**	**3**	**4**
Less:					
Depreciation	368	380	392	403	402
Change in liability for employee entitlements	75	221	88	-46	-66
Other accruals	137	-9	-4	39	-17
Add back:					
Net investing cash flows	376	520	538	554	528
Non-commercial sector PTE accruals not elsewhere excluded	-6	-3	0	0	-4
Operating Result	**-206**	**-71**	**64**	**161**	**209**

The main pressure on outlays comes from 'salaries, wages, annual and sick leave', which is forecast to rise 4.4 per cent (nominal terms) in 1998-99 and 5.5 per cent over the following two years. Commonwealth grants are projected to grow more slowly than inflation, while dividends and distributions fall in nominal terms.

Table 8.1.2 shows the Statement of Financial position for the South Australian Government. This data is still in a developmental stage.

An issue of concern is that the net asset line increases exactly in line with the operating result over the forward estimates period. However, net assets will also change as a result of revaluation. In general we would expect asset prices to move in line with inflation, and consequently the estimated changes in net assets appear to be on the conservative side.

Figure 8.1.2 compares operating results for South Australia, New South Wales, Victoria and Western Australia, expressed as a ratio of total revenue. At face value, New South Wales, Victoria and Western Australia are each in a surplus position in contrast to South Australia's deficit position. However, South Australia shows the most pronounced improvement over the forward estimates period.

The surpluses in States with faster growing populations may reflect the tendency for governments to try to cover social capital expenditures form current budgets. In a fast growing State, social capital spending is more likely to exceed depreciation charges than in a slower growing State. To the extent that State do follow such rules, accrual based financial reporting will show faster growing States more in a deficit direction than slower growing States (other things equal).

Figure 8.1.2
Operating Surplus as Proportion of Total Revenue
Comparisons Between Selected Australian States
1997-98 to 2001-02

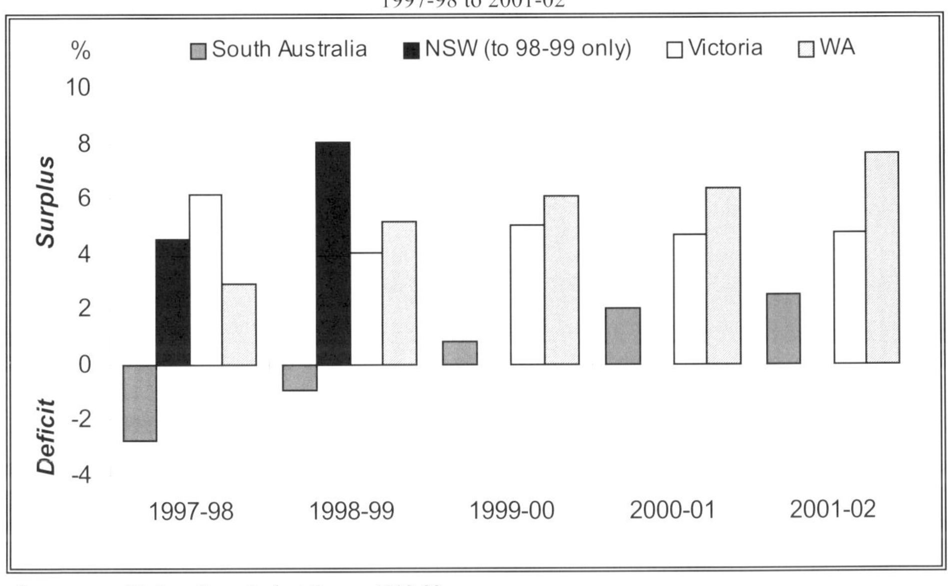

Source: Various *State Budget Papers 1998-99.*

Table 8.1.2
Statement of Financial Position ($M)

	1997-98 Estimated Result	**1998-99 Estimate**	**1999-2000 Estimate**	**2000-01 Estimate**	**2001-02 Estimate**
Assets	14,981	15,163	15,406	15,591	15,802
Liabilities	12,363	12,685	12,899	12,923	12,925
Net assets	**2,618**	**2,478**	**2,507**	**2,668**	**2,877**

8.2 The 1999 South Australian Budget

What normally would have been the State's principal fiscal event in 1999 was overshadowed about two weeks later when MLC Trevor Crothers decided to support a lease deal for South Australia's power sector assets. As a direct result, Treasurer Rob Lucas was left holding a Budget Statement that didn't any longer truly reflect the 1999-2000 likely outcomes. He was, nonetheless, delighted!

Let's be clear. The legislative agreement to (almost) sell our power assets is a great boon to South Australia - one that *should* be rewarded by an upgrade in our credit ratings, signalling to potential investors a more secure fiscal future for the State. However, while both Victoria and Western Australia have regained 'Triple A' status by being bold and determined to correct debt and budget imbalances, South Australia isn't likely to be so lucky. This view reflects the fact that, comparatively, we've temporised, and to an extent fudged and fiddled, to get where we are - namely, a (roughly) balanced budget in underlying terms, and a (potentially) big buy-down in our debt level and debt servicing obligations. In our view, the ratings agencies are likely to consider that South Australia still faces a somewhat 'stressed' budgetary situation, despite approval for the leasing of the former ETSA assets.

This situation of likely continuing budgetary stress flows from several sources. First, and most immediately, the lease deal was met by the Government agreeing to fulfil its commitment to dump the power bill levy. The result is that they've given up about $100 million of guaranteed revenue against an uncertain, but likely small, interest cost saving in 1999-2000 from whenever the lease proceeds start to flow.

Even if we get greater proceeds from the leases than was anticipated earlier, the 1999-2000 Budget currently is probably $80-100 million in estimated deficit, instead of roughly in balance as projected on Budget day 1999. How the Government will attempt to make this up isn't yet known. The Centre offers two guesses about where the Treasurer might be looking:

(i) Stamp duties on the lease deals, which would reduce the contribution to debt reduction by an equivalent amount, but would balance the 1999-2000 Budget and result in a small loss in the level of interest savings in future years.

(ii) A call for extra dividends and/or 'capital returns' from the remaining Government Business Enterprises (GBEs) (SA Water being the only big one once the electricity leases go through).

But, however the current financial year's Budget is brought back into balance, the fact of the matter is that the lease deals will not relieve South Australia of continuing budgetary stress. In the 1998 Budget Statement, the Government announced that its strategy for the following four years had already factored in extra spending financed by *either* the bottom line benefits of an ETSA sale/lease *or* extra revenues raised from increased taxes or levies or whatever. In the event, it announced the levy on domestic power consumers to fulfil this role.

To put it bluntly, the net benefits to annual budgets of debt reduction (lower interest payments *less* lower dividends and other payments into general revenue) - anticipated in 1998 to be at least $100 million a year - had already been committed to fund future spending plans. The reality is, and this has been known to be so for 12 months or more, is that the only budgetary consequence of an ETSA sale/lease was that extra revenue raising measures would be avoided.

Technically, the government can't be faulted on this. Although it is unusual for forward estimates of outlays, revenues and deficits for future years to anticipate future legislative change (in this case either the sale or lease of 'ETSA' or unspecified new revenue measures), this was clearly signalled to be the case in the *1998-99 Budget Statement.*

However, the subsequent confusion about this fact - which saw *The Advertiser* editorialists arguing for the benefits of the lease deals to be used to lower or eliminate the new Emergency Services Levy and letter writers advocating other ideas - was in no small measure contributed to by repeated statements from Government Ministers about what new or additional services *might* be available if a sale or lease proceeded. This clearly suggested that only by the sale/lease proceeding could new opportunities be financed when, in fact, the Government had already committed itself to $100 million of extra spending in each future year whether or not a sale or lease occurred.

There is, moreover, the possibility (if not probability) of more confusion to come when the final arithmetic on the leases is available.

The Premier and the Treasurer have talked about an objective of 'making South Australia a debt-free State'. This was never meant to be taken fully literally. That is, the objective was (as we understand it) intended to refer only to taxpayer-funded debt. Fully self-funding Government Business Enterprises who meet debt repayments out of their internal revenue streams should be free to choose debt levels consistent with sound commercial judgements. But that difference hasn't been carefully explained.

Relatedly, the figure for annual net interest payments quoted by the Government as equivalent to $2 million a day refers to total public sector net interest payments, not to the relevant part of it, namely taxpayer-funded net interest payments.

It is easy to understand the political imperative of keeping messages simple *and* focused on big numbers. But in doing so, the Government may have made a rod for its own back. Unless some extraordinary prices are paid for the electricity leases, the proceeds are not likely to eliminate taxpayer-funded debt (let alone total public sector debt) net of the costs associated with the leasing deals, including paying out existing debt and other liabilities of ETSA. Even allowing for potential proceeds from the sale of some of the other assets still on the table (e.g., SA Ports Corp, the TAB and Lotteries Commission, and SAGRIC) it's highly unlikely that by the time of the next State election we'll be taxpayer-funded-debt free, and substantial sums will still be being paid in net interest.

What will be true will be that taxpayer-funded net debt and interest servicing costs will be back to much more sustainable levels - more like those that existed before the State Bank bail-out. But explaining why, despite all the apparent pain, we aren't yet debt free won't be an entirely easy task, especially with Opposition parties muddying the waters to the best of their abilities.

Finally, so far as issues concerning assets and liabilities are concerned, we shouldn't forget the unfunded past service superannuation liabilities. The Government has received less recognition and credit than it deserves for accepting, in 1994, the recommendation of the Audit Commission that it should establish a schedule of payments to the Superannuation Funds Management Corporation (SFMC) to fully eliminate the accrued and accruing past service liabilities over a 30 year period. The implication was that, while taking politically difficult measures to eliminate a budget deficit of over $300 million a year, it had to also find around an extra $150 million a year to invest in SFMC.

Table 8.2.1
Public Sector Net Debt [(a)] - Real [(b)]
June 1998 to June 2003

As at June	1998	1999	2000	2001	2002	2003
Net Debt						
Including asset sales ($m)	7,663	7,710	7,611	7,483	7,268	7,041
Excluding asset sales ($m)	9,513	9,560	9,461	9,333	9,118	8,891
As a percentage of GSP (%)	19.5	19.0	18.4	17.6	16.6	15.6
Net Debt plus unfunded superannuation						
Including asset sales ($m)	12,253	12,465	12,367	12,258	12,014	11,716
Excluding asset sales ($m)	14,103	14,315	14,217	14,108	13,864	13,566
As a percentage of GSP (%)	29.7	29.3	28.5	27.5	26.2	24.8

Notes: Totals may not add due to rounding.
(a) Excludes asset sales that have occurred since 1 July 1994.
(b) June 1999 prices.
Source: Government of South Australia, *Budget Statement: 1999-2000 Budget Paper No. 2*, p. 2.7.

The logic of the argument for reducing unfunded superannuation liabilities is fairly clear-cut. Allowing these liabilities to grow while selling off assets to reduce what is officially defined as 'net debt' wouldn't see the State's total liabilities reduced and its true financial position improved.

There are two points worth making in this context. The first is to point out that, taking into account unfunded past service superannuation liabilities, the State's total liabilities are currently estimated to be around $12.5 billion, compared to the often quoted net debt figure of only about $7.7 billion. The projected outcomes for each of these debt measures are given in Table 7.1, from the State Budget Papers.

The second point to make is that, even with the provisions now being made to invest in SFMC, the total unfunded liabilities will continue to rise well into the next century. In fact, in the latest Budget the Government has made decisions that will extend the period over which they rise. This has occurred as a result of extending the date at which they'll be eliminated from 2024 to 2034. We have more to say about this in the next section.

Anyone in South Australia who was surprised on Budget day by what was contained in the 1999 State Budget as major initiatives must not have been listening to the radio, watching TV news broadcasts, or reading *The Advertiser*.

Arguably the two biggest initiatives – the Emergency Service Levy arrangements and the (now scrapped) power bill levy – had, in effect, been pre-announced in last year's budget. The likelihood of additional spending on employment programs (especially for youth), on regional development (especially via a regional infrastructure fund and rural roads funding) and on industry and tourism development and attraction had been clearly signalled. And the single largest expenditure initiative, the Government Radio Network, had been much discussed over the year. [The only issue to be resolved (apart from cost-control!) was whether it would be wholly funded from within the Emergency Services Levy revenues: it isn't, which is clearly the principled answer].

For those with an interest in the minutiae and/or longer term trends, however, there was much of interest and, in some cases, surprise. Indeed, there were issues in these details that contribute to a compelling argument that South Australia still faces significant budgetary stress and limited flexibility, and hence our view that the ratings agencies will find it difficult to restore South Australia's public sector to a 'Triple A' credit rating in the near future.

A good starting point in discussing these details/surprises was the revelation that the 1998-99 financial year's non-commercial public sector budget - which had been projected, 12 months ago, to be roughly balanced in underlying terms - was expected, as of Budget day 1999, to record an underlying deficit of around $65 million.

The official explanation has a degree of plausibility. It goes like this. First, the 1997-98 Budget had ended the financial year with an unbudgeted underlying surplus of $44 million, in large part explained by underspending by agencies on projects. That underspending was cancelled out in 1998-99 by allowing agencies to carry over the spending to 'complete' the projects. Second, the non-commercial public sector, in addition, had received $21 million less in dividends from the electricity utilities than originally anticipated.

So far, that explains the $65 million deficit. Or, at least, it does so if you accept that the underspending in 1997-98 had to be allowed to be carried-over in its entirety. Of course, there will be slippage in capital works projects and, sometimes, other program activities. $44 million slippage in a $6.5 billion total budget sounds small. But when you're struggling with consistently keeping budgets not just in underlying balance but, equally importantly, supporting debt reduction strategies, you'd surely expect Budget decision-makers to try to recoup as much as feasible from the previous year's underspending - especially when faced with the prediction that dividends from the electricity utilities were likely to fall short of expectations. Could ***none*** of the dividend shortfall have been offset by cancelling authority to carry-over underspent funds from the previous year - or in other ways?

There is also a third part to the 1998-99 'deficit' outcome story, that adds another intriguing dimension. Faced with this likely underlying deficit outcome for 1998-99, the Government took the discretionary decision to defer 'dividends' from its public sector financial institutions - the SA Assets Management Corporation (SAAMC) especially, but also the SA Financing Authority (SAFA) - until 1999-2000 and 2000-01. Apparently this was 'principally' to reflect the expected slippage of capital works programs from 1998-99 into these later years.

It is understandable at one level that the Government decided that it was better, in terms of public and political perceptions, to use these revenues to keep future budgets in balance than to correct an imbalance in the recent past. Most analysts and commentators would be more interested in the integrity of future budgets than in past period outcomes.

The problem is that the *Budget Statement* (page 2.11, Table 2.5) reveals, in the Forward Estimates Reconciliation Statement, that:

- the slippage of capital works from 1998-99 into 1999-2000 is estimated to be $114 million; and
- the effect in 1999-2000 of the deferred dividends from SAAMC and SAFA is $189 million.

That is, deferral has a net advantage to the 1999-2000 Budget of $75 million (The 2000-01 Budget also benefits, in net terms, by about $36 million). Interestingly, this just happens to be the amount Cabinet has chosen to add to the 1999-2000 Budget for 'outlays increase' (other than capital investment). And the 1999-2000 Budget also indicates that some $24 million of *additional* dividends are being claimed from SAAMC (i.e., additional to those deferred from 1998-99) - almost enough to fund the $26 million of *new* capital investment approved by Cabinet in the 1999-2000 Budget compared with Forward Estimates produced last year.

'So what', you might be asking? Financial years are an arbitrary concept relative to real activity/program delivery, and decisions about when to 'book' deficits when you have discretion over the timing of collecting some revenues, likewise are arbitrary.

The relevant response is 'yes and no!' As will be explained later, we can get a somewhat better fix on the underlying trends from Accruals Based Budget Data. But sticking to 'cash' budget concepts for a while longer, points to a few worthwhile observations.

The most important has to do with 'integrity'. Over the years, the Centre has argued that the post-1994 Budgets have failed to deliver what the (then) Brown/Baker team promised. Particularly because of excessive public sector wage settlements conceded in 1995 and 1996 relative to initial threats and promises, funded through extra revenues (especially from gambling) *plus* deferrals of capital works and opportunistic advantage taken to shift the timing of funding of past-service superannuation liabilities, the Baker Treasureship left us with a Budget balanced in underlying terms, but at much higher levels of annual outlays than originally planned in 1994 - and hence a Budget with less future flexibility than we needed to be able to compete with other States.

Since the Baker/Lucas switch, we have had a switch in the approach to Budgets. Accepting that the community has demanded relief from public sector cuts, the Olsen/Lucas team has promised and delivered more openness and honesty about the need to grow revenues to make expenditure initiatives consistent with balanced budgets, and supportive of debt reduction.

But the suspicion remains that the Government is delivering higher level outlay initiatives, while appearing to balance budgets, through some 'smoke and mirror' strategies.

Several points are pertinent here. The target the Commission of Audit set the South Australian Government was to (at least) restore the Budget of the non-commercial public sector to balance. The Commission accepted that this should be defined in 'underlying terms' - that is, setting aside 'abnormals' that could add to or subtract from the 'bottom line' on a temporary and/or unpredictable basis.

In this connection, two simple points might be made. The first is that given some abnormals were likely to be fairly long-lived - Targeted Separation Packages (TSPs) being the prime example – we now believe that the Commission of Audit should have insisted they be considered either as 'underlying' for the five or six years that they were likely to be significant or, at least, that the target for the underlying budget outcome (net of TSPs) should have been big enough to cover them and other 'regular' abnormals (e.g., costs of asset sales).

Failure to set one or other of these conditions/targets has, in practice, meant that South Australia's non-commercial public sector *actual* deficits have partially offset the benefits to our debt levels of asset sales every year since 1994, and has continued to do so even since 1998 when Budgets were targeted to be in 'underlying balance'. We might not always be talking about large numbers, but the 1998-99 Estimated Outcome suggests that sometimes they might be.

Moving on, the surprise of an estimated *underlying* deficit of $65 million pales into insignificance against an estimated *total* deficit of $142 million - as a result of adding back about $52 million of TSPs and a further $25 million (probably underestimated) of costs associated with asset sales.

Just as important, both the 1999-2000 and 2000-01 Budgets are expected to be in deficit, overall, essentially because of TSPs, compared to claims of (roughly) *underlying* balance.

Another point to be made here is that there has actually been some switching of items from 'abnormal' to 'normal' (underlying). The biggest example is the SAAMC. This, you'll recall, is effectively the 'Bad Bank'. It oversees the assets (and liabilities) the former State Bank took on that proved to be bad or doubtful, and it has been given a mission to 'manage and realise the residual assets of the former State Bank to the best advantage of the State…'.

It is clear that - both in principle and in practice - SAAMC is a source of revenues with both a limited total life and an irregular or unpredictable return to general revenues annually. That should make its status as a revenue source *abnormal* on any reasonable definition. This, indeed, was its status until two or three years ago, but as of 1998-99 and 1999-2000 and beyond, its dividends have been redefined as *underlying*. This highly dubious switch (as explained earlier) has provided the South Australian Government with a way of shifting so-called underlying revenues between years - especially future years - to suit government preferences, in ways that do not conform with appropriate principles (whatever flexibility might be given by the ABS *Government Financial Statistics* (GFS) framework).

If all we had to point to was the timing of the collection of SAAMC/SAFA dividends, the Centre would concede that it was on relatively thin ice. The fact of the matter is, however, that the budget numbers have been 'massaged' in other ways that are somewhat equivalent to complaints the Liberals made prior to the 1993 Election.

In this connection, the Centre draws especial attention to the decision, revealed in the *1999-2000 Budget Statement*, that the schedule for fully funding past service superannuation liabilities has been revised from a 30 year target date to 40 years. As the Government rightly claims, this still will put South Australia ahead of other States, especially New South Wales and Victoria, which have decided to eliminate past accumulated liabilities over 50 years.

But, however you look at it, the Government has found itself a useful source of funding of expanded services not noticed by other than the 'aficionados'. And, it's actually worse than it first sounds, at first. The decision isn't just to add 10 years from 1999-2000 to the investment schedule for eliminating unfunded liabilities. It's recalibrated back to 1994 as a 40 year, rather than 30 year, schedule. The implication is that not only are budget contributions reduced in future (so extra spending is possible) but also that there's a 'premium' (of possibly $150-$180 million) from the years up to and including 1998-99 that can be 'spent' soon as a result of recalculating payments back to 1994.

You can find the estimated benefits in Table 2.5 (p. 2.11) in the *Budget Statement* and in summary form in Table 5.4 which is re-printed here as Table 8.2.2. In 1999-2000, given other initiatives, the Budget proposes only to take an extra $44 million for extra spending. In 2000-01 and 2001-02 their is an extra $118 and $86 million, respectively, available from the revised superannuation contributions.

Our guess is that the recalibration of South Australia's funding of past service superannuation liabilities has had a short-term focus. How it has been done has been about providing space to 'balance' budgets over the next three or four years, rather than focussing on longer term possibilities.

Without putting specific numbers to the magnitude of the claims, the conclusion of this analysis is that:

(i) Even on current definitions of abnormals (including especially TSPs), the South Australian Budget has been in deficit in actual outcome terms since 1994, and will continue to be until at least 2000-01. That is, annual Budget outcomes have been adding to State Debt, offsetting asset sales, and will continue to do so, in cash terms, for at least the next two years.

(ii) The definition of underlying *vs* abnormal items has been modified over time to ensure that *future* budget projections fit the target of at least balanced outcomes in an underlying sense.

(iii) The role of TSPs and SAAMC dividends needs special consideration in relation to this issue of potential inconsistency or incoherence.

Table 8.2.2
Estimates of Past Service Superannuation Liability Payments[a]

	1997-98 $ Million	1998-99 $ Million	1999-2000 $ Million	2000-01 $ Million	2001-02 $ Million	Total $ Million
1998-1999 Budget	214	76	157	258	278	983
1999-2000 Budget	264 [b]	26	113	140	193	736

Notes: Totals may not add due to rounding.
[a] Related to superannuation schemes administered by the State Government with respect to non financial public sector agencies not making provision for superannuation.
[b] Actual.

Source: Government of South Australia, *Budget Statement: 1999-2000 Budget Paper No. 2*, p. 3.4.

Up to this point, our comments have been based on the conventional Budget Statements, which record public sector transactions effectively on a cash-in/cash-out basis. What we have argued is that the capacity to change definitions of, and timing of, cash transactions causes distortion of perceptions about how well the non-commercial public sector is performing in relation to its objectives concerning achieving budget outcomes consistent with debt reduction.

Accruals-based data aren't entirely free from the capacity for manipulation - Professor Bob Walker from UNSW has been challenging the NSW Government's accrual based data for years and the SA *Budget Statement* makes clear that its data are defined on a basis equivalent to the 'underlying' concept in the traditional approach. Nonetheless, the accruals approach, presented in South Australia Budget documents for the first time last year, represents a major step forward in more accurately reflecting the true impact of the South Australian public sector's activities on the State public sector's financial position.

Arguably the most valuable part of the analysis provided relates to the 'operating surplus' of the South Australian non-commercial public sector relative to the target set in the 1998-99 Budget Statement. This target required that the Government:

(i) meets all its operating expenses in the course of each year, including provisions for depreciation and accruing employee entitlements (including super and long service leave); and

(ii) does not need to borrow to fund expenditure on capital investment.

Some might argue that this target is more demanding than is really warranted. Borrowing to fund long-lived assets of value to future generations can be argued to be legitimate. However, with South Australia's current levels of taxpayer-funded debt, the current target is entirely appropriate.

What the data in the *1999-2000 Budget Statement* reveal is that the operating outcome of the non-commercial public sector falls well short of this target in 1999-2000, and isn't expected to do any better than get half-way to achieving it by 2002-03.

In fact, for the just completed financial year (1998-99), the Operating Result was, even before abnormals, $290 million ***in deficit*** - not just below target but actually adding to liabilities. This again largely reflects timing of the SAAMC/SAFA dividends.

Table 8.2.3
Target Operating Surplus

	1999-2000 Budget $ Million	**2000-1 Estimate $ Million**	**2001-2 Estimate $ Million**	**2002-3 Estimate $ Million**
Capital investment in property, plant and equipment	692	588	632	613
Less depreciation	424	436	437	442
Equals Target Operating Surplus	268	152	195	171
Projected Operating Surplus as per 1999-2000 Budget	70	(87)	43	82

Source: Government of South Australia, *Budget Statement: 1999-2000 Budget Paper No. 2,* p. 5.4.

The outlook is for an improvement relative to the target - partly because of improved operating surpluses (with operating revenues expected to grow above the rate of projected outlays) and partly because of a fall in projected capital investment both in gross terms and net of depreciation.

Clearly, the picture painted by this set of projections given at Table 8.2.3 confirms that South Australia's public sector still has some way to go to restore sustainability in a long-term sense. The ETSA lease deals will not fundamentally change the bottom line of these forward projections - they'll switch classifications of expenditures and revenues in a bottom-line neutral fashion unless we receive a much higher payment for the leases than previously has been anticipated.

Unfortunately, given their developmental nature, there is no way of backcasting the accruals data to help measure progress in improving the integrity and sustainability of budgets since the early 1990s. The best guess has to be that the gains have been very substantial. But the punch-line remains that South Australia still has a long way to go to establish Budget outcomes that meet the Government's self-imposed targets - nearly a decade since the State Bank debacle threw us off-track.

The major worry is that, before we can re-establish balance, let alone increase flexibility, other States might start a competitive game of tax cutting. If that happens soon (as Queensland has threatened, and Victoria and New South Wales to some extent have already started), South Australia's 'Budgetary Stress' will intensify.

9 The South Australian Budgets 2000 and 2001

Jim Hancock

This chapter provides a lightly edited version of the analyses which were originally published in SACES *Economic Briefing Reports*, and distributed to the corporate members of SACES a few weeks after the relevant State Budget days of 2000 and 2001. The editing process has *not* been used to make any corrections based on 'the wisdom of hindsight'. The role of the SACES analyses is not to describe the *detail* of a Budget in the way expected of same day (or next day) commentary. The intention has been to 'place' the Budget in the broader economic context of its time. That has meant a strong focus on national saving.

9.1 The 2000 South Australian Budget

In the 1998-99 South Australian Budget, the State Government announced a four year financial plan for the period 1998-99 to 2001-02. The objectives of the plan are summarised in Box 9.1.1

The 2000-01 Budget, brought down in May this year, is the third Budget in the course of this plan, and it is therefore timely to review progress. For some elements of the financial plan, there are indicators which make it possible to conduct an appraisal fairly easily - and in this chapter we focus mostly on those. Other elements - such as meeting service delivery needs efficiently and providing adequate economic and social infrastructure - can only be assessed with a high degree of judgment. While we are not able to draw firm conclusions about performance against these objectives, some relevant observations can be made.

Box 9.1.1
Objectives of the 1998-99 Financial Plan

- to meet the service delivery needs of the South Australian community to a standard and at levels of efficiency at least comparable with other States;
- to maintain the non-commercial sector in underlying balance over the medium term;
- to further reduce non-commercial sector debt in real terms, with the aim of achieving a AA plus rating as soon as possible and AAA in the medium term;
- to eliminate the State's unfunded superannuation liability over 30 years (i.e., by year 2024);
- to ensure the State has a competitive tax regime for business and job creation; and
- to ensure the State has adequate economic and social infrastructure to promote business investment and contribute to social well being.

Source: South Australian Budget Papers.

Key conclusions to emerge from our analysis are:

- while the targets for the 4 year financial plan were set on an accruals basis, the Government has not prepared outcome data on an accrual basis and therefore it is not possible to conclude definitively whether or not the targets have been achieved;
- the available evidence suggests that the Government has had a fairly modest cash *deficit* for the first 3 years of the financial plan, instead of the small *surplus* that was projected;
- the surplus on current operations has been $218 million *smaller* than was projected;
- this has been offset by an increased capital surplus, reflecting reduced capital spending;
- there has been a major reduction in State debt, although this is essentially due to asset sales;
- excluding asset sales, the net debt and superannuation liabilities *increased* moderately over the first 3 years of the financial plan;
- reduced risk exposure has prompted a credit rating upgrade; and
- the State is exposed to the prospect of interstate tax competition.

Our view is that - notwithstanding the declared objectives of the Government and the major recent asset sales - the Budget continues to be in a state of considerable stress. There may be a need for active measures to reduce spending or increase revenue in the near future. Certainly there is no apparent scope to meet any unanticipated calls for new spending or reductions in taxes without offsetting action elsewhere in the Budget.

When we analyse the Budget, an important question is whether the Budget is being managed in a sustainable way. In the short term, a government can spend big on its current activities and tax small, and cover the subsequent shortfall by selling assets, running up debt or cutting levels of capital spending (which represent a prepayment for future services for the community). Of course in the medium term such a strategy is unsustainable - eventually the assets run out and the debt becomes so large that no-one will be prepared to lend any more. It is important therefore to have some measure that indicates the sustainability of the budget strategy.

The best measure of budget sustainability is the 'Operating Result' on an accruals basis. The accruals result is preferable to cash based results for two main reasons. First, it recognises resource consumption which may not show up in cash estimates - such as the depreciation of capital assets. Secondly, accruals results are generally less sensitive to arbitrary timing effects which can significantly influence cash based results (such as the timing of capital investments).

In recognition of the superiority of accruals accounting, the Treasurer began to present budget results and targets on an accruals basis in the 1998-99 Budget, saying that:

> With the 1998-99 budget, the Government moves to a new medium term fiscal planning framework designed to take the State into the next century …
>
> Previously the budget surplus has been measured in accordance with the Australian Bureau of Statistics Government Finance Statistics (GFS) standards. Under the new framework the target becomes the achievement of a non commercial sector operating surplus before depreciation equal to or greater than the total capital investment in the non-commercial sector …
>
> The main benefit of accrual budgeting is that it is easier to see whether the budget strategy is funded in a sustainable manner - that we are living within our means. Accrual financial statements provide the basis for assessing whether this has been achieved, as they reflect the full cost of service provision (including depreciation), and disclose all financial obligations incurred each year (such as superannuation and long service leave liabilities), even if the cash costs come in future years …
>
> … the introduction of accrual accounting will provide the basis for independent assessment of whether Governments are living within their means.

In that Budget, and reflecting these considerations, the targets for budget sustainability included the accruals operating result. A significant deficit was anticipated for 1998-99, but with substantial improvements projected over the forward estimates period. By 1999-2000 the Budget was to be in surplus on an accruals basis, and with much larger surpluses projected for following years. For instance, in 1998-99 the operating result (before abnormals) was to be a $71 million deficit, budgeted to improve to a $64 million surplus in 1999-2000, and to improve further to a $161 million surplus in 2000-01. The medium term objective was for the operating surplus plus depreciation allowances to be sufficiently large to cover capital expenditures on property, plant and equipment. This is tantamount to requiring that the budget balance in cash terms.

The Government has not prepared accrual estimates of the actual outcomes for 1997-98 and 1998-99, and therefore it is not possible directly to confirm whether or not the accrual targets have been met.

The lack of accrual information necessary to monitor performance against the Budget leaves open important questions about the State's finances. In May 1998 significant improvements were projected for the operating result. Have the improvements that were projected in May 1998 for the Budget's deficit on the operating result been achieved? Unfortunately the data do not allow us to answer this question directly. Instead, we turn to an analysis of cash estimates - a second best alternative, since in principle these estimates are less meaningful than accrual based estimates. However, they do exist. Table 9.1.1 summarises projections and estimated outcomes for key cash aggregates.

When the 1998-99 financial plan was introduced, a cash surplus of $10 million was projected for the period 1997-98 to 1999-2000. In the event, a deficit of $46 million is now estimated, implying a deterioration in the outcome of about $56 million.[1]

The most striking feature of the data in Table 9.1.1 is that current outlays are estimated to have been $540 million (3.0 per cent) higher than was initially projected. To some extent this has been accommodated by higher than expected receipts - own source revenues plus grants were $327 million (1.7 per cent) higher than was expected. Still, the combined effect of these largely current items was to push the Budget in a deficit direction by $217 million.

Table 9.1.1
Key Components of the Cash Budget
A Comparison of Mid Term Outcomes and Initial Projections
for the Period 1997-98 to 1999-2000[a]

	1998-99 Budget Estimates[b] ($ million)	**2000-01 Budget Estimates[c] ($ million)**	**Variation ($ million)**	**Variation (Per Cent)**
Current outlays	17,823	18,363	540	3.0
plus: Capital outlays	1,251	1,082	-169	-13.5
less: Own source revenues	9,978	10,059	81	0.8
less: Grants received	8,869	9,115	246	2.8
less: Provisions	226	219	-7	-3.1
Equals: Deficit (Surplus)[d]	1	52	51	
less: Abnormals	8	6	-2	
Equals: Underlying deficit (Surplus)[d]	-10	46	53	
Additional items:				
Current deficit (Surplus)[d]	-1,069	-851	218	
Capital deficit (Surplus)[d]	1,059	896	-163	

Notes:
a totals may not add due to rounding differences.
b sum of 1997-98 estimates and 1998-99 and 1999-2000 projections.
c sum of 1997-98 and 1998-99 actuals and 1999-2000 estimate.
d a positive result indicates a 'deficit'; a negative result indicates a 'surplus'.

Source: South Australian Budget papers.

The impact of this 'deficit push' has mainly been absorbed by means of a sharp reduction in actual capital spending - down $169 million or over 13 per cent. To a lesser extent it has been allowed to flow through into the deficit and, by implication, debt levels.

1 When the 1998-99 Budget was brought down, the 1997-98 financial year was not complete and it was necessary therefore to estimate outcomes. To the extent that any transactions were delayed from 1997-98 - so-called 'slippage' - this would have an impact on 1998-99 results. To represent these effects as deviations from the Budget strategy might be formally correct but would be of little real substance. To abstract from this influence, we have included 1997-98 in the assessment period. Therefore, to the extent that the data in the table indicate deviations from estimates and projections at 1998-99 Budget time, they are not attributable to slippage effects. Furthermore, the analysis refers only to the years 1997-98 to 1999-2000; 2000-01 Budget outcomes are yet to occur.

What these figures indicate is that the budget on current operations has been significantly more in deficit than was intended at the commencement of the current financial plan. The effects of this on the overall budget deficit have largely been attenuated by means of reductions in capital expenditure. These trends suggest that the accrual operating result has been in deficit to a significantly greater extent than was intended. Exactly how much greater is not possible to determine.

The reasons for the worse than expected outcome on the current account must, in a strict accounting sense, lie in either higher than expected spending or lower than expected revenues. However, a more important question is: what are the fundamental drivers of the shortfall? The deterioration in the current balance has occurred in spite of reasonably good economic conditions in South Australia throughout the period of the plan. At the same time, inflation outcomes have been broadly consistent with expectations at the beginning of the financial plan. Therefore, it does not seem possible to explain the variations between budget plans and outcomes in terms of unforeseen cyclical economic conditions. Instead, discretionary items such as tax cuts and new spending initiatives appear to be the explanation.

A significant reduction in the State's net debt has been achieved during the course of the financial plan, mainly reflecting asset sales in 1999-2000. Net debt was reduced from $8.1 billion in mid 1997 to $4.2 billion in mid 2000. The Budget papers note that this was largely attributable to the net proceeds - $3.9 billion - from the ETSA disposal process. The ratio of State net debt to Gross State Product is estimated to have fallen from 21.8 per cent in mid 1997 to 9.9 per cent in mid 2000.

This might be thought of as being the 'headline' outcome for net debt. To properly assess how successful the State Government has been in reducing the State's gross liabilities - which include not only net debt but also other financial obligations which the government is required to meet in future years, notably unfunded superannuation payments to public servants - it is necessary to go behind the headline net debt figures.

Unfunded superannuation liabilities actually rose by about $221 million between June 1997 and June 2000. Net debt *plus* unfunded superannuation liabilities fell from $11.9 billion to $8.3 billion (or from 32.3 per cent to 19.5 per cent as proportions of Gross State Product).

In managing its finances the government has a degree of discretion about whether to apply available funds to reducing net debt or reducing net unfunded super liabilities. However, whatever the choice made, the effects of such a policy on the State's gross liabilities is neutral. In fact, for reasons that are unclear, ratings agencies seem to pay closer attention to debt liabilities than superannuation liabilities in their rating decisions, and it is understandable therefore that a policy of sinking debt rather than super liabilities might therefore be attractive to the Government.

It also needs to be kept in mind that gross liabilities are not the definitive benchmark of the public sector balance sheet. Arguably some net wealth concept, which takes account of the values of assets owned, is more meaningful.

There is of course great emphasis on debt levels in budget commentary, arguably to the neglect of other meaningful indicators such as net wealth of the public sector. It is useful to distinguish between two different types of debt reduction. First, net debt can be reduced through decisions about purchases and sales of assets (which tend to have little impact on net wealth). Secondly, net debt can be reduced through decisions about how much to save (or dissave) from current income streams (saving and dissaving translate directly into impacts on net wealth).

To illustrate the distinction, it is useful to draw an analogy with a homeowner making decisions about paying off a mortgage. Two possibilities are:

- to sell the home, pay off the mortgage and reduce net debt; and
- to show restraint in spending, and make savings to pay off the mortgage and keep the home while reducing net debt.

Obviously the two strategies are very different. While most would regard debt reductions of the second type as likely to be beneficial in the long term, the case for debt reductions of the first type is much less compelling. The first strategy reduces gross liabilities without increasing net wealth. The second strategy reduces gross liabilities and increases net wealth.

The debt reduction achieved in South Australia in recent years has relied on the first strategy. Net debt excluding the proceeds of asset sales fell by $53 million between June 1997 and June 2000. However, unfunded superannuation liabilities rose by about $221 million. Therefore net debt plus unfunded superannuation liabilities (excluding asset sale proceeds) rose from $11.9 billion to $12.1 billion. After allowance for inflation, this amounts to a small fall in real terms.

In conclusion, although net debt has been substantially reduced this is primarily due to disposal of the State's electricity assets. The State's equity in the electricity assets has been surrendered in return. The continuing deficit on the budget for the non-commercial sector actually makes debt levels higher than they otherwise would be.

In fact the primary benefits of electricity asset sales would appear to relate to reduced risk exposure. The national electricity market is now highly competitive. The State is no longer carrying on its balance sheet the risky generation and retailing activities which had a value at risk of the order of $500 million. In addition, it no longer carries the relatively low risk distribution assets - with a market value of over $3 billion. On the basis of these factors, it was concluded in the Budget that:

> … although the sale of revenue producing assets may not immediately produce a significant 'bottom line' impact to the State's finances, it can result in an improvement in the long term through reduction in risks associated with the operations of the assets.

This view appears to be influential with credit rating agencies. In June 1999 Standard and Poors indicated that privatisation of the State's electricity assets could result in a rating upgrade and, in December 1999, they upgraded South Australia to AA+ upon announcement of the sale of ETSA Utilities and ETSA Power. These more positive rating views are important probably not so much for their beneficial impact on the State's interest costs as for their contribution to investment attraction. That is, a higher credit rating sends more positive signals about the economic outlook to potential investors in South Australia.

The Budget forecasts a steady improvement in the accrual operating result over the next few years and a sequence of small cash surpluses. If the improved accrual result can be achieved on current settings, then the budget outlook is positive. However, as we have just discussed, forecasts like this have been made before and not delivered. The question must arise as to how realistic the current set of budget forecasts will prove to be.

In the Budget documents this year, considerable emphasis was placed on cash outcomes, and in particular in the projection of a marginal cash surplus for 2000-01 and subsequent years. This is in spite of the use of accrual based targets in the financial plan and the Treasurer's acknowledgment of the virtues of the accrual based measures (as quoted earlier).

The cash surplus projected for 2000-01 relies on the decision to defer $88 million of SAAMC/SAFA dividends from 1999-2000 into 2000-01.

Taken together, these factors suggest that the Budget is under considerable stress - certainly more stress than is apparent in the sanguine projections of improving accrual budget trends and cash surpluses. One wonders if, by presenting the Budget in the best possible light, the Government has unintentionally increased the calls on the Budget.

For instance, if the Government is serious about the targets which it set out in its 4 year financial plan in the 1998-99 Budget, why did it proceed with reductions in the emergency services levy? The only apparent answer lies in short term political imperative - an imperative which must be more difficult to resist when there is a public perception that the Budget is on track even though, in an underlying sense, it is failing to meet the costs of the public services that it provides.

We think that the Budget outlook, and the Budget management process, will be difficult over the next few years. The Government will have to respond to new revenue and expenditure pressures while at the same time trying to substantially improve the structural balance of the Budget. There is a risk, for instance, that South Australia will face tax competition from other jurisdictions. Victoria has a review of State taxation in progress at the moment. If other States initiated payroll tax cuts, how would South Australia respond? From this point of view, the decision to give up significant amounts of the emergency services levy revenue stream is questionable.

There will also - as always - be new pressures on the spending side of the Budget. Decision makers will have to make choices about what, among the range of possible spending options, are the real priorities. It is, of course, always difficult to establish these priorities and especially difficult to make blanket statements about what sorts of expenditures are not justifiable. However, Government needs to think about this. Some types of spending have a strong equity rationale, but where this is not so there may be room for a greater degree of user pays approaches. For instance, what degree of priority should be given to (say) health services and spectator sporting stadiums when both call on the budget? We do not suggest an answer, but decision makers do need to grapple with issues like this.

9.2 The 2001 South Australian Budget

In May 1998 the South Australian Treasurer announced a four year financial plan for the period 1998-99 to 2001-02. Three years into the Plan, it is apparent that:

- in cash terms, and excluding asset sales proceeds, the Budget has been approximately in balance to date;
- achievement of this result has been by means of reduced payments in respect of past service superannuation and lower than expected capital spending;
- accrual budget information, although incomplete, suggests that the Government's ongoing operations have made a small draw on the State's net wealth since the Plan commenced;
- gross liabilities have been significantly reduced, but this has been achieved by privatisations which at best guess are likely to have been broadly neutral on the State's net worth; and
- South Australia's public sector has low net worth in per capita terms.

The net result is that South Australia's budgetary position remains fragile and stressed. The low net worth of the South Australian public sector means that, unless the South Australian Government can lift the efficiency of its own budgetary operations above national average levels, it will need to levy above average taxes just to provide average levels of services. In these circumstances, it is essential that the Government gives careful consideration to all decisions concerning the provision of services, but especially decisions regarding the mix and manner of delivery of services, so as to ensure efficient outcomes.

This report identifies and analyses the above issues. In the analysis that follows it is important to bear in mind the distinction between the 'whole of government' and government 'non-commercial sector' accounting entities. 'Whole of government' means the entire State public sector as a consolidated entity. This comprises both non-commercial and commercial entities. Publicly owned entities which operate in the commercial sector tend to have relatively narrow commercial objectives (although these may sometimes be influenced by means of so-called 'community service obligation' payments by government) and their financial results tend to reflect market conditions. In contrast, the government non-commercial sector is generally subject to more direct management control by government. It involves most taxation and social services spending choices, and is the component of the Budget by which the government gives force to most of its broad social and economic agenda.

It is established practice to focus on the Budget outcomes of the non-commercial sector for understanding trends in discretionary revenue and spending policies. In May 1998 the South Australian Treasurer announced a four year Financial Plan for the period

1998-99 to 2001-02. Outcomes projections to the end of 2000-01 suggest that the non-commercial sector cash targets set out in the Plan have been approximately met. However, there is a significant shortfall against accrual targets. To that extent the results are disappointing – especially when one takes into account a quite benign economic climate since the Plan was set.

Ideally an analysis of Budget outcomes to date would consider the accrual results against the targets announced in 1998. In fact, although the Budget papers provide forward estimates on an accruals basis, historic accruals data is incomplete. Instead, therefore, it is necessary to consider historic cash outcomes data. This is regrettable, since the accruals data would be more meaningful, in that they net out the impact of lumpy capital transactions on the cash budget, and include important non-transacted costs and revenues – e.g. depreciation.

A stylised reconciliation of the cash and accrual presentations is as follows:

	Operating result
+	Depreciation
+	Accruing employee entitlements
+	Other accruals
-	Capital expenditures
=	*Underlying cash result*

Table 9.2.1 compares cash outcomes to the end of 2000-01 with the projections made when the Financial Plan was announced in May 1998. The comparison relates to the four year period 1997-98 to 2000-01. By using an aggregated period, the analysis is able to avoid discretionary timing effects. (For instance, a decision to defer a SAAMC dividend payment from one year to the next would affect the year by year deficits in a quite arbitrary manner.)

When the 1998-99 Financial Plan was introduced, an underlying cash surplus of $10 million for the non-commercial sector was projected for the period 1997-98 to 2000-01. A deficit of $27 million is now estimated, implying a deterioration in the outcome of about $37 million.[2] In itself this is a very minor sum, amounting to just 0.1 per cent of current outlays for the period. A reasonable interpretation is that the non-commercial sector was approximately in balance in underlying cash terms over the period 1997-98 to 2000-01. The $27 million deficit contrasts with a deficit of $397 million for the triennium 1994-95 to 1996-97.

[2] When the 1998-99 Budget was brought down, the 1997-98 financial year was not complete and it was necessary therefore to estimate outcomes. To the extent that any transactions were delayed from 1997-98 - so-called 'slippage' - this would have an impact on 1998-99 results. To represent these effects as deviations from the Budget strategy might be formally correct but would be of little real substance. To abstract from this influence, 1997-98 is included in the assessment period. Therefore, to the extent that the data in the table indicate deviations from estimates and projections at 1998-99 Budget time, they are not attributable to slippage effects. Furthermore, the analysis refers only to the years 1997-98 to 2000-01; 2001-02 financial year estimates are not included.

Although cash balance has been approximately achieved, it was necessary to reduce sinking payments in respect of past service superannuation liabilities and capital outlays to get there. Payments in respect of past service superannuation liabilities have been $75 million less than was originally anticipated. The amount of these payments is discretionary, and the Government has extended the repayment schedule from 2024 to 2034 so as to accommodate smaller sinking payments.

Table 9.2.1
Comparison of Mid Term Outcomes and Initial Projections for the Period 1997-98 to 2000-01[a]

	1998-99 Budget Estimates[b] ($ million)	2001-02 Budget Estimates[c] ($ million)	Variation ($ million)	Variation (Per Cent)
Own source revenues and grants received	25,444	26,280	836	+3.3
less: Current outlays	23,933	24,959	1,026	+4.3
less: Capital outlays	1,817	1,726	-91	-5.0
plus: Provisions	308	288	-20	-6.5
Equals: Surplus (Deficit)[d]	2	-117	-119	
plus: Abnormals	8	90	82	
Equals: Underlying surplus (deficit)[d]	**10**	**-27**	**-37**	
Information item:				
Past service super sinking payments[e]	705	630	-75	-10.6

Notes:
[a] totals may not add due to rounding differences.
[b] sum of 1997-98, 1998-99, 1999-2000 and 2000-01 projections.
[c] sum of 1997-98, 1998-99 and 1999-2000 actuals and 2000-01 projections.
[d] a positive result indicates a 'surplus'; a negative result indicates a 'deficit'.
[e] included as current outlays

Source: South Australian Budget papers.

In addition, capital spending was $91 million less than originally planned. Current spending, on the other hand, was $1,026 million higher than planned, while revenues were up by $836 million.[3]

The practical implication of this is that the *accrual operating result*, which represents the non-commercial sector's earnings of resources less its consumption of resources, remains in deficit – well short of the targets set for it three years ago (see Figure 8.4.1). For instance, a surplus of $64 million was intended for 1999-2000, while the eventual outcome was a deficit of $330 million. A surplus of $161 million was projected for 2000-01, but a deficit of $221 million is now expected.

[3] The introduction of *A New Tax System* brought about some reductions in own source revenues — in particular the loss of franchise fee replacement revenue which has been treated as an "own revenue and reductions in some gambling taxes.

The implication is that the Government has achieved cash balance primarily by restraining capital expenditures. The fact that cash balance has been achieved suggests some stabilisation of the budget position, and to that extent is to be welcomed. However, the continuing accrual deficits mean that the Government has failed to consolidate the State's financial position nearly as much as it originally had intended, in spite of a quite benign economic climate. In 2000-01, for instance, favourable 'parameter effects' – such as higher than anticipated Commonwealth grants and mining royalties – contribute $150m to the bottom line (this equates to over 2 per cent of total revenues).

Figure 9.2.1
The Accrual Operating Surplus ($ million)

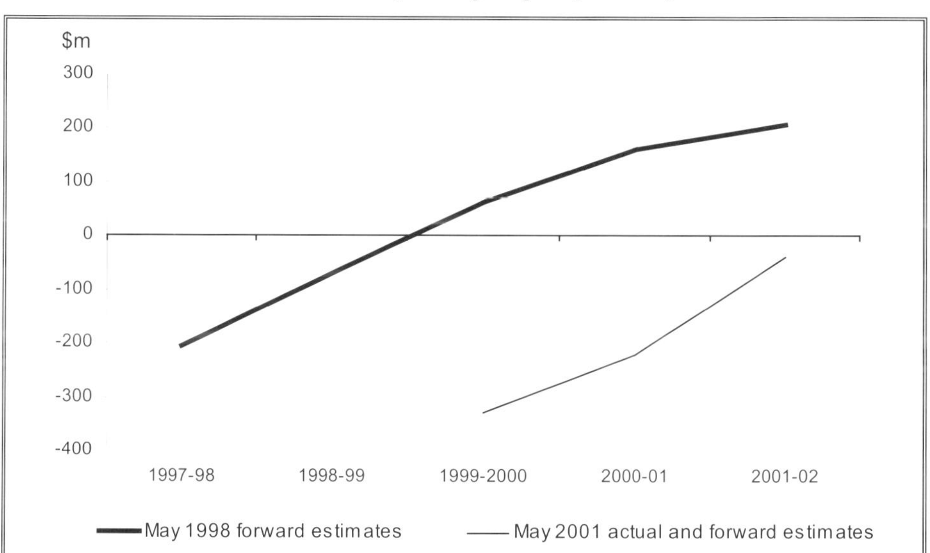

Source: South Australian Budget Statements, various years.

Turning to the balance sheet position, a significant reduction in the State's net debt has been achieved during the course of the financial plan, mainly reflecting electricity lease payments received in 1999-2000. Net debt for the South Australian whole of government sector has been reduced from $8.1 billion in mid 1997 to $3.3 billion in mid 2001, with $4.9 billion of this debt reduction arising from the privatisation of electricity assets. Over this period the ratio of State net debt to Gross State Product is estimated to have fallen from 21.8 per cent to 7.2 per cent.

In addition to net debt, the other major component of the State's gross liability position is unfunded superannuation liabilities in respect of public employees, which at mid 2001 still amounted to about $3.3 billion. The aggregate of net debt and unfunded superannuation has fallen from $11.9 billion (32.3 per cent of GDP) in mid 1997 to an estimated $6.6 billion (14.5 per cent of GDP) in mid 2001.

These falls in gross liabilities are attractive at face value, but have been achieved by means of major asset sales. The ordinary activities of the consolidated public sector have not contributed anything to debt reduction – in accrual terms the public sector was in deficit by $89 million in the three financial years to 1999-2000. Furthermore, a deficit of $190 million for the non-financial public sector is expected for 2000-01.

Because debt reductions have arisen solely from asset sales, there has not been a corresponding improvement in the State's net worth. And, in fact, figures in the Budget papers show that the South Australian public sector's net worth compares relatively poorly with other States (Table 9.2.2). In per capita terms South Australia's 'net financial worth' is third lowest of all the States. South Australia's 'net worth' – a measure that encompasses the value of the general government sector's holdings of physical assets as well as its holdings of financial assets – is lowest of all the States ($8,324 per capita compared with a six State average of $12,668).[4]

Differences between the States are generally more pronounced in terms of 'net worth', reflecting the fact that States with low net financial worth generally have low physical asset holdings. An important extension to this observation is that differences in net financial worth are not explained in terms of current day choices about holdings of physical assets – i.e. low net financial worth levels are not generally a product of decisions to hold high levels of physical assets.

The net worth measures raise some interesting questions, for instance:

- How did the differences arise?
- Are the differences important?
- Are the differences likely to disappear?

One source of differences in net worth is past policy decisions about Budget balances – i.e. choices about whether to run surpluses or deficits. A second cause has been differences in the success of investment policies from State to State. This includes both 'entrepreneurial' investments – such as state banks, state insurance companies and economic development corporations – and investments in assets which are needed for the delivery of core government services, such as roads, schools, water supply and sewerage infrastructure. The large losses of the State Banks of South Australia and Victoria are notable examples of unsuccessful entrepreneurial investments which have reduced the net worth of these States.[5]

A final factor which may to some extent account for these variations is differences in land price trends from between the States. Relatively strong land price trends probably tend to boost net worth, because State Governments have land holdings within their own jurisdictions.

---

4 Net financial worth is the sum of holdings of financial assets such as cash and tradable instruments, plus equity in public sector commercial enterprises, less liabilities such as debt and unfunded superannuation liabilities. Net worth is the sum of net financial worth and non-financial assets (mainly land and fixed assets). Net financial worth is probably the best measure of the 'liquid' component of net worth, while net worth itself is an encompassing concept.

5 In Victoria a temporary State Deficit Levy was introduced to claw back some of the slippage in the State's financial position.

Table 9.2.2
Per capita Net Worth of General Government Sector ($)

	Net Financial Worth	Non-Financial Assets[b]	Net Worth[b]
New South Wales	3,492[a]	10,054	13,617
Victoria	1,192[a]	7,241	8,469
Queensland	4,335[a]	11,730	16,167
Western Australia	4,615[a]	12,434	16,822
South Australia	1,994[a]	6,318	8,324
Tasmania	980[b]	11,837	12,817
Six States average	3,027[b]	9,641	12,668

Source: a) *South Australian Budget Statement*, 2001-02.
b) ABS Cat. Nos. 5512.0, 3101.0, SACES calculations.

In general, changes in net worth have not been a reflection of privatisation decisions. Privatisations affect net worth only when privatisation proceeds differ from a government's own valuation of privatised assets as previously shown on its balance sheet. When valuation differences do become apparent after a sale process, one would need to question the validity of the pre-sale valuation.[6] In the South Australian context, privatisation decisions probably have limited, if any, power to explain the differences apparent in Table 9.2.2.

The implication of differential levels of net worth is that if State Governments provide similar levels of public services, then they will almost certainly need to charge different levels of taxes. For instance, South Australia's low level of net financial worth suggests that the Budget has available to it net income about $90 million per annum *below* the per capita adjusted average of the other States (assuming a 6 per cent rate of return).

The difference is substantially greater when one takes into account holdings of physical assets and assumes that these assets provide services which would otherwise need to be financed from recurrent expenditure. The combination of physical assets and financial assets is aggregate net worth. Assuming returns to net worth of 6 per cent of asset value implies that South Australia would have to raise revenues about $390 million per annum *above* what it would need to raise if per capita net worth was around the average of other States - if a similar level of services it to be provided at average efficiency.[7]

These figures are indicative but rely on some guesswork about rates of returns to financial and physical asset holdings. Precise budgetary impacts cannot be calculated. What can be said with confidence is that the South Australian public sector, because of its low net worth, is at a financial disadvantage to other State Governments. To provide

---

6 This is not to rule out that genuine reasons for valuation differences from one owner to another may sometimes exist. Those differences would typically arise because of different owners' varying abilities to run enterprises profitably and because of taxation anomalies. However, pre-sale valuations of government assets are often highly imprecise and cannot necessarily be assumed to represent the true degree of 'value adding' that occurs with a privatisation. For instance, historic book values are sometimes used.

7 This analysis assumes that these differences are treated as 'policy' factors by the Commonwealth Grants Commission and therefore excluded from the fiscal equalisation process.

any particular level of government services (at average levels of efficiency), South Australia must tax harder than other States.

There is really no prospect that this disadvantage will disappear in the short to medium term. To reverse the situation, South Australia would need a protracted run of budget surpluses greater than those recorded in other States. To return South Australia to the average, for instance, would require that the South Australian government 'save' about $6.5 billion (Victoria $20 billion) over the chosen adjustment period. This would need to be done by higher taxes, lower services, or a combination of both. Queensland could 'dissave' about $12.5 billion.

Whether government should attempt to remove this disadvantage however, now that it exists, is a question to which there is not a conclusive answer. The matter relates partly to intergenerational equity. Should higher taxes, or lower services, be put in place in respect of the current generation of taxpayers, so as to rebuild net worth to the advantage of future generations? Or should priority be given to the existing South Australian community, recognising that South Australia's low net worth already implies a need for higher taxes just to provide standard service levels? That is, to what extent should a policy of saving be adopted to restore net worth, given that it constrains the government and the community from potentially justified present day uses of resources?[8]

Also in this context, South Australia's continued relative attractiveness as a place to live will be influenced by the choices that are made today. Low net worth, and the associated need for high taxes to provide standard service levels, will tend to deter people living here.

It is likely in addition that low net worth, and the associated financial vulnerability, undermines South Australia as a potential investment location. A stronger balance sheet may be seen as indicating a lesser prospect of tax increases or other threats to investment returns.

It is interesting in this context to note that net worth has a positive correlation with relative economic strength over recent years. Queensland and Western Australia are well above average and New South Wales is a little above average, while Victoria and South Australia are below average. Tasmania is an anomaly on the net worth measure, but fits the pattern on the net financial worth measure.[9] Of course the direction of causation is not clear.

The above analysis makes it clear that South Australia's Budget position remains fragile and under stress. What is the least painful way for South Australia to deal with its stressed budgetary situation?

---

8 From the national perspective, to the extent that there is an interest in efficient interstate migration decisions, there is a case for having the States equalise their per capita net worth. Differences in net worth provide incentives to migration that are quite unrelated to the underlying efficiency of jurisdiction choices.

9 It would not be surprising to see low per capita net worth in regions with strong population growth because with strongly growing populations the aggregate net worth would be diluted across a larger population. But, in fact, this appears not to happen.

The Financial Plan includes the objectives:

- to meet the service delivery needs of the South Australian community to a standard and at levels of efficiency at least comparable with other States; and
- to ensure the State has a competitive tax regime for business and job creation.

These are worthy objectives, but as noted previously South Australia's balance sheet position is such that if the South Australian Government is to provide average levels of service at average levels of efficiency, it will need have above average levels of taxes. There is no way around this in the short term. What the Government can do, however, is to *minimise* the need for above average taxes, by ensuring efficient production of government services and by ensuring that the mix of services provided is efficient. This involves two tests for government service provision choices.

The *productive efficiency* test requires a consideration of the most efficient way to provide a given service. This decision needs to be taken in an all-encompassing sense; for instance, in out-sourcing the provision of a particular public service it might be justified to select a provider that trains a substantial number of apprentices, even if that provider charged more to the government to provide those services than some other provider that did not train apprentices.

The importance of a well framed service definition can hardly be overstated – use of a narrow or excessively short term set of indicators may lead to a mistaken choice. The choices about productive efficiency may involve choices of production technologies, or choices of suppliers – e.g., in-house provision or contracting out. To maximise productive efficiency, decisions need to be taken on their merits, on a case by case basis. The assessments of efficiency need to be from a whole community point of view, taking into account factors such as the costs of worker displacement.

The *allocative efficiency* test requires a consideration of what is the right mix of services provided by government to the community. The mix of services provided will be allocatively efficient if the recipients of the services value them at as least as much as the alternative of a cash transfer equal to the costs of provision. This may not be the case when governments bundle together distributive decisions and service provision decisions. Bundling creates an environment in which service delivery becomes a surrogate for the achievement of particular distributive outcomes, but is actually an inefficient means of achieving them.[10]

The separation of distributive outcomes and service provision is straightforward in principle, and often (although not always) feasible in practice. For instance, in recent years the identification of 'community services obligation' payments for non-viable commercial activities has increased the transparency of bundled distributive and service level decisions.

---

10 The approach taken here draws on Stephen Coate (2000) 'An Efficiency Approach to the Evaluation of Policy Changes', *Economic Journal,* 110 (April), pp. 437-55. An example might be the provision of public infrastructure on a non-charged basis where the infrastructure costs more than the benefits to intended beneficiaries. Because beneficiaries pay a zero cost, the decision is attractive to them regardless of true costs, although it would not be if they paid true costs.

There may also be scope to improve the institutional structure to support better decision making. For instance, decisions about service levels are more likely to be taken according to their costs and benefits if they are devolved to lower level decision units in which there is a better correspondence between payees and beneficiaries. At the margin, spending by those decision units would have a dollar for dollar impact on the taxes or charges to their constituents.[11] Obviously the degree of devolution needs to be determined cognisant of the costs of the low level decision units.

For instance, more infrastructure could be charged to local beneficiaries according to local costs. This would involve moving away from state-wide pricing policies, with prices being set instead at the local level according to service level choices. It would be quite consistent with the operation of such a model for government to continue to provide financial support to those decentralised decision units, but not to tie financial support to the level of service chosen. To a significant degree local government operates on this basis.

The Treasurer forecasts a steady improvement in the accrual operating result over the next few years and, from 2002-03, a sequence of small cash surpluses. However, as discussed previously, forward estimates like this have been made before and not delivered.

The forward estimates imply a continued net lending requirement, and this is at odds with the Financial Plan's target. The Plan intended that the operating surplus should be large enough to cover capital investment net of depreciation. Figure 9.2.2 shows forward estimates of the net lending requirement at the beginning of the Plan and from this year's Budget. At the beginning of the Plan, it was intended that the net lending requirement be reduced from $356 million in 1998-99 to zero by 2000-01. In the event, the net lending requirement for 2000-01 is estimated to have been $346 million. A gradual improvement is predicted, but the no-net-lending target is now not even on the horizon of the forward estimates period.

So long as the deficit on the operating result continues, the State's net asset position is unlikely to show a systematic improvement. Even with the projected moderate surpluses, any improvement will be very gradual. And it is hard, on the basis of past performance in meeting targets, to be confident that the surpluses forecast for the future will be achieved. In fact the current state of approximate cash balance seems likely to continue unless an argument emerges that is convincing enough to create a multi-partisan view that a significant surplus is desirable.

---

11 Decision processes could be reinforced by empowering the beneficiaries, who are also the payers, to accept or reject spending proposals - for instance by means of ballots. These could be at a local government level for local government type services, or at the level of small groupings of collective beneficiaries for infrastructure provided by other organisations.

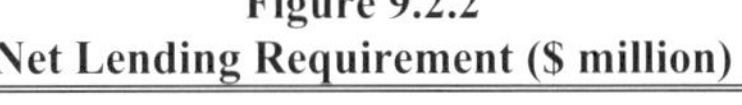

Figure 9.2.2
Net Lending Requirement ($ million)

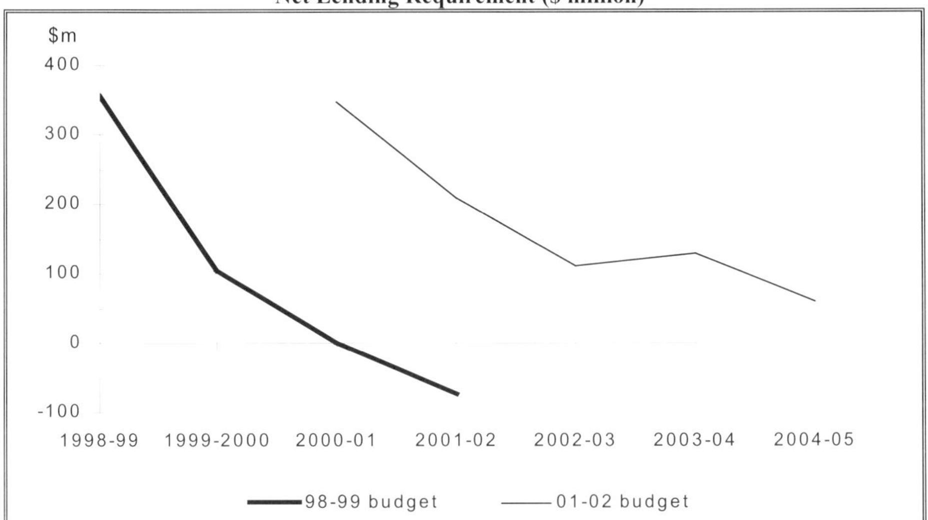

Source: South Australian Budget Statements, various years.

10 Concluding Comments

Owen Covick

Australia's National Saving level had been an issue of economic policy debate before the FitzGerald Inquiry of 1993. The *Australian Financial Review* had devoted its editorial of 2 April 1992 to a call for a federal government White Paper on the issue. Successive Commonwealth Budget and *mini*-Budget documents in the second half of the 1980s repeatedly stressed the objective of lifting the level of national saving, and the role of a tight Commonwealth fiscal policy in furthering that objective. But the FitzGerald Inquiry clearly brought focus to the debate. And it is useful to conclude this book by considering some of the main points arising from preceding chapters in the context of the recommendations made by FitzGerald nine years ago.

When the then Treasurer John Dawkins announced that he had commissioned former senior public servant Dr Vince FitzGerald to produce a national saving strategy for Australia, he did so in his first major speech after the Australian Labor Party had won the March 1993 federal election. At the centre of that federal election campaign had been the two 'plans': the Coalition's *Fightback* offering major personal income tax cuts to be funded by the introduction of a broad-based consumption tax of the European VAT type (GST) and substantial cuts in government spending; the ALP's *One Nation* offering almost as generous personal income tax cuts, divided into two tranches, without the discomforts of a GST or substantial cuts in government spending. The ALP won what had been widely described as an *unwinnable* election for the party. Treasurer Dawkins was left with the challenge of putting together a Budget which combined responsible economics and compatibility with the election promises. Announcing the commissioning of the FitzGerald Report, Dawkins stated it would focus on four issues in particular:

(a) the factors affecting household saving over the medium term;
(b) the ability of retirement incomes policy to further contribute to national saving;
(c) the factors affecting the ability of the business sector to generate additional internal funds to help meet its investment needs; and
(d) the scope for the Commonwealth and State governments' fiscal strategies to provide an improved level of national saving.[1]

When he presented his report Dr FitzGerald argued for a national saving goal of 22 to 23 per cent of GDP and advised the Treasurer: 'The more immediate and major part of the further lifting of national saving clearly must come from the public sector … Essentially, of course, a medium term lift in public sector saving means reducing the

[1] Speech by the Treasurer, the Hon. John Dawkins, MP to the Australian Society of Certified Practising Accountants, Friday 2 April 1993, Treasurer Press Release, No. 27, p. 1 and pp. 7-8.

general government budget deficit nationally (Commonwealth and State combined).' Of the ten concrete policy proposals Dr FitzGerald put forward to the Treasurer the first four were recommendations for ways Australian governments could directly increase their contribution to national saving by raising additional tax revenues. The four can be summarised:

- postpone or cancel the second round of personal income tax cuts from *One Nation*;
- consider measures to broaden the income tax base and/or reintroduce inheritance taxes;
- through negotiation with the States, and in conjunction with reducing *vertical fiscal imbalance*, seek to broaden the payroll tax base and the base of services taxation, and to consider also increasing the tax rates in areas where Australia's tax effort is relatively low (e.g., fuels); and
- introduce a temporary personal income tax surcharge.[2]

The Government made public FitzGerald's list of recommendations on Budget night of 1993 when it was able to announce also that it had rejected the fourth proposal and much of the second and third. The Budget as set out on 17 August 1993 adopted proposal one, announced some fairly modest income tax base-broadening and a program of increases in sales tax rates, petrol excise and tobacco excise. To sugar the pill, the first round of *One Nation* tax cuts was brought forward. When the pill still proved unpalatable to the minority parties in the Senate (and to some in the ALP Caucus) some of its components were negotiated down or out – and partly offset by still higher tobacco excise increases.

FitzGerald's remaining six recommendations can be summarised as follows:

- reinforce the SGC arrangements by a series of measures including: introducing an additional employee 3 per cent requirement on top of the employer 9 per cent; bringing forward the increase in the preservation age; setting as an ultimate goal an SGC contribution rate of 18 per cent;
- allow banks and other financial institutions to offer superannuation saving vehicles directly, without the requirement for a separate trust structure, or life insurance subsidiary;
- resist proposals to allow people early access to their compulsory superannuation saving for use towards house purchase;
- increase the tax rate on compulsory superannuation contributions so as to finance increased taxation concessions for voluntary contributions;
- introduce a new type of tax-advantaged saving vehicle 'applicable to a range of life-cycle purposes' (i.e., not just retirement income); and
- actively pursue information and education programs to promote saving.

Nine years on, what is the situation? The general government sector's direct contribution to the national saving position, as we saw in Chapter One, has been dramatically improved over that period. This has been the result of three forces:

---

2 Treasurer Press Release No. 97, 17 August 1993, *Release of Dr FitzGerald's Policy Proposals and Government Response.*

restraint in government spending programmes at both Commonwealth and State levels; restraint in providing reductions in overall real taxation levels (the 1998-2000 Commonwealth tax reforms involved little real change in overall revenue raising, strident publicity suggesting the opposite notwithstanding); and the impact of eight years in the non-recessionary part of the economic cycle. As has been discussed in Chapters Seven, Eight and Nine the first of these three factors has been playing a diminishing role over the last four years. The third factor is now largely responsible for the general government sector's bottom line continuing to look so good in national saving terms. Until one can enjoy the wisdom of hindsight (in combination with the discomforts of the next major economic recession) it is very difficult to distinguish how much of that overall government saving performance is *structural* and how much *cyclical.*

Turning to private sector saving: the clock on the SGC minimum contribution requirements has ticked on and the hand now points to 9; there have been some tightenings of preservation requirements; what might be described (if one was being very kind) as an attempt at providing a FitzGerald type broad-based tax advantage for saving, the 'savings rebate' scheme, was terminated after one year of being 'phased-in'; early access to super for housing purposes has been successfully resisted; and banks (and other deposit taking institutions) have been authorised to offer retirement savings accounts (RSAs) which provide the same tax advantages as the more traditional forms of superannuation. Apart from that, the picture is still pretty much the same as it was in 1993 – and the private sector's contribution to national saving continues to look 'low' (see Chapters One and Two).

If it is accepted that Australia's national saving level is *still* not as high as could reasonably be considered to be in the overall best interest of the Australian community, the discussion of the issue in the preceding chapters of this book would suggest that the following points may be useful in considering the various approaches that might be viewed as available policy options:

- Legislating for the SGC minimum standard to be increased to a level greater than the current 9 per cent, by one percentage point stages set to take effect on two-yearly intervals commencing on 1 July 2004 ought to be fairly straightforward for the community to digest. It should also require minimal *additional* compliance costs (and compliance-ensuring costs) compared with the present situation. Since the actual incidence of the additionally required superannuation contributions would be likely to be the same whether the legal obligation to contribute was on an employee's employer or on the employee themselves (see Chapter 5), it would not seem worth the effort of finding an appropriate Commonwealth Constitutional power, drafting a whole new body of legislation, and setting up a new set of payment arrangements simply to mollify some of the least mentally-alert employer-interests in the country that the new requirement was for 'employee contributions'.
- The issue of extending compulsory retirement-saving arrangements to Australia's self-employed should *not* be ignored. But nor should it be treated as a simple matter. Where a self-employed person is demonstrably building

up personal net wealth for their retirement at a rate above the SGC prescribed minimum, and on a basis that inspires reasonable confidence that the 'prescribed-minimum' element is not at too much risk of disappearing prior to preservation age being reached, there would seem to be sense in giving this appropriate recognition (see Chapter 3). But the mere fact that *some* self-employed persons are behaving so commendably should not be used to argue that self-employed persons who *choose* to save little for their retirement should be treated differently from equivalent-income wage/salary earners who would prefer to do the same. Similarly there should be some reasonable equivalence of preservation requirements as between the two categories of workers' retirement savings. More work is required in designing how to extend compulsory minimum saving requirements to Australia's self-employed.

- Instead of worrying further about the appropriate level of the preservation *age* for superannuation in Australia (currently 55, but to rise to 60 by the year 2025), the focus should be shifted to the broader issue of requiring that a defined minimum of each person's superannuation savings be accessed as a retirement income stream which includes compulsory longevity insurance. Policy-makers would need to take steps to ensure that life annuities (and appropriate variants thereof[3]) were available for purchase at actuarially justified prices before making such purchase mandatory. But the whole *raison d'etre* of compulsory saving for retirement would seem to be confounded by maintaining a system of rules which, once a citizen has reached a prescribed age, removes *all* requirements for the prudent marshalling of the monies thus far accumulated to see the citizen through their remaining years of life? This issue is discussed more thoroughly in Bateman, Kingston and Piggott's *Forced Saving: Mandating Private Retirement Incomes*, Cambridge University Press, 2001.
- Policy-makers should resist special 'tax-breaks for saving' proposals (and government subsidies for saving proposals). The bottom line here is that *real* saving is about thrift. It has never been a particularly exciting or glamorous activity to participate in and is unlikely to become so. Any special new tax advantaged savings vehicles which are perceived by citizens as so attractive that they voluntarily and enthusiastically sign up for them, and then feel very pleased about having done so, almost certainly involve overall national saving going backwards as a result (when the full public sector saving consequences are considered as well as the full private sector consequences – see Chapter 5).
- If governments allocate even a relatively modest amount of proceeds from major privatisations to additional government current-purpose spending and/or additional low-return government 'investment' projects which do not satisfy reasonable social benefit to cost tests, the whole exercise is likely to

---

[3] It should be noted that the typical 'allocated pension' product available in Australia today is almost entirely devoid of any significant element of longevity insurance. Allocated pensions are thus little more than tax-preferred unit trusts. Paring back these largely unwarranted tax preferences might help encourage retirees to place their retirement savings in products which *do* guarantee an income stream for life.

worsen the nation's saving-investment imbalance rather than improve it (see Chapter 6).

- Governments should not ignore the capacity of public-education campaigns to help lift national saving. Professional economists have traditionally been skeptical about 'increased awareness' or 'moral suasion' campaigns. And the 'watering-can' television ads promoting the SGC in 1992-93 no doubt bolstered such skepticism. But it is truly stunning how poorly acquainted most Australians are in regard to how long an Australian adult currently of the same age as themselves, can expect to live for if 'statistically average'. Many seem to believe life-expectancy at birth is the only figure you need to remember to do this exercise, with you simply subtracting your current age from that figure. Helping people understand just how many years they are (if 'statistically average') likely to live for after retirement, is clearly a first step in helping people appreciate the likely value to them of current period saving. The work of Richard Thaler discussed in Chapter 3 provides additional reasons for supporting policies to increase awareness about personal saving. The Fitzgerald Report's recommendation on public education should not be confused with a recommendation for more 'watering-can' adverts.
- The nation's taxation system and the arrangements under which social security benefits (and other government services subject to means testing) are delivered influence the quantum and pattern of private sector saving. But assessing the precise nature of those influences is a very complex matter. At the present stage of knowledge it would be premature to conclude that the present Australian arrangements lead to overinvestment in owner-occupied housing or that heavier effective tax rates on housing would improve Australia's saving/investment performance. The same applies to propositions about bias as between debt financing and equity financing. Chapters 3 and 4 attempted to highlight where further research is needed in these (and similar) areas.
- Lastly there is the issue of what represent the appropriate longer-term guidelines (or 'objectives') for the stance of fiscal policy. Over the last twenty years there has been a significant shift in Australian public policy, away from single-year cash-focussed budgeting to a medium-term focus guided by published forward estimates and accruals-based accounting methodologies. That has occurred at both Commonwealth and State levels and has represented, overall, a significant improvement in the public policy framework. But the *medium*-term framework, combined with our current *accruals* accounting methodologies may not have taken us far enough. The essence of the medium-term framework was spelt out succinctly in the 1999 Commonwealth Budget Papers (p. 1.14).

> The primary objective of the Government's medium-term fiscal strategy is to achieve fiscal balance, on average, over the course of the business cycle. This will ensure that, over time, the Commonwealth general government sector makes no net call on private sector saving and therefore does not contribute to the national saving-investment imbalance (i.e., the current account deficit).

Thus, in the parlance of present day fiscal policy making, medium-term means 'over the course of the economic cycle' and the objective is no *direct* general government sector contribution to saving-investment imbalance over that time-frame. The three factors of a bulge of baby-boomers moving along the age-spectrum, increasing life expectancy, and increasing community expectations of what represents a socially-acceptable minimum standard of living for the elderly (with the public purse called upon to underwrite that standard) may mean that the Australian public sector is accruing significant future expenditure liabilities, year-by-year, which are not being picked up by today's accruals figuring. We need a clearer picture of what represents *fiscal balance* in such a broader *accruals* framework. We need further debate on the consequences of simply allowing the 'missing' currently accruing expenditure liabilities to be unfunded and unrecorded.

References

Atkinson, A.B. (1974), *Unequal Shares: Wealth in Britain*, Penguin Books, Harmondsworth, England.

Asian Development Bank, *Asian Development Outlook*, (various issues), Oxford University Press.

Australian Bureau of Statistics (ABS) (2000), *The Australian National Accounts: Concepts, Sources and Methods*, Cat. No. 5216.0.

____________________, *Australian National Accounts: State Accounts*, Cat. No. 5220.0, (various issues).

____________________, *Australian National Accounts*, Cat. No. 5204.0, (various issues)

Baekgaard, H. (1998), "The Distribution of Household Wealth in Australia, 1986 and 1993", National Centre for Social and Economic Modelling, Discussion Paper No. 34, University of Canberra.

Bateman, H., J. Frisch, G. Kingston and J. Piggott (1991), "Demographics, Retirement Saving and Superannuation Policy", in Centre for Economic Policy Research *Saving and Policy: Proceedings of a Conference*, P.J. Stemp (ed.), Australian National University.

Bateman, H., G. Kingston and J. Piggott (2001), *Forced Saving: Mandating Private Retirement Incomes*, Cambridge University Press, Cambridge, UK.

Bosworth, B.P. (1991), "The Global Decline in Saving: Some International Comparisons", in Centre for Economic Policy Research *Saving and Policy: Proceedings of a Conference*, P.J. Stemp (ed.), Australian National University.

Brown, A. (1996), "Should Telstra be Privatised?", Working Paper No. 8, Griffith University, School of Economics Working Papers.

Chapman, B. (1997), "Labour Market Programmes", in Industry Commission, *Changing Labour Markets: Prospects for Productivity Growth, Workshop Proceedings*, Industry Commission, Melbourne.

Coate, S. (2000), "An Efficiency Approach to the Evaluation of Policy Changes", *Economic Journal*, Vol. 110, No. 463, April, pp. 437-55.

Commonwealth of Australia (1997), *Savings: Choice and Incentive*, Statement by the Treasurer and the Minster for Social Security, 13 May, AGPS, Canberra.

Commonwealth Treasurer (1998), *A New Tax System*, AGPS, Canberra.

Commonwealth Treasury (1999), "The Measurement of Saving in Australia", *Economic Round-Up*, Spring, pp. 21-50.

__________ (2001), "Australian net private wealth", *Economic Round-Up*, Centenary Edition, March, pp. 137-152.

Covick, O. (1986), "Wages As a Component of Total Remuneration", in J. Niland (ed.), *Wage Fixation in Australia*, Allen and Unwin, Sydney, pp. 217-243.

__________ (1987), *A Measure of Total Labour Costs*, Report prepared for the Advisory Committee on Prices and Incomes, AGPS, Canberra.

__________ (1995), "The Treatment of Casualty Insurers in the Australian National Accounts", paper presented to the 24th Conference of Economists, Adelaide, September.

__________ (1996), "Demutualisation, Privatisation and National Saving", *Economic Papers*, Vol. 17, December.

__________ (1997a), "Regulation and Labour Market Flexibility", in Industry Commission, *Changing Labour Markets: Prospect for Productivity Growth*, Industry Commission, Melbourne.

__________ (1997b), "The Australian Labour Market – September 1997", *Australian Bulletin of Labour*, Vol. 23, No. 3.

__________ (1998), "Self-Employment as Disguised Unemployment", in T. Lange (ed.), *Unemployment in Theory and Practice,* Edward Elgar, London, 1998.

Covick, O. and B. Higgs (1995), "Will the Australian Government's Superannuation Initiatives Increase National Saving"?, Paper presented to 24th Conference of Economists, September.

Covick. O. and M.K. Lewis (1996), "Insurance, Superannuation and Managed Funds", in Lewis, M.K. and Wallace, R.H. (eds) *The Australian Financial System*, Longman, Melbourne.

Covick. O. and B. Vickers (1995), *Saving in Australia, A Report to the Credit Union Services Corporation (Australia) Limited*, South Australian Centre for Economic Studies, October.

Dawkins, J. (1993a), "Speech to the Australian Society of Certified Practising Accountants", Treasurer Press Release No. 27, 2 April.

__________ (1993b), "FitzGerald Report on National Saving: Release of Dr FitzGerald's Policy Proposals and Government Response", Treasurer Press Release No. 97, 17 August.

Edey, M. and M. Britten-Jones (1990), "Saving and Investment", in Stephen Grenville (ed.) *The Australian Macro-Economy in the 1980s*, Reserve Bank of Australia, Sydney, pp. 79-145.

Fisher, I. (1930), *The Theory of Interest*, London, Macmillan.

FitzGerald, V.W. (1993), *National Saving, A Report to the Treasurer*, AGPS, Canberra.

_____________ (1996), *Reform of Australia's Taxation System*, in CEDA Information Paper No. 46, October.

FitzGerald, V.W. and I. Harper (1991), "Super Preferred or 'Level Playing Field': Implications for Saving and the Financial System", paper presented to the Third Annual Melbourne Money and Finance Conference.

Freebairn, J. (1995), "Some Strengths and Weaknesses of the Compulsory Superannuation Scheme", Paper presented to the Round-Table on *The New Compulsory Superannuation Scheme*, ANU, 8 November.

Gale, W.G. and J.K. Scholz (1994), "Inter-generational Transfers and the Accumulation of Wealth", *Journal of Economic Perspectives*, Vol. 8, Fall, pp. 145-160.

Green, F. (1991), "Institutional and Other Unconventional Theories of Saving", *Journal of Economic Studies*, March.

_______ (1984), "A Critique of the Neo-Fisherian Consumption Function", *Review of Radical Political Economics*, Vol. 16, pp. 95-114, Summer.

_______ (1981), "The Effect of Occupational Pension Schemes on Saving in the United Kingdom: A Test of the Life Cycle Hypothesis", *Economic Journal*, Vol. 91, March, pp. 136-144.

Gravelle, J.G. (1994), *The Economic Effects of Taxing Capital Income*, The MIT Press, Cambridge, Massachusetts.

Hirshleifer, J. (1985), "The Expanding Domain of Economics", *American Economic Review*, December, pp. 53-68.

INDECS (1990), *State of Play 6: The Australian Economic Policy Debate*, Allen and Unwin, Australia, Sydney.

_______ (1995), *State of Play 8: The Australian Economic Policy Debate*, Allen and Unwin Australia, Sydney.

Industry Commission (1991), *Availability of Capital*, Report No. 18, AGPS, Canberra, December.

Keynes, J.M. (1936), *The General Theory of Employment, Interest and Money*, Macmillan, London.

Latham, M. (1998), *Civilising Global Capital*, Allen & Unwin, Australia.

Lindsey, L.B. (1987), "Rates, Realizations, and Revenues of Capital Gains", in Martin Feldstein (ed) *Taxes and Capital Formation*, University of Chicago Press, Chicago.

Loewenstein, G. and R.H. Thaler (1989), "Intertemporal Choice", *Journal of Economic Perspectives*, pp. 191-193.

McKissack, A. and P. Sedgley (1993), "The Effective Taxation of Personal Savings in Australia", Paper presented to the Conference of Economists, 27-30 September.

McLean, I.W. (1991), "Australian Saving Since 1861", in Centre for Economic Policy Research *Saving and Policy: Proceedings of a Conference*, P.J. Stemp (ed.), Australian National University.

Menger, K. (1892), "On the Origin of Money", *Economic Journal*, Vol. 2, No. 6, pp. 239-255.

Minarik. J.J. (1992), "Capital Gains Taxation, Growth, and Fairness", *Contemporary Policy Issues*, July, Vol. 10, No. 3.

Modigliani, F. (1986), "Life Cycle, Individual Thrift and the Wealth of Nations", *American Economic Review*, pp. 297-313.

Murphy, C. (1991), "Saving Policy Issues Examined With a Macroeconomic Model", in Centre for Economic Policy Research *Saving and Policy: Proceedings of a Conference*, P.J. Stemp (ed.), Australian National University.

Musgrave, R.A. and P.B. Musgrave (1984), *Public Finance in Theory and Practice*, McGraw-Hill, New York.

OECD (1990), *The Personal Income Tax Base, A Comparative Survey*, OECD, Paris.

_____ (1994), *Taxation and Household Saving*, OECD, Paris.

_____ (1997), *Technology and Industrial Performance*, OECD, Paris.

Office of the Economic Planning Advisory Council (EPAC) (1988), *Trends in Private Saving*, Council Paper No. 36, December.

Olekalns, Nilss (1997), "Has Financial Deregulation Revived the Permanent Income/ Life Cycle Hypothesis?", *Australian Economic Review*, Vol. 30, June.

Pender, H. and S. Ross (1993), *Income Tax and Asset Choice in Australia*, EPAC Research Paper No. 3, March.

Review of Business Taxation (1998), *A Strong Foundation: Establishing Objectives, Principles and Processes*, AGPS, Canberra.

________________________ (1998), "An International Perspective: Examining How Other Countries Approach Business Taxation", an information paper commissioned from Arthur Andersen, AGPS, Canberra.

________________________ (1999), *A Platform for Consultation: Building On a Strong Foundation*, AGPS, Canberra.

Ryan, S. (1995), "Superannuation Funds: Global Perspectives and Globalisation", Lend Lease Presentation, 24 August.

Smith, P. (1991), "Saving and Taxation", in Centre for Economic Policy Research *Saving and Policy: Proceedings of a Conference*, P.J. Stemp (ed.), Australian National University.

Stemp, P.J. (1991), "Saving, Policy and Growth", in Centre for Economic Policy Research *Saving and Policy: Proceedings of a Conference*, P.J. Stemp (ed.), Australian National University.

Summers, L. and C. Carroll (1987), "Why is US National Saving So Low?", *Brookings Papers in Economic Activity*, Vol. 2.

Thaler, R.H. (1987), "The January Effect", *Journal Of Economic Perspectives*, pp. 197-201.

Thomson, D. (1995), "Stock versus Mutual Ownership Structure: Building Societies to Banks", paper presented to the Eighth Annual Australasian Finance and Banking Conference.

Toohey, B. (1995), "Cautious Capitalists", *Australian Financial Review*, 22 August, p. 13.

Vickers, J. and G. Yarrow (1988), *Privatisation: An Economic Analysis*, MIT Press, Cambridge, Massachusetts.

Vickery, W.S. (1992), "Meaningfully Defining Deficits and Debt", *American Economic Review*, May, Vol. 82, No. 2, p. 305(6).

Index